D0841128

# Amphibians and Reptiles of Louisiana

JEFF BOUNDY AND JOHN L. CARR

# Amphibians
# & Reptiles
## *of Louisiana*

## AN IDENTIFICATION AND REFERENCE GUIDE

LOUISIANA STATE UNIVERSITY PRESS

BATON ROUGE

Publication of this book is made possible in part by the support of the
John and Virginia Noland Fund of the Baton Rouge Area Foundation.


Published by Louisiana State University Press
Copyright © 2017 by Louisiana State University Press
All rights reserved
Manufactured in the United States of America
LSU Press Paperback Original
First printing

Designer: Barbara Neely Bourgoyne
Typeface: Ingeborg
Printer and binder: Sheridan Books

All maps and line drawings are by the authors.


Library of Congress Cataloging-in-Publication Data

Names: Boundy, Jeff. | Carr, John L. (John Lee), 1957–
Title: Amphibians and reptiles of Louisiana : an identification and reference guide /
Jeff Boundy and John L. Carr.
Description: Baton Rouge : Louisiana State University Press, [2017] |
Includes bibliographical references and index.
Identifiers: LCCN 2016041285| ISBN 978-0-8071-6548-5 (pbk. : alk. paper) | ISBN
978-0-8071-6549-2 (pdf) | ISBN 978-0-8071-6550-8 (epub) | ISBN 978-0-8071-6551-5
(mobi)
Subjects: LCSH: Amphibians—Louisiana. | Amphibians—Louisiana—Identification. |
Reptiles—Louisiana. | Reptiles—Louisiana—Identification.
Classification: LCC QL653.L6 B68 2017 | DDC 597.909763—dc23
LC record available at https://lccn.loc.gov/2016041285


The paper in this book meets the guidelines for permanence and durability of the Committee
on Production Guidelines for Book Longevity of the Council on Library Resources. ∞

For my parents, John and Carolyn, who encouraged me to stay out in the woods and look for venomous snakes;

to Douglas Rossman, who got me to come to Louisiana;

and to Johnnie Tarver, who gave me a job as a herpetologist so that Pearl wouldn't be a weekend widow.

—JB

For my incredibly patient wife, Christina Tweet.

—JLC

# Contents

# Preface and Acknowledgments

If you live in or travel to Louisiana, you are almost certain to encounter amphibians and reptiles. Visitors may find strange lizards outside of motel rooms or lose sleep from an annoying, squawking frog outside their window. Tourists may wish to see an alligator or, whether they like it or not, encounter large, frightening snakes lurking about shorelines. Urbanites may discover little brown snakes in their flowerbeds or find big eel-like creatures stranded in their carports after a heavy rain. Rural folk may wonder if the orange-headed lizard living in the woodpile is poisonous or wish to learn a little about why "chicken snakes" do what they do. Experts may have a need to check some distinguishing feature for "look-alike" species or use the range maps to confirm a range extension. Some species of amphibians and reptiles have legal protection, collecting seasons, or bag limits, and correct identification of them is necessary. The purpose of this book is to facilitate a quick identification of Louisiana's native and established species of amphibians and reptiles, as well as provide basic natural history information about each. With this book in hand, it is hoped that anyone can find the answers to "What is it?" and "What does it do?"

One of the vital aspects of any field guide is a comprehensive, illustrative portrayal of each species, which was achieved through the talents of the following people and sources: Christopher C. Austin, Todd Baker, Amity Bass, Charles D. Battaglia, David Beamer, Richard Bejarano, Kurt Buhlmann, Dave Butler, Donna L. Dittman, Kyle Elmore, Ruth Elsey, Kevin Enge, Dino Ferri, Andy Ford, Kathy Gault, Brad M. Glorioso, Beau

Gregory, David Heckard, Jeromi Hefner, Timothy Herman, Sam Holcomb, Brian J. Hutchinson, John Jensen, Judy Jones, Robert Jones, Jennifer Y. Lamb, Keri Landry, James R. Lee, Stephanie D. Lee, Peter V. Lindeman, the Louisiana Natural Heritage Program of the Louisiana Department of Wildlife and Fisheries, Jacob Loyacano, Morrison Baker Mast, Roderic B. Mast, Armin Meier, Mickey Miller, Brad R. Moon, W. Parke Moore III, Donald Newman, Matt Pardue, Wayne Parker, Christopher Reid, Kory Roberts, Michael Seymour, Don Shepard, Steve Shively, Greg Sievert, Kimberly Terrell, John Tupy, United States Fish & Wildlife Service, and Chris Williams. Specific attributions for each photograph are listed at the back of this guide.

The following people offered their expertise to the accounts for certain subjects: Thomas Arnold (snake bite), Ruth Elsey (alligators), Deborah Fuller (sea turtles), James Lee (Black Pine Snake), and Peter Lindeman (map turtles).

A great many students have helped me (JLC) learn about the herpetofauna, and I gratefully acknowledge them here: Mark Antwine, Amity Bass, Mike Baranski, Charles Battaglia, Lauren Besenhofer, María Blanco, Josh Brown, Lisa Brown, Matt Brown, Darah Coley, Jason Courtney, Clayton Faidley, Eli Greenbaum, Mike Harrell, Jason Hatfield, Sam Holcomb, Ashley Hudson, Marcie Kapsch, Justin Martin, Sonia Morrone, Sarah Nix, Matt Pardue, Michelle Rachel, Mitch Ray, Matt Reid, Chris Rice, Amanda Rosenzweig, Brandon Smith, Nora Smith, Stephanie Sorensen, Cody Townsend, Ashley Triplett, and Lori White. I also thank many colleagues: Peter Aku, Chris Austin, Dennis Bell, Brett Bennett, Joydeep Bhattacharjee, Jacoby Carter, Sean Chenoweth, Brian Crother, Sean Doody, Neil Douglas, Harold Dundee, Bob Eisenstadt, Mike Ewert, Mark Feldman, Ricky Fiorillo, Cliff Fontenot, Steven George, Mac Hardy, Brent Harrel, Peter Lindsey, Ernie Liner, Theron Magers, Martha Ann Messinger, Brad Moon, Amy Ouchley, Kelby Ouchley, George Patton, Frank Pezold, Larry Raymond, Bob Rickett, Steve Shively, Ann Bloxom Smith, Robert A. Thomas, and Kim M. Tolson. Funding for various field studies has facilitated work across the state, and for that I thank the Louisiana Wildlife and Fisheries Foundation, US Geological Survey—Biological Resources Division, the Nature Conservancy of Louisiana, the Howard Hughes Medical Institute, the Kitty DeGree Endowed Professorship in Biology, the Friends of Black Bayou, the Louisiana Department of Wildlife and Fisheries, and the US Fish and Wildlife Service, Division of Federal Aid, through the State Wildlife Grants Program.

Along with mutual associates cataloged above, I (JB) thank the following individuals for accompanying me afield and/or casting nuggets of knowledge in my direction: Karla Allen, Rich Anderson, Eric Baka, Todd Baker, Kyle Balkum, David Beamer, Tom Blanchard, Ron Bonett, Leanne Bonner, John-Paul Boundy, Scot Boundy, Matt Brandley, Bonnie Brit, Frank Burbrink, Joel Carlin, Dane Cassady, Ryan Chabarria, Kevin Chapman, Bryan Christy, Don Church, Lindsey Coldiron, David Cyr, Chris Davis, Jim Delahoussaye, Alan De Queiroz, Tom Devitt, Jeff Duguay, Mike Duran, Danny Edler, Jimmy Ernst, Brad Glorioso, David Good, Beau Gregory, John Haydel, Jeromi Hefner, Keith Hemsteader, Matthew Herron, Wayne Higginbotham, Owen Holt, Brian Horne, Cybil Huntzinger, Kelly Irwin, Steve Jenkins, Robert Jones, Walter Joyce, Steve Karsen, Curtis Kennedy, Ramona Kent, Harvey Kliebert, Jen Lamb, Shanna Lambert, Brennan Landry, James Lazell, Adam Leaché, Emile LeBlanc, Jim Lecour, Holly LeGrande, Jacob Loyacano, Tom Mann, Frank Marabella, Richard Martin, Gordon Matherne, Jim McGuire, Bruce Means, Albert Meier, Armin Meier, Aaron Mitchell, Mike Monlezun, Gary Morrow, Jamie Oaks, Darrel O'Quinn, the Perrys, Buck Prima, Ben Puckett, Jim Ragland, Phil Ralidis, Chris Reid, Virginia Rettig, John Ritchie, Douglas Rossman, Craig Rudolph, Alec Sabo, David Sever, Jaclyn Shanly, Tom Sinclair, Joe Slowinski, Gerald Soderstrum, Jimmy Stafford, Travis Taggert, Jeff Tamplin, Johnnie Tarver, Sairah Teta, Bill Vermillion, Dan Vicknair, Laura Vogel, Wen Wa, Peter Warney, Brian Warren, Mark Waters, Bill Watts, Avery Williams, Chris Williams, Kenneth Williams, Blair Wolf, and Tiffany Wolf.

# Amphibians and Reptiles of Louisiana

# Introduction

Louisiana's native amphibians and reptiles (herpetofauna) comprise 23 species of salamanders, 30 frogs and toads (anurans), 27 turtles, 12 lizards, and 47 snakes, as well as the American Alligator. As of late 2016, three species of frogs, one turtle, three lizards, and one snake not native to Louisiana have or may have become established here as introduced species. Several species are presumed extirpated, but several others occur near Louisiana's borders in adjacent states and may be undetected here. What follows is an illustrated synopsis of the herpetofauna of the state, with guidance for the identification of each species, and with basic natural history information about habitat, feeding, reproduction, habits, and distribution. To facilitate identification of animals in hand, use the "Identification" sections to determine to what genus the animal belongs, then use the bold highlights under the "Descriptions" to distinguish between species in each genus.

## IDENTIFYING AMPHIBIANS AND REPTILES

Louisiana's amphibians all lack scales and claws, and have relatively membranous skin that supplements, or replaces, the lungs or gills for respiration. Such skin is readily susceptible to water loss, and all amphibians require near-constant or daily hydration. Amphibian skin may be very smooth or granular in texture and may be adorned with warts, tubercles, or glands. All Louisiana amphibians possess four limbs, except for Sirens, which lack hind limbs. The eyes of Sirens, Amphiumas, and Waterdogs are small, lidless, and flush with the surface of the head. Otherwise, amphibians have protruding eyes that bear lids and usually have horizontally oval or round pupils. External ear openings are absent, but most anurans possess an external tympanum that is visible in the skin on the sides of the head. Most amphibians remain out of the water for much of their lives, but the Sirens, Amphiumas, and Waterdogs must remain in water at all times or may leave only under saturated conditions. The four species of Woodland Salamanders and the two nonnative Rain Frogs do not enter water bodies and must dwell in, and deposit their eggs in, damp soil, rotting logs, and/or burrows. The remaining species of amphibians must at a minimum use water in order to deposit their eggs, which are covered by a transparent membrane and gelatinous coating. Poorly developed, gilled larvae hatch from eggs that are deposited in water. The larvae of anurans, known as tadpoles, resorb their external gills within a day or so of hatching, and subsequently respire by pumping water over internal gills and out an opening (spiracle) on one side of the body. Salamander larvae retain their external gills until they are ready to leave the water, at which time their bodies undergo a metamorphosis, and the resulting animals are gill-less with the exception of some permanently aquatic species. Anuran tadpole metamorphosis involves the growth of four limbs and resorption of the tail. The postmetamorphic salamanders and anurans are called metamorphs. Identification of larvae is not dealt with in this book; see Altig and McDiarmid (2015).

Reptile skin contains epidermal outgrowths—scales—that abut or overlap to cover the entire body in lizards and snakes, most of the body in the alligator, and portions of the limbs and head in turtles. Except for Softshells and adult Leatherbacks, turtles also possess epidermal shields, or scutes, on their shells. All Louisiana reptiles with limbs possess claws. All bear four external limbs, except for the snakes and Glass Lizards. All possess external eyes, except for the Brahminy Blind Snake, and the eyes tend to be flush, or nearly so, with the skull, except for those of the alligator. The eyes are lidded, except those of the snakes and geckos, and the pupil is round in most, though vertically oval in a few species. An external ear opening is present in the alligator and all lizards, but is absent in snakes. There is no external ear opening in turtles, but the tympanic membrane may be seen flush with the head, or it may be indistinguishable from the head skin. All Louisiana reptiles lay shelled eggs or give birth to live young on land. The hatchlings or newborns are called neonates.

## VARIABILITY

Most amphibians and reptiles are variable within each species, due to ontogenetic changes, sexual dimorphism, geographic variation, and individual variation (such as the ability to change color in species like Squirrel Tree Frogs and Anoles). All Louisiana amphibians (postmetamorphic) and reptiles undergo ontogenetic changes; that is, their coloration and/or form change as they age and grow. Change in form usually involves nothing more than change in the relative size of the eyes and head (larger in neonates; compare figs. 119b and 119f for the Western Ribbon Snake). It also includes a reduction (e.g., Stinkpot) or exaggeration (e.g., Alligator Snapping Turtle) of shell ridges in turtles and an increase in gland and cranial crest formation in toads (compare figs. 28f and 28h for the Fowler's Toad). Changes in color between neonates and adults may not be evident in some species (e.g., Bronze Frog, Glossy Swamp Snake), but can be complete in others, with adults retaining no elements of the neonate color pattern (compare figs. 123d and 123k for the North American Racer).

Many species of amphibians and reptiles exhibit external sexual dimorphism, often seen as size or coloration differences. One sex averages larger in size than the other in most species, and in some species of turtles and snakes the differences can be obvious (see fig. 60d for the Pearl River Map Turtle). In some species of anurans, males possess a larger tympanum than do the females, and in most species the throat of males is darker than that of females, due to the presence of elements of the vocal sac used for calling. Male anoles possess an extendable dewlap, and adult male skinks have a head that is broader at the rear of the jaws, and usually a more obscured color pattern, than do females.

Variation from one part of a species' range to another is common across distances of several hundred miles or more. Geographic variation has been documented for most species that occur in Louisiana, which has led to the recognition of subspecies for some. Morphological differences may be subtle—such as the change in relative toe web extent in Blanchard's Cricket Frogs between the Florida Parishes and northwestern Louisiana—or readily apparent, such as the color patterns of the North American Racer. Differences may occur along a gradient of many miles or along specific boundaries. For example, along the north shore of Lake Pontchartrain, Racers inside the forest boundary are black, while those at the marsh margin are gray. Genetic (DNA) differences have been studied within numerous Louisiana species, and in some the differences were sufficient to indicate that more than one species was involved (e.g., Fowler's and East Texas Toad, Black King Snake and Speckled King Snake). Unfortunately, with these species pairs, while genetic differences may be clear, there may be no parallel external differences to distinguish between them.

Mutations such as albinism or aberrant color patterns can occur in any species and in some may occur with regularity. Populations of the Glossy Swamp Snake around Lake Pontchartrain contain a high percentage of melanistic (entirely black) individuals, and two Copperheads with longitudinal, rather than transverse, bands have been found in the Atchafalaya Basin. Blue individuals of normally green species of frogs result from an absence of yellow pigment in the skin. Other abnormalities result from a developmental defect: compare the scute patterns in the two hatchling Loggerhead Sea Turtles (fig. 75d).

## LANDSCAPE AND HABITATS

Louisiana is situated in the Gulf Coastal Plain and has a highly irregular coastline composed of a combination of marsh and beach. Most of the southern part of the state, the Gulf Coast Prairies and Marshes, is flat and poorly drained, with few areas over 70 feet (21 m) in elevation. Elevated areas north of the prairies and marshes are separated by the Mississippi River Alluvial Plain, which runs north to south from the northeastern corner of the state to the southeastern river deltas. The area to the east of the river in the southeastern part of the state, the Eastern Gulf Coastal Plain, is referred to as the Florida Parishes. To the west of the lower Mississippi River are the extensive swamp and bottomland forests of the Atchafalaya Basin, beyond which lies the Cajun Prairie district. The Western Gulf Coastal Plain, west of the upper Mississippi River Delta in northern and central Louisiana, is mostly forested uplands between 100 and 300 feet (30–91 m) in elevation, bisected from northwest to southeast by the Red River Valley.

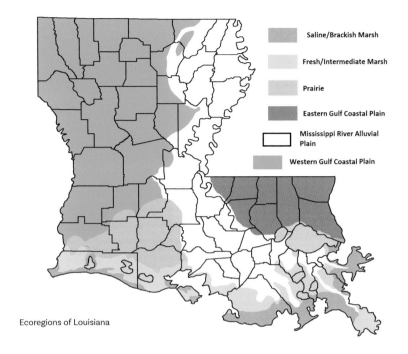

Saline/Brackish Marsh

Fresh/Intermediate Marsh

Prairie

Eastern Gulf Coastal Plain

Mississippi River Alluvial Plain

Western Gulf Coastal Plain

Ecoregions of Louisiana

Detailed descriptions of habitats are found in Holcomb et al. (2015). The Coastal Marshes consist of (in order of increasing salinity) freshwater, intermediate, brackish, and salt marsh. The number of amphibian and reptile species decreases as salinity increases, although the Diamondback Terrapin and Salt Marsh Snakes are salt marsh specialists. The Coastal Prairie is currently reduced to small, remnant tracts due to agricultural conversion. Isolated woodland along the coast occupies cheniers, which are long ridges of slightly higher ground that were prehistoric coastal beaches.

North of the Coastal Prairie and Marshes, the Eastern and Western Gulf Coastal Plains begin as pine or hardwood flatwoods, or longleaf pine savanna, mingled with riverine hardwood forests. Dominant forests in uplands on either side of these river floodplains consist of shortleaf pine-hickory, upland longleaf pine, and loblolly-hardwood slope forest. Rarer habitats in the Western Gulf Coastal Plain include sandstone glade and calcareous prairie.

Most of Louisiana's herpetofaunal diversity is found in the Eastern Gulf Coastal Plain (eastern Florida Parishes), with a tendency for a decrease in

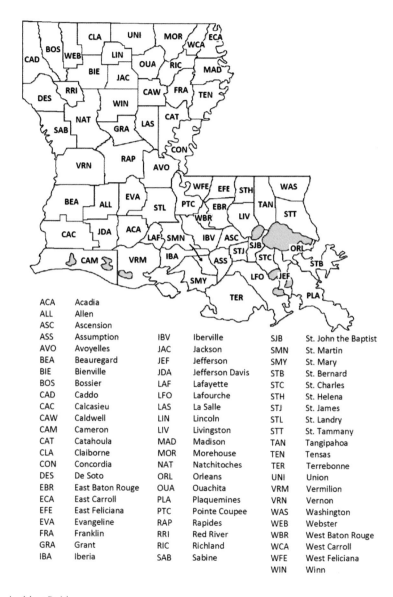

| | | | | |
|---|---|---|---|---|
| ACA | Acadia | | | |
| ALL | Allen | | | |
| ASC | Ascension | | | |
| ASS | Assumption | IBV | Iberville | SJB | St. John the Baptist |
| AVO | Avoyelles | JAC | Jackson | SMN | St. Martin |
| BEA | Beauregard | JEF | Jefferson | SMY | St. Mary |
| BIE | Bienville | JDA | Jefferson Davis | STB | St. Bernard |
| BOS | Bossier | LAF | Lafayette | STC | St. Charles |
| CAD | Caddo | LFO | Lafourche | STH | St. Helena |
| CAC | Calcasieu | LAS | La Salle | STJ | St. James |
| CAW | Caldwell | LIN | Lincoln | STL | St. Landry |
| CAM | Cameron | LIV | Livingston | STT | St. Tammany |
| CAT | Catahoula | MAD | Madison | TAN | Tangipahoa |
| CLA | Claiborne | MOR | Morehouse | TEN | Tensas |
| CON | Concordia | NAT | Natchitoches | TER | Terrebonne |
| DES | De Soto | ORL | Orleans | UNI | Union |
| EBR | East Baton Rouge | OUA | Ouachita | VRM | Vermilion |
| ECA | East Carroll | PLA | Plaquemines | VRN | Vernon |
| EFE | East Feliciana | PTC | Pointe Coupee | WAS | Washington |
| EVA | Evangeline | RAP | Rapides | WEB | Webster |
| FRA | Franklin | RRI | Red River | WBR | West Baton Rouge |
| GRA | Grant | RIC | Richland | WCA | West Carroll |
| IBA | Iberia | SAB | Sabine | WFE | West Feliciana |
| | | | | WIN | Winn |

Louisiana Parishes

number of species as one travels west from there. In fact, 31 species are found nowhere else in Louisiana, their westward occurrence limited by the Mississippi River floodplain.

The Mississippi River Alluvial Plain is wooded with bottomland hardwood forests and cypress-tupelo swamps. In the southern portions of the floodplain, relatively high ground following rivers is wooded by coastal live oak–hackberry forest. Upstream, rivers are bordered much of their length by batture forest, which grows in low areas that are routinely inundated.

Aside from marsh, permanently aquatic habitats include bayheads, rivers, streams, lagoons, lakes, estuaries, and continental-shelf marine. Ephemeral wetlands such as gum ponds and woodland sloughs are important breeding habitats for many amphibians.

Much of the nonaquatic habitat in Louisiana has been impacted by agricultural use and, to a lesser extent, by urbanization. Some uses (e.g., clearing of bottomland hardwood forest for conversion to sugarcane or soybean fields) have eliminated both the habitat and the resident herpetofauna, but other uses (e.g., conversion of upland mixed forest to pine plantation) appear to have a negative impact on some species or are detrimental to one species cohort while beneficial to others (e.g., conversion of prairie to rice/crawfish impoundments).

Intermediate marsh (St. Tammany Parish)

Salt marsh (St. Bernard Parish)

Coastal prairie (Calcasieu Parish)

Pine flatwood (St. Tammany Parish)

Hardwood flatwood (St. Tammany Parish)

Longleaf pine savanna (St. Tammany Parish)

Shortleaf pine–hickory (Lincoln Parish)

Upland longleaf pine (St. Tammany Parish)

Loblolly pine–hardwood slope (Rapides Parish)

Calcareous prairie (Caldwell Parish)

Bottomland hardwoods (Ascension Parish)

Cypress-tupelo swamp (Tangipahoa Parish)

Coastal liveoak (Orleans Parish)

Batture (Orleans Parish)

Bayhead (St. Tammany Parish)

River (Livingston Parish)

Stream (East Baton Rouge Parish)

Lake (St. Martin Parish)

Gum pond (East Baton Rouge Parish)

Woodland slough (St. Landry Parish)

Abandoned sugarcane field (Iberville Parish)

Loblolly pine plantation (LaSalle Parish)

# OBSERVING AMPHIBIANS AND REPTILES

In general, amphibians and reptiles are secretive, and when they venture from shelter, they will typically retreat if approached. Many species are primarily aquatic and seldom leave the familiarity of the water, except to perform certain activities. For example, female sea turtles come on shore to nest, as do freshwater aquatic turtle species that only leave the water when females go on land to lay their eggs. Certain species are active during the day and bask or forage in the open: turtles sun on logs; lizards forage on vines, tree trunks, or the rails of boardwalks; snakes prowl along shorelines. Others give away their presence only when they go for cover, as when frogs jump into water from a stream bank or lizards run up and around the back side of a tree trunk. Some species only leave shelter in darkness, and then perhaps only during rain. Thus, there is a range of observability among amphibians and reptiles, from those species that are obvious on the landscape to those that are nearly impossible to locate. (In fact, after twenty-three years of searching for amphibians and reptiles in Louisiana, Boundy still has not found 17 of the 147 species covered in this book.)

General advice for finding amphibians and reptiles includes searching appropriate sites, searching at the right time of day or year, and searching under the appropriate climatic conditions, as well as using a variety of search techniques. Within these guidelines, the individual choice of options depends on whether the objective is to see large numbers of species or animals, or to focus on one or a few species of interest.

Locating an appropriate site is relatively simple—the habitat should accommodate the species or cohorts of species that you are seeking. Habitats with dense grass cover are difficult to search, whereas shaded, open ground with scattered water bodies, found in bottomland hardwood forest, is easily searched. A number of species are fairly easy to see in many habitats (e.g., Bronze Frogs, Little Brown Skinks, and Pond Sliders) and will be observational "by-catch" during routine searches.

Amphibians and reptiles can be found throughout the year. Many amphibian species are active in winter, when cool, wet conditions allow surface activity, and many salamander and several anuran species (e.g., Chorus Frogs and Leopard Frogs) are winter breeders. In cold weather, many species of reptiles shelter in shallow refuges, from which they may emerge during relatively warm, sunny periods. During spring, another cohort of anurans, and most reptiles, are reproductively active and are more likely to venture into the open as they thermoregulate, forage for food, and search for mates. Their visibility is enhanced during this time because the animals are active during the day, and plants are not fully in leaf. As nighttime temperatures increase to levels that permit routine activity, most species become crepuscular or nocturnal, and diurnal species are easily concealed by extensive foliage. Diurnal species adopt dual activity periods in early morning and late afternoon. During fall, springtime activity patterns are revived, though animals are not as apparent, due to abundant foliage and decreased movements. Regardless of season, immediate climatic factors will dictate amphibian and reptile activity. Amphibians will migrate to breeding sites only if there has been sufficient rainfall to partially fill them, and they may move only on rainy nights. Heavily overcast days will prolong diurnal reptile activity, whereas wind during periods of low humidity will diminish it.

The art of discovering an animal (i.e., determining its microhabitat) requires some understanding of the physical needs and behavior of each species. They will change their activity patterns during the day or night, and either be exposed or concealed depending on a particular activity. Many species use logs or burrows as shelter; others conceal themselves under stream banks or inside dead, standing trees. Many use artificial cover such as boards, sheet metal, and discarded roofing shingles or appliances. Those searching in or under such objects should be careful to replace them precisely as found. Other concealment sites include brush piles, leaf beds, dense aquatic vegetation, and muck. Nocturnal species may be encountered while slowly driving remote roads at night.

## SNAKE BITE

The seven species of venomous snakes in Louisiana inject venom through muscular contraction of paired venom glands. Once injected, the venom travels in a diffuse manner via the lymphatic or, rarely, the vascular system. Once venom enters these systems, it cannot be extracted. Thus, cutting and sucking the wound serves no benefit and may worsen the injury. Additional first aid, such as applying ice or a tourniquet, also provides no benefit to the snake bite victim. Usually, these measures cause negative complications and delay appropriate medical care. **The first priority if bitten by a venomous snake is to obtain medical treatment without delay**. Remain calm, keep the affected extremity immobile, remove rings and tight clothing from the injured area, and **call ahead to your chosen medical facility** so that they can prepare for your arrival. Poison Control can provide real-time, around-the-clock instructions and assistance in finding an appropriate medical facility. They may be contacted by calling 1-800-222-1222.

## OVERVIEW OF THE SPECIES ACCOUNTS

The sequence of species accounts, as well as of the checklist below, is based on the authors' understanding of the evolutionary relationships of the major groups of amphibians and reptiles down to the level of families. Within family groups and genera, species are grouped by relatedness and/or similarity of appearance.

**Other names**. If the species is or has been known by other names in common use in the past decade, then its other Standard English names are capitalized, and scientific names are italicized. Colloquial, including Cajun French, names are in lower case. Our taxonomic treatment is based on Crother (2012), Fouquette and Dubois (2014), and Van Dijk et al. (2014), as well as subsequent taxonomic revelations based on publications and input from colleagues.

**Subspecies**. Forty-nine of the 147 species of Louisiana's amphibians and reptiles contain subspecies, although in most cases only one is found in the state. Two box turtle subspecies are provided separate accounts, due to their different morphologies and natural histories, as well as recent taxonomic instability. For the ten other polytypic species, the differences between the subspecies are provided either under Description or in the Subspecies section.

**Description**. The summary and keys for identification within each group (salamanders, anurans, turtles, lizards, and snakes) are designed to enable the reader to determine to which genus a particular animal belongs. Characteristics that distinguish between species in the same genus or similar genera are highlighted in bold. The description of each species provides the general form, the color and color pattern for adults and juveniles, and numeric values for diagnostic characters: costal groove counts for salamanders, and number of scale rows for snakes. Also, particular features such as skin texture, scalation, webbing, and pupil shape are included where pertinent.

**Size**. Lengths are provided in inches and their metric equivalents. Lengths given for the alligator, salamanders, and snakes are the total length from snout to tail tip. The maximum total length and maximum snout-vent length (SVL) are given for lizards, but only the SVL is given for the usual adult and hatchling lengths (except for the Texas Horned Lizard, for which only the total length is provided). Anuran measurements are the snout-urostyle length, which is the distance from the tip of the snout to the posterior end of the urostyle ("tailbone"). Turtle lengths are the straight-line carapace length (CL) measured in the middle of the top shell (but not over the curve).

**Voice**. For anurans, the general tone and duration of the call is described.

**Habitat**. Habitat describes the general terrain and vegetative- or water-body type in which the particular species occurs (see above, Landscape and Habitats).

**Natural history**. Information on the general behavior, activity patterns, microhabitat use, reproductive output, and food and feeding habits is provided. Occasional vignettes relate to the discovery of some species.

**Distribution and status**. A description of the geographic area within Louisiana that each species inhabits supplements the visual information provided by each distribution map. The distribution on each map is in most cases the known or estimated historic range and does not show regions from which a species may be extirpated, unless otherwise stated. The general population trend (stable, declining, etc.) is provided, as well as legal protected status if available. Species of Conservation Concern is a formal but not legally binding categorization for species whose occurrences are tracked by the Louisiana Natural Heritage Program (LNHP).

**Photographs.** The selection of photographs is meant to portray the range of dorsal color pattern variation in each species, as well as coloration of the underside, close-ups of certain features, and appearance of juveniles. An effort was made to use photographs of Louisiana specimens, but that was not possible in every case. All specimens that are portrayed from outside of Louisiana resemble those that would be found in the state.

# Checklist of Louisiana Amphibians and Reptiles

## SALAMANDERS (ORDER CAUDATA)

Sirens (Family Sirenidae)
    Lesser Siren (*Siren intermedia*)

Newts (Family Salamandridae)
    Eastern Newt (*Notophthalmus viridescens*)

Mole Salamanders (Family Ambystomatidae)
    Spotted Salamander (*Ambystoma maculatum*)
    Marbled Salamander (*Ambystoma opacum*)
    Mole Salamander (*Ambystoma talpoideum*)
    Small-mouthed Salamander (*Ambystoma texanum*)
    Eastern Tiger Salamander (*Ambystoma tigrinum*)

Waterdogs (Family Proteidae)
    Gulf Coast Waterdog (*Necturus beyeri*)
    Red River Waterdog (*Necturus louisianensis*)

Amphiumas (Family Amphiumidae)
    Two-toed Amphiuma (*Amphiuma means*)
    Three-toed Amphiuma (*Amphiuma tridactylum*)

Lungless Salamanders (Family Plethodontidae)
Louisiana Slimy Salamander (*Plethodon kisatchie*)
Mississippi Slimy Salamander (*Plethodon mississippi*)
Southern Red-backed Salamander (*Plethodon serratus*)
Webster's Salamander (*Plethodon websteri*)
Southern Dusky Salamander (*Desmognathus auriculatus*)
Spotted Dusky Salamander (*Desmognathus conanti*)
Four-toed Salamander (*Hemidactylium scutatum*)
Southern Two-lined Salamander (*Eurycea cirrigera*)
Three-lined Salamander (*Eurycea guttolineata*)
Dwarf Salamander (*Eurycea quadridigitata*)
Mud Salamander (*Pseudotriton montanus*)
Red Salamander (*Pseudotriton ruber*)

## ANURANS (FROGS AND TOADS, ORDER ANURA)

North American Spadefoots (Family Scaphiopodidae)
Eastern Spadefoot (*Scaphiopus holbrookii*)
Hurter's Spadefoot (*Scaphiopus hurterii*)

True Toads (Family Bufonidae)
Dwarf American Toad (*Bufo [Anaxyrus] charlesmithi*)
Southern Toad (*Bufo [Anaxyrus] terrestris*)
Fowler's Toad (*Bufo [Anaxyrus] fowleri*)
East Texas Toad (*Bufo [Anaxyrus] velatus*)
Oak Toad (*Bufo [Anaxyrus] quercicus*)
Gulf Coast Toad (*Bufo [Incilius] nebulifer*)

Tree Frogs (Family Hylidae)
Blanchard's Cricket Frog (*Acris blanchardi*)
Eastern Cricket Frog (*Acris crepitans*)
Southern Cricket Frog (*Acris gryllus*)
Spring Peeper (*Pseudacris crucifer*)
Cajun Chorus Frog (*Pseudacris fouquettei*)
Ornate Chorus Frog (*Pseudacris ornata*)
Strecker's Chorus Frog (*Pseudacris streckeri*)

Eastern Gray Tree Frog (*Hyla versicolor*)
Cope's Gray Tree Frog (*Hyla chrysoscelis*)
Bird-voiced Tree Frog (*Hyla avivoca*)
Pine Woods Tree Frog (*Hyla femoralis*)
Green Tree Frog (*Hyla cinerea*)
Squirrel Tree Frog (*Hyla squirella*)
Barking Tree Frog (*Hyla gratiosa*)
Cuban Tree Frog (*Osteopilus septentrionalis*) [Introduced]

Rain Frogs (Family Eleutherodactylidae)
Greenhouse Frog (*Eleutherodactylus planirostris*) [Introduced]
Rio Grande Chirping Frog (*Eleutherodactylus cystignathoides*)
[Introduced]

Narrow-mouthed Frogs (Family Microhylidae)
Eastern Narrow-mouthed Toad (*Gastrophryne carolinensis*)

True Frogs (Family Ranidae)
Crawfish Frog (*Rana [Lithobates] areolata*)
Dusky Gopher Frog (*Rana [Lithobates] sevosa*)
Pickerel Frog (*Rana [Lithobates] palustris*)
Southern Leopard Frog (*Rana [Lithobates] sphenocephala*)
Bronze Frog (*Rana [Lithobates] clamitans*)
Pig Frog (*Rana [Lithobates] grylio*)
Bullfrog (*Rana [Lithobates] catesbeiana*)

## CROCODILIANS (ORDER CROCODILIA)

Alligators (Family Alligatoridae)
American Alligator (*Alligator mississippiensis*)

## TURTLES (ORDER TESTUDINES)

Softshells (Family Trionychidae)
Florida Softshell (*Apalone ferox*) [Introduced]

Spiny Softshell (*Apalone spinifera*)
Smooth Softshell (*Apalone mutica*)

Freshwater Turtles (Family Emydidae)
Chicken Turtle (*Deirochelys reticularia*)
Ringed Sawback (*Graptemys oculifera*)
Pearl River Map Turtle (*Graptemys pearlensis*)
Northern Map Turtle (*Graptemys geographica*)
False Map Turtle (*Graptemys pseudogeographica*)
Ouachita Map Turtle (*Graptemys ouachitensis*)
Sabine Map Turtle (*Graptemys sabinensis*)
Diamondback Terrapin (*Malaclemys terrapin*)
Southern Painted Turtle (*Chrysemys dorsalis*)
River Cooter (*Pseudemys concinna*)
Pond Slider (*Trachemys scripta*)
Gulf Coast Box Turtle (*Terrapene carolina major*)
Three-toed Box Turtle (*Terrapene carolina triunguis*)
Ornate Box Turtle (*Terrapene ornata*)

Tortoises (Family Testudinidae)
Gopher Tortoise (*Gopherus polyphemus*)

Sea Turtles (Family Cheloniidae)
Green Sea Turtle (*Chelonia mydas*)
Hawksbill Sea Turtle (*Eretmochelys imbricata*)
Loggerhead Sea Turtle (*Caretta caretta*)
Kemp's Ridley Sea Turtle (*Lepidochelys kempii*)

Leatherback Sea Turtle (Family Dermochelyidae)
Leatherback Sea Turtle (*Dermochelys coriacea*)

Snapping Turtles (Family Chelydridae)
Common Snapping Turtle (*Chelydra serpentina*)
Alligator Snapping Turtle (*Macrochelys temminckii*)

American Mud Turtles (Family Kinosternidae)
Common Mud Turtle (*Kinosternon subrubrum*)

Razor-backed Musk Turtle (*Sternotherus carinatus*)
Loggerhead Musk Turtle (*Sternotherus minor*)
Stinkpot (*Sternotherus odoratus*)

## SCALY REPTILES (ORDER SQUAMATA)

### Lizards (Suborder Sauria)

True Geckos (Family Gekkonidae)
Sri Lankan House Gecko (*Hemidactylus parvimaculatus*)
[Introduced]
Mediterranean Gecko (*Hemidactylus turcicus*) [Introduced]

Anoles (Family Dactyloidae)
Carolina Green Anole (*Anolis carolinensis*)
Cuban Brown Anole (*Anolis sagrei*) [Introduced]

North American Scaly Lizards (Phrynosomatidae)
Texas Horned Lizard (*Phrynosoma cornutum*)
Prairie Fence Lizard (*Sceloporus consobrinus*)

Lateral-fold Lizards (Family Anguidae)
Slender Glass Lizard (*Ophisaurus attenuatus*)
Eastern Glass Lizard (*Ophisaurus ventralis*)

Racerunners (Family Teiidae)
Six-lined Racerunner (*Aspidoscelis sexlineatus*)

Skinks (Family Scincidae)
Little Brown Skink (*Scincella lateralis*)
Coal Skink (*Plestiodon anthracinus*)
Southern Prairie Skink (*Plestiodon obtusirostris*)
Common Five-lined Skink (*Plestiodon fasciatus*)
Southeastern Five-lined Skink (*Plestiodon inexpectatus*)
Broad-headed Skink (*Plestiodon laticeps*)

## Snakes (Suborder Serpentes)

Weak-jawed Blind Snakes (Family Typhlopidae)
  Brahminy Blind Snake (*Indotyphlops braminus*) [Introduced]

Swivel-jawed Snakes (Family Dipsadidae)
  Ring-necked Snake (*Diadophis punctatus*)
  Common Worm Snake (*Carphophis amoenus*)
  Western Worm Snake (*Carphophis vermis*)
  Red-bellied Mud Snake (*Farancia abacura*)
  Rainbow Snake (*Farancia erytrogramma*)
  Eastern Hog-nosed Snake (*Heterodon platirhinos*)
  Pine Woods Snake (*Rhadinaea flavilata*)

Water Snakes (Family Natricidae)
  Dekay's Brown Snake (*Storeria dekayi*)
  Red-bellied Snake (*Storeria occipitomaculata*)
  Rough Earth Snake (*Haldea striatula*)
  Smooth Earth Snake (*Virginia valeriae*)
  Glossy Swamp Snake (*Liodytes rigida*)
  Graham's Crawfish Snake (*Regina grahamii*)
  Mississippi Green Water Snake (*Nerodia cyclopion*)
  Diamond-backed Water Snake (*Nerodia rhombifer*)
  Plain-bellied Water Snake (*Nerodia erythrogaster*)
  Salt Marsh Snake (*Nerodia clarkii*)
  Southern Water Snake (*Nerodia fasciata*)
  Common Water Snake (*Nerodia sipedon*)
  Western Ribbon Snake (*Thamnophis proximus*)
  Eastern Ribbon Snake (*Thamnophis saurita*)
  Common Garter Snake (*Thamnophis sirtalis*)

Typical Snakes (Family Colubridae)
  Rough Green Snake (*Opheodrys aestivus*)
  North American Racer (*Coluber constrictor*)
  Coachwhip (*Masticophis flagellum*)
  Southeastern Crowned Snake (*Tantilla coronata*)
  Flat-headed Snake (*Tantilla gracilis*)

Red Corn Snake (*Pantherophis guttatus*)
Slowinski's Corn Snake (*Pantherophis slowinskii*)
Texas Rat Snake (*Pantherophis obsoletus*)
Gray Rat Snake (*Pantherophis spiloides*)
Eastern Pine Snake (*Pituophis melanoleucus*)
Louisiana Pine Snake (*Pituophis ruthveni*)
Scarlet Snake (*Cemophora coccinea*)
Scarlet King Snake (*Lampropeltis elapsoides*)
Eastern Milk Snake (*Lampropeltis triangulum*)
Western Milk Snake (*Lampropeltis gentilis*)
Yellow-bellied King Snake (*Lampropeltis calligaster*)
Black King Snake (*Lampropeltis nigra*)
Speckled King Snake (*Lampropeltis holbrooki*)

Fixed-fang Snakes (Family Elapidae)
Harlequin Coral Snake (*Micrurus fulvius*) **VENOMOUS**
Texas Coral Snake (*Micrurus tener*) **VENOMOUS**

Vipers (Family Viperidae)
Copperhead (*Agkistrodon contortrix*) **VENOMOUS**
Cottonmouth (*Agkistrodon piscivorus*) **VENOMOUS**
Pygmy Rattlesnake (*Sistrurus miliarius*) **VENOMOUS**
Eastern Diamondback Rattlesnake (*Crotalus adamanteus*)
   **VENOMOUS**
Timber Rattlesnake (*Crotalus horridus*) **VENOMOUS**

SPECIES ACCOUNTS

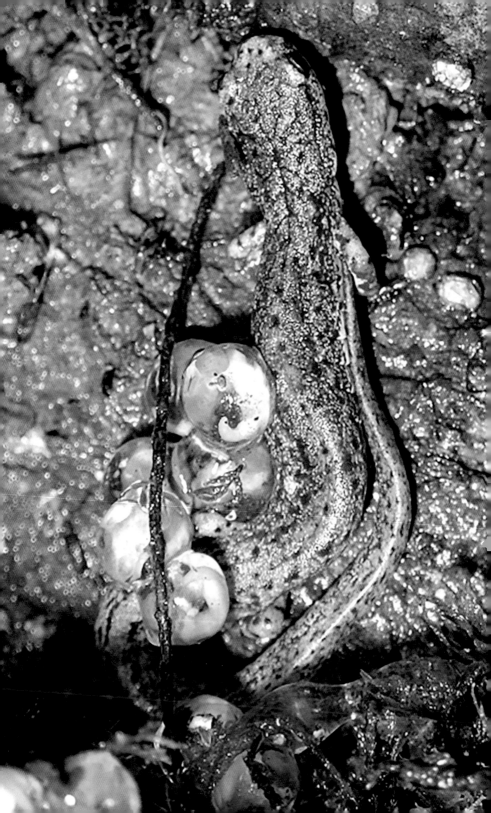

# Salamanders

## IDENTIFICATION

Most salamanders possess a somewhat elongated body, four limbs, and a tail. All Louisiana salamanders, except those of the genus *Plethodon,* deposit their eggs in or near water, and the eggs hatch into aquatic larvae. *Plethodon* deposit their eggs in damp areas below the ground or in or under logs, and these hatch into miniature versions of the adults. All of the aquatic larvae possess feathery, external gills, which are resorbed in all species except for the Sirens (*Siren*) and Waterdogs (*Necturus*).

Key characters: Most salamander species have costal grooves on their sides that correspond with each trunk vertebra and rib. Costal groove counts vary among species. The presence or absence of a nasolabial groove is diagnostic, as well as the cross-sectional shape of the tail.

a. normally-proportioned salamander

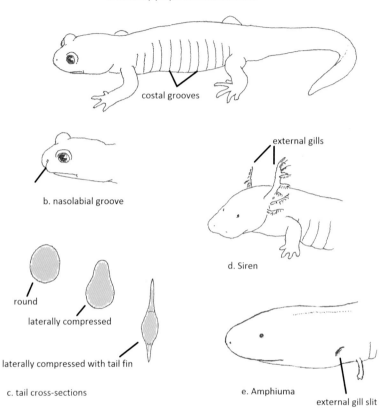

costal grooves

b. nasolabial groove

external gills

d. Siren

round

laterally compressed

laterally compressed with tail fin

c. tail cross-sections

e. Amphiuma

external gill slit

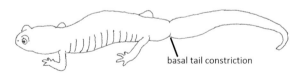

basal tail constriction

f. Four-toed Salamander

# KEY TO SALAMANDER GENERA

**1a.** External gills present (fig. d) . . . . . **2**

**1b.** No external gills (fig. a) . . . . . **3**

**2a.** Long, eel-like body with only the front limbs (fig. d) . . . . . *Siren,* pp. 38–39

**2b.** Normally shaped body with all four limbs and four toes on hind feet, and lives in large, flowing streams and rivers . . . . . *Necturus,* pp. 52–55

**2c.** Normally shaped body with all four limbs, five toes on hind feet (except Four-toed and Dwarf Salamanders), less than four inches (100 mm) long, and not found in a large flowing stream or river; larva of a species that loses the external gills . . . . . **4**

**3a.** Long and eel-like with four tiny, spindlelike limbs (fig. e) . . . . . *Amphiuma,* pp. 56–59

**3b.** Normally proportioned body and limbs (fig. a) . . . . . **4**

**4a.** No nasolabial groove . . . . . **5**

**4b.** Nasolabial groove present (fig. b) . . . . . **6**

**5a.** No costal grooves and grainy texture to the skin . . . . . *Notophthalmus,* pp. 40–41

**5b.** Costal grooves present and has smooth skin . . . . . *Ambystoma,* pp. 42–51

**6a.** Tail rounded throughout in cross-section (fig. c) . . . . . **7**

**6b.** Tail laterally compressed, at least at the tip (fig. c) . . . . . **8**

**7a.** Tail lacks a basal constriction, and venter is dark or finely speckled . . . . . *Plethodon,* pp. 60–67

**7b.** Tail has a basal constriction (fig. f), and venter is white with a few black spots . . . . . *Hemidactylium,* pp. 72–73

**8a.** Black dots on the back and a pink venter . . . . . *Pseudotriton,* pp. 80–83

**8b.** Black lines on the body, at least between the dorsal and lateral color . . . . . *Eurycea,* pp. 74–79

**8c.** Irregular dark markings on the upper sides, and a pale bar from the eye to the angle of the jaw . . . . . *Desmognathus,* pp. 68–71

## Lesser Siren (*Siren intermedia*)

**Other names**: sole

**Subspecies**: Western Lesser Siren (*S. i. nettingi*)

**Description**: Lesser Sirens are **eel-like** in appearance, with **forelimbs only** and with **external gills** present throughout their lives. The eyes are tiny and set flush with the head. They are olive, dark brown, or dark gray above, covered with tiny black dots. A pale yellow or dull white band runs across the top of the mouth toward the gills, often extending posteriorly beyond the forelimbs, where it fades into the ground color. The lower sides are usually slightly paler than the back. The underside is palest on the throat and chest, which are covered with mingled pale and dark flecks. There is often a dark midventral band. Juveniles are very dark gray, nearly black, and the labial stripe is very distinct yellow to orange and may run along the sides of the body. There is an orange vertebral stripe, and a transverse orange mark on the back of the head. Costal grooves number 32–37.

**Size**: Maximum length 20.2 inches (514 mm); adults usually 7.2–17.8 inches (182–453 mm); larvae 0.4–0.5 inches (11–12 mm) long at hatching.

**Habitat**: Lesser Sirens are completely aquatic, favoring lacustrine waters and bayous with a bottom layer of muck, leaves, and/or sticks. Ideal sites also possess submerged or emergent aquatic vegetation. They occupy many habitats in Louisiana, provided that permanent wetlands or ephemeral ponds are present. They have been reliably reported in slightly brackish waters in coastal marshes.

**Natural history**: Lesser Sirens seem to be nocturnal; at night they may be found moving about in shallow water. By day they are usually encountered in muck, leaf mats, and dense aquatic vegetation. In ephemeral wetlands they take refuge in mud pockets, and if the mud dries sufficiently prior to rains, they will secrete a cocoon about their bodies to retain moisture. During mid- to late winter, females produce clutches of 100–1,500 (usually 200–1,000) eggs, which are deposited in pockets in the substrate. Sexual maturity is reached in about two years. Lesser Sirens feed on aquatic vegetation, aquatic insects, and other small, aquatic arthropods, small clams and snails, worms, and occasionally tadpoles. When captured, they often emit clicks or squeals of distress.

**Distribution and status**: Lesser Sirens occur statewide, except in coastal marshes with a moderate to high salinity content. Their populations have not been evaluated, but they remain fairly easy to locate in their habitats, which are abundant.

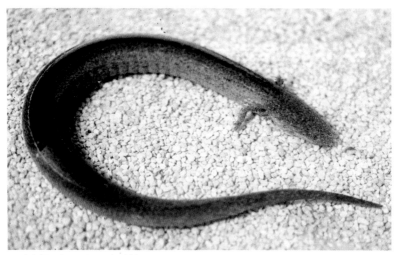

1a adult (East Baton Rouge Parish)

1b venter (East Baton Rouge Parish)

1c anterior (Caldwell Parish)

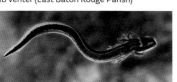

1d larva/juvenile (Sevier Co., AR)

## Eastern Newt (*Notophthalmus viridescens*)

**Other names**: Spotted Newt, red eft

**Subspecies**: Central Newt (*N. v. louisianensis*)

**Description**: Eastern Newts are small salamanders with well-proportioned limbs and a slightly compressed to finlike tail. Unlike other Louisiana salamanders, the **skin has a slightly grainy texture**. The upper part of the body and tail is olive (aquatic stage) to reddish or dark brown (terrestrial stage, "eft"), and the lower half is dull yellow to orange. The entire body is sprinkled with black dots, and a dark stripe may pass through the eye along each side of the head. Newts often possess a row of a half dozen small red spots, encircled by black, on the upper sides. During the aquatic stage, newts acquire a caudal fin that is yellow with black dots. Juvenile coloration is similar to that of terrestrial adults. There are **no costal grooves**.

**Size**: Maximum length 4.9 inches (125 mm); adults usually 2.5–4.0 inches (64–100 mm); metamorphs 1.3–1.6 inches (33–40 mm).

**Habitat**: Eastern Newts occur in cypress lakes, ponds, freshwater marshes, and ephemeral wetlands, such as woodland sloughs, gum ponds, and swamps. During the terrestrial stage, they occupy forests in the vicinity of these aquatic sites.

**Natural history**: Adult Eastern Newts gather at aquatic breeding sites during winter. Females attach single eggs to submerged vegetation; the total number that a female deposits each season is unknown. Larvae metamorphose as ephemeral wetlands dry from midspring to early summer. However, in permanent wetlands, larvae may skip the terrestrial life stage and reach adult size after over a year in the water. Typically, following metamorphosis, juvenile newts, called efts, disperse into woodlands, spending most of their time under logs, in leaf litter, or below the surface of the ground. In permanent wetlands, adults may remain aquatic throughout their lives. Eastern Newts eat invertebrates, including worms, insects, spiders, juvenile clams, and crawfish.

**Distribution and status**: Eastern Newts occur over most of Louisiana, except in coastal areas of brackish and salt marsh. Due to their widespread distribution and continued observations throughout the state, their populations are considered stable.

2a terrestrial adult with red spots (St. Martin Parish)

2b adult without red spots (Atchafalaya Basin)

2c adult (Ouachita Parish)

2d adult male, aquatic stage (Sebastian Co., AR)

2e terrestrial eft (Catahoula Parish)

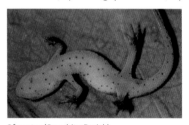
2f venter (Ouachita Parish)

2g juvenile (St. Martin Parish)

## Spotted Salamander (*Ambystoma maculatum*)

**Description**: Spotted Salamanders are of moderately robust build with a tail that is somewhat laterally compressed. The **back is dark gray to black with a row of 5–8 large, circular yellow spots on each upper side**. The yellow spots continue onto the sides of the tail. The head is also adorned with a few spots, and these may be orange. The entire underside and lower sides are pale pinkish gray or lavender gray, often with tiny white dots. Juveniles are colored similar to adults, though the yellow spots may be smaller and less well developed. There are usually 12, but occasionally 11 or 13, costal grooves.

**Size**: Maximum length 9.8 inches (248 mm); adults usually 4.7–7.2 inches (120–182 mm); metamorphs 1.1–2.0 inches (27–52 mm).

**Habitat**: Spotted Salamanders occur in forested habitats from hardwood bottoms to pine-dominated uplands. They are most often found in mixed pine-hardwood forest in the vicinity of breeding ponds.

**Natural history**: Spotted Salamanders spend most of their lives in burrows and other underground chambers. During cool seasons they may be found under logs. They breed in ephemeral wetlands, from puddles and flooded ruts to small swamps, which they migrate to when such areas begin to fill with early winter rains. Reproduction takes place during early to midwinter. Females deposit several gelatinous clumps with 20–330 eggs in each. Spotted Salamanders feed on arthropods, worms, and slugs.

**Distribution and status**: Spotted Salamanders occur over most of the state, except in the nonforested coastal zones and extensive bottomlands such as the Atchafalaya Basin. They do not occur south of Lake Pontchartrain, nor along riverine forests that extend through coastal marsh and prairie. Little is known of their current population levels, but because they continue to be found in numbers over much of the state, their populations are considered stable.

3a adult (Grant Parish)

3b adult (Ouachita Parish)

3c venter (Grant Parish)

3d juvenile (Grant Parish)

## Marbled Salamander (*Ambystoma opacum*)

**Description**: Marbled Salamanders are somewhat stout, robust salamanders. The tail is slightly compressed on the sides. The underside and sides are black up to the level of the eyes, and the upper portion of the head and back is silvery white. There is a black patch on the crown, and **large black blotches or saddles connect with the black of the sides to interrupt the white zone from the neck to the tail tip.** Juveniles are gray above, covered in pale flecks, and have a row of pale spots along the sides. Within a year of metamorphosis, the pale spots begin to coalesce and enlarge until the adult color pattern develops. There are 11 or 12 costal grooves.

**Size**: Maximum length 5.0 inches (127 mm); adults usually 3.0–4.3 inches (77–108 mm); metamorphs 1.8–2.7 inches (45–68 mm).

**Habitat**: Marbled Salamanders inhabit woodlands, usually hardwood dominated, from bottomland hardwoods and swamp margins to forested uplands.

**Natural history**: Marbled Salamanders spend most of their lives underground in burrows but can be found under logs during all but the hottest months of summer. As temperatures begin to drop in late September, adults migrate to breeding areas prior to their filling from rainfall. Females deposit clutches of 40–120 eggs in damp depressions, where they tend the clutch until the pond or swamp begins to fill. Larvae metamorphose as the wetlands dry in midspring, at which time the metamorphs disperse into the surrounding forest. Marbled Salamanders eat arthropods, worms, and snails. When perturbed, Marbled Salamanders may arch their bodies and tails, and exude a sticky, milky, noxious substance from glands on the top of the tail.

**Distribution and status**: Marbled Salamanders occur in forested areas over most of Louisiana, except in the coastal zone. They are absent from south of Lake Pontchartrain and from the lower Atchafalaya Basin. They remain widely distributed in the state, and their populations are considered stable.

4a adult (Catahoula Parish)

4b adult (Atchafalaya Basin)

4c venter (Sabine Parish)

4d juvenile (East Baton Rouge Parish)

4e metamorph (East Carroll Parish)

## Mole Salamander (*Ambystoma talpoideum*)

**Description**: Mole Salamanders have a stocky build. The **head is relatively oversized**, the **trunk is short**, and the tail is laterally compressed. The dorsum is brown to very dark gray, **covered by pale blue-gray flecks and patches that are densest on the sides, producing a frosted, lichenlike appearance**. The underside is gray, almost completely covered with pale blue or gray flecks. Juveniles are brown, mottled with black, speckled with blue flecks on the sides, and often have a pale line along each side of the body. There are usually **10, rarely 11, costal grooves**.

**Size**: Maximum length 4.8 inches (122 mm); adults usually 3.2–4.4 inches (82–113 mm); metamorphs 1.8–2.8 inches (46–70 mm).

**Habitat**: Mole Salamanders occur in wooded and forested areas, including bottomland hardwoods, pine flatwoods, and upland mixed pine-hardwood forests.

**Natural history**: Mole Salamanders are primarily fossorial, living in burrows. They come to the surface during the breeding season as ponds begin to fill (late fall to late winter), but surface activity may last only a week or two each year. Breeding sites are typically ephemeral ponds and ruts that retain water for at least several months. Females lay a total of 205–505 eggs, which they deposit in several to dozens of small clumps on submerged objects. If breeding sites retain water for a year or more, larvae may remain in the ponds, reaching lengths that equal those of terrestrial adults. Presumably the adults and larvae feed on invertebrates.

**Distribution and status**: Mole Salamanders occur statewide except for the coastal zone, the region south of Lake Pontchartrain, the Atchafalaya Basin, and most of southwestern Louisiana. Their distribution is spotty, often with dozens of miles between known sites. However, new sites have been discovered since the 1980s, and declines at previously known sites are not evident. For those reasons, Mole Salamander populations are considered secure.

5a adult (St. Tammany Parish)

5b adult (East Feliciana Parish)

5c adult (Caldwell Parish)

5d venter (Union Co., AR)

5e juvenile (Hancock Co., MS)

## Small-mouthed Salamander (*Ambystoma texanum*)

**Description**: Small-mouthed Salamanders have a **long trunk** and a **relatively small head** in relation to the body. The tail is rounded at its base but gradually becomes laterally compressed toward the end. The back is dark gray to brown, and the sides are pale to medium gray. **Nearly the entire upper body down to the sides of the belly is covered by brown or speckled pale gray patches that reduce the ground color to irregular fragments, giving the salamander a frosted or lichen-covered appearance**. The underside is dark brown or dark gray with scattered pale spots. Juveniles are dark with pale dots that increase in size as they age, until the adult color pattern is achieved. There are **14 or 15 costal grooves**.

**Size**: Maximum length 7.0 inches (178 mm); adults usually 4.0–5.3 inches (101–134 mm); metamorphs 1.9–2.4 inches (48–60 mm).

**Habitat**: Small-mouthed Salamanders occur in forested low areas, preferably those dominated by hardwoods and often those with a palmetto understory. They occur sparingly in uplands in the vicinity of isolated swamps and large gum ponds.

**Natural history**: Small-mouthed Salamanders spend most of their time in underground burrows, coming to the surface only after fall and winter rains begin to fill breeding ponds. Breeding takes place from December to February, and adults may be found under logs near breeding sites until early spring. Females produce 250–800 eggs, which they attach singly or in groups of two or three to submerged objects. They feed on worms and arthropods.

**Distribution and status**: Small-mouthed Salamanders occur throughout Louisiana, except for open country in the coastal zone, and areas of extensive uplands. Their population status in Louisiana is unknown. They seem to have disappeared from many sites in southeastern Louisiana, and adult numbers appear to be reduced at some breeding sites.

6a adult (Vermilion Parish)

6b adult (St. Martin Parish)

6c adult (East Baton Rouge Parish)

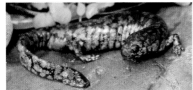

6d adult (Harris Co., TX)

6e adult (Caldwell Parish)

6f venter (East Baton Rouge Parish)

6g juvenile (East Baton Rouge Parish)

## Eastern Tiger Salamander (*Ambystoma tigrinum*)

**Description**: Tiger Salamanders are of moderately robust build, and the tail is laterally compressed. They are **black or dark gray, slightly paler on the underside, and except for the middle of the belly, are covered with numerous, large rounded or oval spots that are yellow or tan**. The juveniles are similar in color, but the yellow spots are smaller and more diffuse. There are usually 12 costal grooves.

**Size**: Maximum length 12.9 inches (327 mm); adults usually 6.3–8.3 inches (160–210 mm); metamorphs 2.9–3.7 inches (73–93 mm).

**Habitat**: In Louisiana, Tiger Salamanders occur or occurred in semi-open pine woodlands or mixed flatwoods, in the vicinity of ephemeral breeding ponds.

**Natural history**: Tiger Salamanders seem to leave their underground retreats only for one or two annual breeding events that may last only a few days each. Such events occur during winter, when passing rain fronts fill breeding sites. Known sites are ephemeral ponds and adjacent roadside ditches, which cover a half acre or less and reach a maximum depth of under two feet. Females deposit egg masses containing 13–165 (usually 30–70) eggs, which are attached to submerged stems. Larvae feed on aquatic invertebrates and tadpoles. The diet of adults in Louisiana is unknown, but in the northern United States it includes worms, insects, and other arthropods, as well as small amphibians and reptiles. Tiger Salamander larvae are often sold as fish bait or as aquarium pets called "axolotls." These larvae originate from the Great Plains and may escape and metamorphose, appearing in the vicinity of fishing places.

**Distribution and status**: Tiger Salamanders are known from several sites in Louisiana. There is a specimen collected at Gayle, Caddo Parish, from the 1920s, but none have been found there since. A series of larvae were found at a gum pond in St. Tammany Parish in 1964, but despite considerable survey effort between 1990 and 2005, they have not been found there since. The only sites from which they are currently known are in the vicinity of a half-dozen, closely spaced ephemeral ponds in western Vernon Parish. Due to its limited distribution, the Tiger Salamander is considered a Species of Conservation Concern.

7a adult (Vernon Parish)

7b adult (Vernon Parish)

7c venter (Benton Co., AR)

7d metamorph (Vernon Parish)

## Gulf Coast Waterdog (*Necturus beyeri*)

**Description**: Waterdogs are salamanders of medium build with a laterally compressed tail fin and **external red gills**. There are **four toes on the hind feet**. The eyes are tiny and set flush with the head. The dorsum and sides of the tail are tan or medium brown to dark gray, grading to gray or dull yellow on the lower sides, with irregular black spots or blotches, and mingled with many yellow dots. The **underside is dull white or pale gray to brown gray, also with large dark spots**. A black stripe passes through each eye from the snout to the rear of the jaws. **Juvenile color pattern is similar to that of adults**, but the dark spots are fewer in number. There are no costal grooves.

**Size**: Maximum length 10.1 inches (256 mm); adults usually 6.5–8.4 inches (164–214 mm); larvae 0.6–1.1 inches (16–27 mm) long at hatching.

**Habitat**: Waterdogs are permanently aquatic and occur in lotic streams and rivers, preferably those with relatively clear water. Streams must have adequate shelter, such as overhanging banks with root tangles, and complex stream bottom topography with ample leaf beds and submerged logs.

**Natural history**: Waterdogs are nocturnal and are most active during winter when water temperatures are coldest. By day the adults conceal themselves in cavities beneath tree roots and overhanging stream banks, or under submerged logs. Larvae and juveniles reside in submerged leaf beds. In late April through May, females deposit clutches of 27–76 eggs in depressions beneath submerged logs, and they may tend the nest for a portion of the incubation period. Waterdogs feed on small clams, aquatic insects, and other aquatic arthropods, especially crawfish.

**Distribution and status**: Gulf Coast Waterdogs are separated into two populations by the Red-Mississippi Alluvial Valley. One population is found in the Florida Parishes, the other in upper reaches of the Calcasieu and Sabine River watersheds. The population status of waterdogs has not been evaluated since the early 1980s. Due to a lack of population trend data and on account of extensive degradation of some stream habitats due to sand mining, it is considered a Species of Conservation Concern.

8a adult (Washington Parish)

8b adult (St. Tammany Parish)

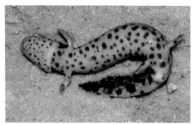

8c venter (St. Tammany Parish)

8d juvenile (St. Tammany Parish)

## Red River Waterdog (*Necturus louisianensis*)
**Other names**: mudpuppy, *Necturus maculosus louisianensis*

**Description**: Waterdogs are salamanders of medium build with a laterally compressed tail fin and **external red gills**. There are **four toes on the hind feet**. The eyes are tiny and set flush with the head. The dorsum is tan, medium brown, or gray brown, with numerous irregular black spots or blotches, mingled with many pale flecks. The **underside is pale gray to brown gray, with a pale gray to whitish midventral region that has few or no spots**. The sides are usually darker than the back and overlain by large dark blotches. A black stripe passes through each eye from the snout to the rear of the jaws. **The juvenile color pattern is very different from that of the adults**: the back is yellow with a wide black or dark gray band down the middle and another along each side of the body and tail. There are no costal grooves.

**Size**: Maximum length 12.1 inches (307 mm); adults usually 6.4–9.6 inches (163–243 mm); larvae 0.9–1.0 inches (23–25 mm) long at hatching.

**Habitat**: Waterdogs are permanently aquatic and occur in lotic streams and rivers, preferably those with relatively clear water. They may also occur in impoundments. Streams must have adequate shelter such as overhanging banks with root tangles, and complex stream bottom topography with ample leaf mats and submerged logs.

**Natural history**: Waterdogs are nocturnal and are most active in winter when water temperatures are coldest. By day the adults conceal themselves in cavities beneath tree roots and overhanging stream banks, or under submerged logs. Larvae and juveniles reside in submerged leaf beds. In late April through May, females deposit clutches of 22–91 eggs in depressions beneath submerged logs, and they may tend the nest for a portion of the incubation period. Waterdogs feed on small clams and fish, worms, aquatic insects, and other aquatic arthropods, especially crawfish.

**Distribution and status**: Red River Waterdogs are found in the Red and Ouachita River watersheds, except in the downstream reaches below Evangeline and Caldwell Parishes. The population status of Waterdogs has not been evaluated. Due to a lack of population trend data, and due to extensive degradation of some stream habitats from sand mining and siltation from forestry practices, it is considered a Species of Conservation Concern.

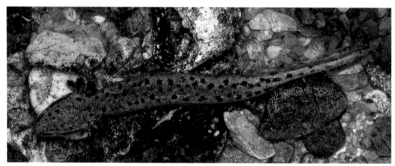

9a adult (Clark Co., AR)

9b adult (Clark Co., AR)

9c venter (Randolph Co., AR)

9d juvenile (Grant Parish)

## Two-toed Amphiuma (*Amphiuma means*)
**Other names**: ditch eel

**Description**: Amphiumas are elongate, **eel-like** salamanders with four **minute limbs** and external gill slits but **no visible gills**. The Two-toed Amphiuma has **two toes on each limb**. The eyes are tiny and set flush with the head. The back is very dark gray to nearly black, the **underside and lower sides dark gray**. The middle of the throat bears a dark patch. Juveniles resemble the adults in coloration.

**Size**: Maximum length 45.7 inches (1,162 mm); adults usually 18.1–36.5 inches (460–926 mm); hatchlings 1.9–2.5 inches (50–64 mm).

**Habitat**: Two-toed Amphiumas occur in flatwoods habitats, especially in slash pine woodland and bayheads. They are also known from poorly drained uplands of mixed pine-hardwood forest. They inhabit ditches, swamps, oxbows, shallow streams, gum ponds, and pothole ponds.

**Natural history**: Two-toed Amphiumas are primarily aquatic and nocturnal, spending the day submerged in crawfish burrows or other holes, chambers, and shelters near or below the water level. They will crawl overland on rainy nights. They feed on a variety of aquatic invertebrates (including snails and aquatic insects), as well as fish and frogs, but they favor crawfish. Females produce clutches of 25–210 eggs in damp depressions in swamps, under logs, or in cavities and holes, and they remain coiled about the eggs until they are submerged by rainfall events. The eggs are thought to be laid in January. Amphiumas can deliver a powerful bite when handled.

**Distribution and status**: Two-toed Amphiumas occur only in the Florida Parishes. There are numerous records in the flatwoods north of Lake Pontchartrain, but there are few, scattered records north of the flatwoods and west of the Tangipahoa River. Two-toed Amphiumas continue to be found at historic localities, as well as at a number of newly discovered sites. For that reason, its populations are considered stable.

10a adult (St. Tammany Parish)

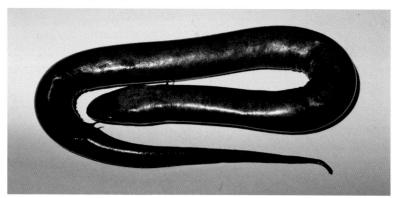

10b venter (St. Tammany Parish)

10c anterior (St. Tammany Parish)

10d juvenile (Wake Co., NC)

## Three-toed Amphiuma (*Amphiuma tridactylum*)
**Other names**: congre, Congo eel, ditch eel

**Description**: Amphiumas are elongate, **eel-like** salamanders with four **minute limbs** and external gill slits but **no visible gills**. They have **three toes on each limb**, though one or more may be missing due to injury. The eyes are tiny and set flush with the head. The back is dark brown or gray, distinctly set off from the **pale gray underside and lower sides**. The middle of the throat bears a dark patch. Juveniles resemble the adults in color pattern but tend to be darker.

**Size**: Maximum length 41.7 inches (1,060 mm); adults usually 18.1–39.8 inches (460–1,010 mm); hatchlings 1.7–2.5 inches (43–64 mm).

**Habitat**: Three-toed Amphiumas occur in most freshwater habitats in Louisiana, including permanent and ephemeral wetlands, and ditches.

**Natural history**: Three-toed Amphiumas are primarily aquatic and nocturnal, spending the day submerged in crawfish burrows or other holes, chambers, and shelters near or below the water level. They appear to favor shallow (less than five feet deep), lentic waters with silt, clay, or muck bottoms. They will crawl overland on rainy nights. They are often observed at night in shallow ditches and ponds. They feed on a variety of aquatic invertebrates (including worms, snails, and aquatic insects), as well as occasional small fish, but they favor crawfish over other prey. Females produce clutches of 40–350 eggs, which they lay in damp depressions in swamps, under logs, or in cavities and holes, and they remain coiled about the eggs until they are submerged by rainfall events. The eggs are thought to be laid in fall and brooded for up to five months. Amphiumas can deliver a powerful bite when handled.

**Distribution and status**: Three-toed Amphiumas occur statewide, except for extensive areas of brackish and salt marshes. Amphiuma populations can be remarkably dense, as evidenced by kills from chemical flushing and dredging of ditches. Due to the wide geographic range and population sizes, they are considered secure.

11a adult (St. Charles Parish)

11b venter (Faulkner Co., AR)

11d juvenile (East Baton Rouge Parish)

11c anterior (Reelfoot Lake, TN)

## Louisiana Slimy Salamander (*Plethodon kisatchie*)

**Description**: Slimy Salamanders are of medium build with a tail that is round in cross-section. Adults are black above and black to dark gray below. The back and sides have scattered **white spots, about half the size or more of the eye, which may be especially dense along the sides**. The **spots often have a vague brassy tint** and become larger and more numerous in older adults. The underside is not (or sparsely) spotted, and the throat is gray. Juveniles are dark overall and covered above with numerous tiny, metallic flecks. Adult males possess a grayish pink, oval gland under the chin. There are 15 costal grooves.

**Size**: Maximum length 5.8 inches (148 mm); adults usually 4.0–5.5 inches (101–140 mm); hatchling size is unknown.

**Habitat**: Slimy Salamanders occur in well-drained uplands in mixed pine-hardwood forest with a closed canopy. Known sites consist of mature forest with little or no ground or midstory vegetation.

**Natural history**: The Louisiana Slimy Salamander was discovered in 1965 by Dr. Neil Douglas of the University of Louisiana at Monroe and has since been found at a little over thirty sites. They are most frequently observed under fallen logs during cool, wet weather. When exposed, Slimy Salamanders use leaf litter and burrows to escape. During warm and dry conditions, they retreat under the surface, using the same burrows to reach underground chambers. Females lay 14–23 eggs, probably in the fall and probably underground or in damp, rotting logs. Known prey includes insects (ants, beetles) and centipedes. When captured, Slimy Salamanders exude from skin glands a sticky mucus that leaves a gluey mess on one's hands.

**Distribution and status**: The core range of the Louisiana Slimy Salamander is the forested uplands from northeastern Rapides Parish north to the vicinity of Ruston. Isolated populations occur in the Sicily Island Hills and a few miles east of Coushatta. A single individual was collected near Gorum and is the only known specimen recorded west of the Red

River. This Slimy Salamander is relatively difficult to find, even at known sites and under optimum conditions. Surveys conducted for this species during 2001 and 2007 found fewer individuals than surveys conducted in the 1970s. For those reasons, and because of its spotty distribution, it is considered a Species of Conservation Concern in Louisiana.

12a adult (Rapides Parish)

12b adult (Catahoula Parish)

12c venter (Rapides Parish)

## Mississippi Slimy Salamander (*Plethodon mississippi*)

**Description**: Slimy Salamanders are of moderate build with a tail that is rounded in cross-section. Adults are black above and black to dark gray below. The **back and sides are covered with white spots, those on top of the back less than half the size of the eye.** The white spots may be large and densely packed along the sides. The spots become larger and more numerous in older adults, but in some populations they are nearly absent. The underside is not (or sparsely) spotted, and the throat is gray. Juveniles are dark overall and covered above with a fine sheen of metallic flecks and scattered white dots. Adult males possess a grayish pink, oval gland under the chin. There are 15 costal grooves.

**Size**: Maximum length 5.6 inches (142 mm); adults usually 2.8–5.1 inches (72–130 mm); hatchlings 0.8–1.0 inches (20–26 mm).

**Habitat**: Slimy Salamanders occur in closed-canopy forest, preferably dominated by hardwoods, but also in mixed pine-hardwood forest and marginally in old-growth pine stands. They range from well-drained uplands to bottomland forest.

**Natural history**: Slimy Salamanders are most frequently observed under fallen logs during cool, wet weather. When exposed, they use leaf litter and burrows to escape. During warm and dry conditions, they retreat under the surface, using the burrows to reach underground chambers. Females lay 14–23 eggs, probably in late summer and probably underground or in damp, rotting logs. They probably feed on arthropods and other small invertebrates. When captured, Slimy Salamanders exude from skin glands a sticky mucus that leaves a gluey mess on one's hands.

**Distribution and status**: The Mississippi Slimy Salamander occurs throughout much of the Florida Parishes, except in the Mississippi River floodplain. There appears to be a general decrease in the number of observations since the 1990s, and ongoing surveys should determine whether this is a cyclic trend or true decline.

13a adult (Chickasaw Co., MS)

13b adult (Pearl River Co., MS)

13c adult, spotless (East Feliciana Parish)

13d venter (St. Tammany Parish)

13e juvenile (West Feliciana Parish)

## Southern Red-backed Salamander (*Plethodon serratus*)

**Description**: Southern Red-backed Salamanders are somewhat slender in form, with small limbs and a tail that is round in cross-section. They possess a **distinct red band or zones of red markings over the top of the back, from neck to tail tip**. The **edges of the red band on the trunk possess serrate margins**. Red patches may also be present on the top of the head, neck, and base of the forelimbs. The sides and underside are speckled with dark gray and white to produce a "salt-and-pepper" appearance. The chin and throat are dull white. The young are colored like the adults. There are 18 or 19 costal grooves.

**Size**: Maximum length 4.1 inches (105 mm); adults usually 3.2–4.0 inches (80–100 mm); hatchlings 0.8–0.9 inches (20–23 mm).

**Habitat**: Red-backed Salamanders occur in upland mixed pine-hardwood forests and longleaf pine woodland where rocks are exposed at or near the surface.

**Natural history**: Red-backed Salamanders spend most of their lives below the surface but can be found under rocks and logs during cold, wet conditions from December to March. In the summer, females deposit a clutch of 4–9 eggs in logs or below the surface and guard them until they hatch in August. They feed on small arthropods (ants, beetles, spiders), small snails, and worms. The Red-backed Salamander was first found in Louisiana in 1968 by members of a Southwestern Louisiana University field trip led by Ed Keiser and Paul Conzelman.

**Distribution and status**: Red-backed Salamanders have been found in five separate localities in DeSoto, Natchitoches, Rapides, and Catahoula Parishes. Their Louisiana range roughly follows that of the Catahoula Formation, and they probably occur in intervening locations. One such site was discovered in 2014 by Eric Rittmeier. Due to its limited range, it is considered a Species of Conservation Concern.

14a young adult (Catahoula Parish)

14b old adult (Catahoula Parish)

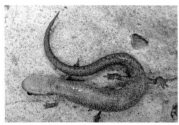

14c venter (Natchitoches Parish)

14d juvenile (LeFlore Co., OK)

## Webster's Salamander (*Plethodon websteri*)

**Description**: Webster's Salamanders are some- what slender in form, with small limbs and a tail that is round in cross-section. They possess a **reddish or orange band on the top of the back**, from neck to tail tip. The **edges of the red band on the trunk possess dark, irregular wavy margins**. Orange patches may also be present on the neck and base of the forelimbs. The sides are flecked with dark gray and white to produce a "salt-and-pepper" appearance. In older salamanders the orange color of the back may break into patches that are obscured by darker color, though the top of the tail remains brightly colored. The underside bears an irregular pattern of pale gray and dark gray vermiculations. The young are colored like the adults, but the band on the dorsum is more distinct. There are 18 costal grooves.

**Size**: Maximum length 3.2 inches (82 mm); adults usually 2.5–3.1 inches (63–80 mm); hatchlings 0.8–0.9 inches (20–23 mm).

**Habitat**: Webster's Salamanders occur in upland hardwood forest, cut by steep ravines, where sandstone outcrops are present on or near the surface.

**Natural history**: Webster's Salamanders spend most of their lives below the surface but can be found under rocks and logs during cold, wet con- ditions from December to March. In February and March, they migrate to areas of sandstone, where they remain underground until cool weather and rain bring them to the surface in late fall. During the summer, females deposit a cluster of 3–8 eggs in logs or underground and guard them until they hatch in late summer. They feed on small arthropods (insects, mites, centipedes, spiders), small snails, and worms. The Webster's Salamander was first found in Louisiana in 1978 by A. J. Meier.

**Distribution and status**: Webster's Salamanders have been found in Lou- isiana only in the headwaters of Polly Creek, West Feliciana Parish. All of those found in Louisiana have come from an area of less than five acres. Due to its limited range in the state, it is considered a Species of Conser- vation Concern.

15a adult (West Feliciana Parish)

15b adult (Hinds Co., MS)

15c adult (Hinds Co., MS)

15d venter (West Feliciana Parish)

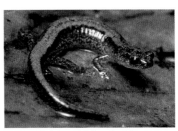
15e juvenile (West Feliciana Parish)

## Southern Dusky Salamander (*Desmognathus auriculatus*)

**Description**: Dusky Salamanders are of moderately robust build with a laterally compressed tail beyond the base. The upper half of the body is brown or gray, usually with vague, irregular dark markings. A row of white dots, one spot between each costal groove, runs along the upper and lower sides of the body, with that of the lower sides continuing onto the tail. The **crest of the tail bears a pale dull orange to tan stripe that is connected to several pale spots for a short way back from the hind limbs**. There is a dull orange or pale tan bar from the rear of the eye to the corner of the mouth. The sides of the body are paler than the back, and the underside is dark gray and covered with pale flecks. Adults are often very dark brown when captured but will lighten appreciably if retained for several hours. **Juveniles have a broad, reddish brown or tannish orange band down the back, with slightly scalloped edges where pale spots connect**. The band color continues onto the tail, where it breaks into pale spots separated by the tail crest. There are 13 or 14 costal grooves.

**Size**: Maximum length 5.0 inches (128 mm); adults usually 2.9–4.6 inches (74–118 mm); metamorphs 1.6–1.9 inches (41–47 mm).

**Habitat**: Southern Dusky Salamanders have been found in swamp margins, riverine forests, ephemeral woodland sloughs, boggy flatwoods, and bayheads. Currently, they seem to be limited to the latter.

**Natural history**: Southern Dusky Salamanders remain close to the waterline, living under logs, leaf mats, and piles of sticks and mud deposited along streams. They prefer sites with wet, mucky soil and retreat into burrows as water tables drop. Females deposit a clutch of 9–26 eggs in small chambers in the ground or under logs and leaf mats within a few feet of water. They guard the nest during the summer. The eggs hatch after fall rains provide a suitable habitat for the larvae. They feed on worms, snails, arthropods, and smaller salamanders. When uncovered, Dusky Salamanders quickly dash for nearby burrows.

**Distribution and status**: Southern Dusky Salamanders once ranged from the western edge of the Atchafalaya Basin eastward, including low forested extensions from Terrebonne Parish to Jefferson and Orleans Parishes. They disappeared from most of this range during the 1970s and 1980s, and since 1990 have only been found at several localities in St. Tammany Parish (indicated on the map in dark red). They have similarly declined or disappeared from many seemingly pristine sites in the remainder of their range from Mississippi to the Carolinas. The cause of the disappearances is unknown. It is considered a Species of Conservation Concern.

Recent genetic studies have shown that the true Southern Dusky Salamander is restricted to the Coastal Plain east of the Apalachicola River in Florida and into the Carolinas. What has been called the Southern Dusky Salamander from western Florida into eastern Louisiana consists of one or more undescribed species.

16a adult (St. Tammany Parish)

16b adult (St. Tammany Parish)

16c adult (Forrest Co., MS)

16d venter (St. Tammany Parish)

16e venter (St. Tammany Parish)

16f juvenile (Forrest Co., MS)

## Spotted Dusky Salamander (*Desmognathus conanti*)

**Description**: Dusky Salamanders are of moderate to moderately robust build with a laterally compressed tail beyond the base. The upper surface is tan or brown with six very large, irregular orange or tan patches on either side of the midline that bear dark outer margins. The patches become obscure with age, and adults often display only the irregular black outlines of the patches along the upper sides. A row of white dots, one spot between each costal groove, may run along the upper and lower sides of the body, with that of the lower sides sometimes continuing onto the tail. The **top of the tail bears a pale dull orange to tan stripe that is broad at the base with wavy margins**. (Unfortunately, this character bears resemblance to the Southern Dusky Salamander in many individuals from central and northern Louisiana, and identification of these must rely on geography.) There is a dull white or pale tan bar from the rear of the eye to the corner of the mouth. The sides are slightly paler than the back, grading to a pale to medium gray underside that is covered with pale specks. Adults are often very dark brown when captured, but will lighten appreciably if retained for several hours. **In juveniles, the large spots on the back are bright orange or reddish and may coalesce to form a reddish dorsal band**. There are 13 or 14 costal grooves.

**Size**: Maximum length 5.0 inches (127 mm); adults usually 2.2–3.7 inches (55–94 mm); metamorphs 1.3–1.6 inches (33–42 mm).

**Habitat**: Spotted Dusky Salamanders occur in closed canopy forests, primarily in upland terrain, near and along streams, springs, and seepages.

**Natural history**: Spotted Dusky Salamanders remain close to the water line, especially where there is a film of clear water over muck, sand, or gravel substrates. They live under logs and leaf mats, as well as in soft, saturated substrates, and retreat into burrows as water tables drop. Females deposit a clutch of 13–41 eggs in small chambers in the substrate or under logs and leaf mats within a few feet of water. They guard the nest during the summer. The eggs hatch after fall rains provide a suitable habitat for the larvae. They feed on snails and arthropods. When uncovered, Dusky Salamanders often dive into nearby, submerged burrows.

**Distribution and status**: Spotted Dusky Salamanders occur in the Florida Parishes and in upland portions of western Louisiana from northern Calcasieu and Evangeline Parishes northward. They are absent from the upper Mississippi Delta, and there are no records from west of the Red River north of southern De Soto Parish. Unlike the Southern Dusky Salamander, populations of this species remain fairly abundant at many of their historic localities. Given this abundance and the species' extensive range, its populations are considered stable.

17a adult male (Washington Parish)

17b adult (West Feliciana Parish)

17c adult (Wilkinson Co., MS)

17d venter (Washington Parish)

17e venter (Forrest Co., MS)

17f juvenile (Catahoula Parish)

### Four-toed Salamander (*Hemidactylium scutatum*)

**Description**: Four-toed salamanders are of medium build with **four toes on all limbs**. The **tail is rounded in cross-section and bears a basal constriction**. The upper side is reddish tan to dull orange, usually overlaid by fine, dark markings on the top of the head and back, and with a scattering of black dots. The snout, shoulders, limb bases, and top of the tail are tan or dull orange, paler than the back. The sides are sprinkled dark gray and white. The **underside is porcelain white with scattered black spots**. Juveniles are colored like the adults. There are **13 or 14 costal grooves**.

**Size**: Maximum length 4.0 inches (102 mm); adults usually 2.0–3.5 inches (51–90 mm); metamorphs usually 0.7–0.9 inches (18–24 mm).

**Habitat**: In Louisiana, Four-toed Salamanders have been found in slash pine flatwoods and in flatwood stands of spruce pine, magnolia, beech, and oak forest in the vicinity of gum ponds.

**Natural history**: Four-toed Salamanders are rarely found at the surface except during the mating and nesting period in fall and winter. They can be found under logs or in mats of moss near water. Females deposit clutches of 25–57 eggs in the latter, sometimes communally, and at least one will guard the eggs until they hatch in late February or early March. The nests are typically positioned on raised ground or low root balls so that the newly hatched larvae can wriggle downward into shallow water. The adults feed on snails, worms, and arthropods. When disturbed, Four-toed Salamanders may make a flat coil with their body and tail, and may turn upside down to expose the white underside. They will also drop their tails by breakage at the basal constriction.

**Distribution and status**: Until recently, Four-toed Salamanders were known from a pair collected north of Baton Rouge in 1924 and another one collected in St. Tammany Parish in 1964. In 1995 a population was discovered in Ascension Parish by Frank Marabella. Subsequently, several more populations have been discovered on the east side of Baton Rouge and in

East Feliciana Parish. Because Four-toed Salamanders are strongly associated with gum ponds that have moss beds, and have recently been found at only three such sites, they are considered a Species of Special Concern.

18a adult (East Feliciana Parish)

18b adult (East Baton Rouge Parish)

18c venter (Ascension Parish)

18d metamorph (Adair Co., KY)

## Southern Two-lined Salamander (*Eurycea cirrigera*)

**Description**: Two-lined Salamanders are moderately slender salamanders with a tail that is rounded in cross-section but becomes thin and bladelike near its tip. There are **five toes on the hind feet**. The dorsum is yellowish or metallic gold, with the color darkest around the midline and brightest on the top of the tail. The middle of the **back and top of the head bear a number of small black spots**. **A black band passes along the upper sides, originating on the snout, passing through the eye, and continuing to near the tail tip**. The sides below the band are dull yellow and usually unmarked. The underside is bright yellow, though somewhat translucent, and the chin and throat have a pink tint. Juveniles are colored like the adults. There are 13 or 14 costal grooves.

**Size**: Maximum length 4.3 inches (110 mm); adults usually 2.6–4.0 inches (67–101 mm); metamorphs 2.0–2.8 inches (52–72 mm).

**Habitat**: Two-lined Salamanders occur in forests, primarily in uplands, with clear streams and seeps. They follow riparian forests into flatlands.

**Natural history**: Two-lined Salamanders occur in and near clear seeps and streams, and can be found under surface objects and leaf mats over a film of water. They can also be found on slopes where springs and seeps originate, away from surface water. During winter, females deposit clutches of 15–115 (usually 40–50) eggs on the bottom of submerged objects or in submerged debris mats. The larvae may require at least a year to metamorphose. The adults and larvae feed on small invertebrates, both terrestrial and aquatic. Adults also feed on small worms and snails.

**Distribution and status**: Two-lined Salamanders occur in the Florida Parishes, except in the Mississippi River floodplain. Their populations are largest in Washington and northern Tangipahoa Parishes, where spring-fed seeps and streams are abundant. Populations appear to be stable.

19a adult (Tishomingo Co., MS)

19b adult (Washington Parish)

19c venter (Tangipahoa Parish)

## Three-lined Salamander (*Eurycea guttolineata*)

**Description**: Three-lined Salamanders are relatively slender with a laterally compressed tail. There are **five toes on the hind feet**. The back and top of the head and tail are yellow to very dull yellow, with a **black stripe down the middle of the back** that stops just beyond the hind limbs. The top of the head usually has several black spots. **A black band runs along each side from the side of the snout to the tail tip, and is often invaded by yellow or white spots.** The lower sides are white or yellow, covered with irregular black markings and spots. The underside is white to pale pinkish or yellowish white, with irregular gray markings. The juveniles are colored like the adults. There are 13 or 14 costal grooves.

**Size**: Maximum length 7.9 inches (200 mm); adults usually 4.0–6.3 inches (100–160 mm); metamorphs 1.7–2.1 inches (44–54 mm).

**Habitat**: Three-lined Salamanders occur in forested areas, both upland and lowland, primarily near streams that are fed by springs or seeps. They can also be found sparingly along swamp margins.

**Natural history**: Three-lined Salamanders occur near water, especially stream margins that have a permanent or near-surface water supply. They are usually found in leaf mats or under logs but seem to favor piles of leaves and sticks left by high water around the bases of trees. In late fall and early winter, females deposit clumps of 8–14 eggs, but the total number of clumps produced by a single female is unknown. They feed on small invertebrates, primarily insects and spiders, but also on small snails and worms.

**Distribution and status**: Three-lined Salamanders occur in the Florida Parishes. They appear to have disappeared from some suburban regions but remain fairly common at numerous other sites. For that reason, their populations are considered stable.

20a adult (Wilkinson Co., MS)

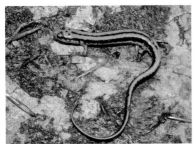

20b adult (Wilkinson Co., MS)

20c adult (East Baton Rouge Parish)

20d venter (Tangipahoa Parish)

20e juvenile (West Feliciana Parish)

## Dwarf Salamander (*Eurycea quadridigitata*)

**Description**: Dwarf Salamanders are somewhat slender in build with small limbs and a tail that is laterally compressed toward the tip. There are **four toes on each hind foot**. The top of the back has a broad, dull yellow tan, brassy, or dull reddish band that extends to the tail tip. The band usually bears a **thin, broken stripe or row of dark dots down the center** and is bordered on the **upper sides by a black stripe from the snout to near the tail tip**. The sides are dark gray, sprinkled with pale dots to create a "salt-and-pepper" appearance. The underside is pale pinkish gray on the throat, pale gray to yellow under the body, and yellow under the tail. Metamorphs are colored like the adults. There are 15–17 costal grooves.

**Size**: Maximum length 3.5 inches (90 mm); adults usually 2.1–3.0 inches (54–75 mm); metamorphs 1.0–1.6 inches (26–41 mm).

**Habitat**: Dwarf Salamanders occur in forested areas from swamp margins, bottomland hardwoods, and pine flatwoods to upland forests of mixed pine and hardwoods. They are usually found close to seeps, streams, and ponds but are occasionally encountered on hilltops and ridges.

**Natural history**: Dwarf Salamanders are most often found in marginally wet sites such as seepages and margins of flatwood ponds and swamps. There they can be found under logs or in wet leaf and sphagnum mats. Females deposit a clutch of 13–36 eggs during early winter in or near shallow or ephemeral water, such as at the base of sphagnum mats. They feed on small invertebrates including spiders, worms, mites, and ants.

**Distribution and status**: Dwarf Salamanders occur in the forested portions of Louisiana and are absent from the open coastal marsh and prairie. They are widely distributed and commonly found, and their populations are considered stable.

21a adult (Natchitoches Parish)

21b adult (Natchitoches Parish)

21c adult (Evangeline Parish)

21d adult (Natchitoches Parish)

21e venter (St. Tammany Parish)

21f juvenile (St. Tammany Parish)

## Mud Salamander (*Pseudotriton montanus*)

**Subspecies**: Gulf Coast Mud Salamander (*P. m. flavissimus*)

**Description**: Mud Salamanders are of slightly robust build with a tail that is round at the base and laterally compressed toward the tip. They are overall orange tan to orange red, though the dorsal surface may turn orange brown in older adults. The **upper surfaces, including the limbs, bear a scattering of black spots**, which are sparse or absent underneath. The **iris of the eye is dark**. Juveniles resemble the adults in coloration. There are 16 or 17 costal grooves.

**Size**: Maximum length 4.7 inches (119 mm); adults usually 3.1–4.4 inches (80–112) mm; metamorphs 2.5–3.0 inches (62–75 mm).

**Habitat**: Mud Salamanders are found in forested bogs and bayheads fed by seeps, usually near the bases of slopes and outward into spring-fed bottomland forest.

**Natural history**: Mud Salamanders have been found under logs on or near mucky seeps and streamlets in winter and spring. Presumably, they spend much of their time in subterranean chambers or in muck near the water table. Females lay their clutch of up to 30 eggs in fall, probably in submerged cavities or in springheads. Their feeding habits are unknown. Mud Salamanders are rarely encountered. At known sites and under optimal conditions, it may require a dozen or more hours of searching to find a single individual—if they are at the surface.

**Distribution and status**: Mud Salamanders are known from Washington and northern St. Tammany Parishes. Since the 1990s, they have been found at one site in the Talisheek drainage and one along the Bogue Chitto River. Because little is known of the species' life history and habits, and because it is currently known from only two sites in Louisiana, it is considered a Species of Conservation Concern.

22a adult (St. Tammany Parish)

22b venter (St. Tammany Parish)

# Red Salamander (*Pseudotriton ruber*)

**Subspecies**: Southern Red Salamander (*P. r. vioscai*)

**Description**: Red Salamanders are of moderately robust build with tails that are rounded at the base and laterally compressed toward the tip. They are salmon red above, deep pink below. They are **covered above by black spots**, which are reduced to dots on the underside, and the sides may also be frosted with white flecks. The **muzzle is marked by black and white flecks**. The back of older adults may darken to purple brown. The **iris of the eye is yellow**. Juveniles are bright red with black spots. There are 16 costal grooves.

**Size**: Maximum length 6.4 inches (162 mm); adults usually 3.9–5.8 inches (98–146 mm); metamorphs 2.4–3.1 inches (60–78 mm).

**Habitat**: Red Salamanders occur in the vicinity of springs and seeps, on or at the base of pine-hardwood forested slopes.

**Natural history**: Red Salamanders live in and near springheads and seeps, and are most often found under logs on or near such seeps, usually on slopes. Presumably, they spend the hotter months in subterranean zones of such seeps. Females lay 30–130 eggs in late summer or fall underneath submerged objects or in subterranean chambers in or over water. The larval stage lasts about 1.5–2 years. They feed on small salamanders, snails, worms, millipedes, spiders, and insects. When uncovered, Red Salamanders will bolt down water-filled burrows into their subterranean refuges.

**Distribution and status**: Red Salamanders are known only from a dozen or so sites in Washington Parish. Due to the limited range and restrictive habitat association in Louisiana, it is considered a Species of Conservation Concern.

23a adult (Washington Parish)

23b adult (Washington Parish)

23c old adult (Washington Parish)

23d venter (Washington Parish)

# Anurans
## (Frogs & Toads)

### IDENTIFICATION

All native frogs and toads (anurans) in Louisiana lay their eggs in water, and these hatch into aquatic larvae (tadpoles). After a period of development, the larvae metamorphose into juveniles (metamorphs) that bear the tailless, long-legged form of the adults. All have four toes on the front legs and five on the hind legs. However, certain features such as color pattern, warts, and glands may not begin to appear for weeks or months after metamorphosis. Unique calls of the males distinguish species.

Key characters: Anuran species can be distinguished by presence or absence of skin features, including toe webbing, texture, parotoid and pectoral glands, warts, cranial crests, dorsolateral folds, and tarsal spades. Color and color pattern are useful identification characters, but many anuran species come in a variety of colors and patterns, and individuals of some species can change color and pattern.

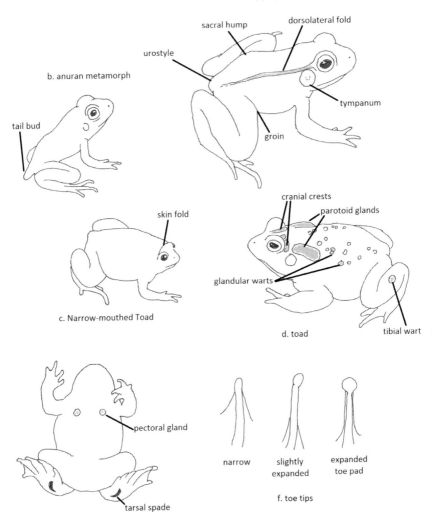

a. normally proportioned frog

sacral hump

dorsolateral fold

urostyle

b. anuran metamorph

tympanum

tail bud

groin

cranial crests

parotoid glands

skin fold

glandular warts

c. Narrow-mouthed Toad

d. toad

tibial wart

pectoral gland

narrow

slightly expanded

expanded toe pad

tarsal spade

f. toe tips

e. ventral view of Spadefoot

# KEY TO ANURAN GENERA

**1a** Lacks webs between the toes of the hind feet . . . . . **2**

**1b** Webs present between toes of hind feet . . . . . **3**

**2a** Skin fold present across the back of a small, pointed head (fig. c) . . . . . *Gastrophryne,* pp. 134–135

**2b** Lacks a skin fold, has a relatively wide, blunt head, and has a dark line down the middle of the belly . . . . . *Eleutherodactylus,* pp. 130–133

**3a** Parotoid glands and a dark spade on the heel are present (fig. e) . . . . . **4**

**3b** Lacks parotoid glands and dark spade on each heel . . . . . **5**

**4a** Eye has a horizontal pupil, and there are no pectoral glands (fig. d) . . . . . *Bufo,* pp. 92–101

**4b** Eye has a vertical pupil, and there are pectoral glands (fig. e) . . . . . *Scaphiopus,* pp. 88–91

**5a** Tips of the toes have expanded round disks that are wider than the rest of the toe (fig. f) . . . . . **6**

**5b** Disks on toe tips not or scarcely (slightly expanded) wider than the rest of the toe (fig. f) . . . . . **7**

**6a** Skin of head loose from skull, without a distinction from the skin of the back . . . . . *Hyla,* pp. 114–127

**6b** Skin of the head fused (co-ossified) to the skull, with a distinct zone behind the head where the skin becomes free of attachment . . . . . *Osteopilus,* pp. 128–129

**7a** Tympanum is indistinct or not visible, there are a half-dozen warts in irregular rows on the flanks and sides of the back, and the frog is never over 1.6 inches (41 mm) long . . . . . *Acris,* pp. 102–105

**7b** Tympanum is distinct, there are no warts, the webbing on the hind foot is less than a third the length of the longest toe, and the frog is never over 1.9 inches (49 mm) long . . . . . *Pseudacris,* pp. 106–113

**7c** Tympanum is distinct, warts may or may not be present, the webbing on the hind foot is over half the length of the longest toe, and only juveniles are under 1.5 inches (39 mm) long . . . . . *Rana,* pp. 136–149

## Eastern Spadefoot (*Scaphiopus holbrookii*)

**Description**: Eastern Spadefoots are squat-bodied, short-legged, and have **vertical pupils**. The parotoid glands are circular, and small reddish to dark brown warts are scattered on the back and sides of the body. They are **medium to dark brown to purple brown**, with a yellow to dull white, **hourglass-shaped mark** running from behind the eyes, narrowing at the shoulders, widening along the sacral ridge, and joining on the tailbone. The face and sides of the body are yellow to dull white, often with dark mottling on the sides and a **dark patch beneath each eye**. The underside is white under the throat, grading to pale gray or lavender under the body and limbs. The young are a little paler than the adults.

**Size**: Maximum length 2.9 inches (73 mm); adults usually 1.9–2.5 inches (48–63 mm); metamorphs 0.4–0.7 inches (9–16 mm).

**Voice:** A disgorging bleat that lasts several seconds.

**Habitat**: Spadefoots occur in wooded areas from pine flatwoods to upland mixed pine-hardwood forest, including riverine forest bordering sandy streams and rivers. They are absent from bottomland hardwood forest.

**Natural history**: Spadefoots seem to be entirely nocturnal, and adults are rarely encountered, except during rainy nights. They are explosive breeders and usually only breed when at least 2.5 inches of rain have fallen in a 24-hour period and temperatures are at least 60° F. Breeding events may occur from February through July. Favored breeding sites are ephemeral ponds, but they also use ditches and overflow ponds along streams and rivers. Females deposit 1,180–5,500 eggs in strings, strands, and clusters attached to submerged plants and sticks. They feed on arthropods. Spadefoots spend most of their lives in burrows that they construct by digging backward into the soil. Their skin secretions have a distinct odor and will cause burning if rubbed into one's eyes.

**Distribution and status**: Eastern Spadefoots occur in the Florida Parishes, except for the Mississippi River floodplain and swampy bottomlands.

Because of a spotty distribution and the infrequency of observations, it is considered a Species of Conservation Concern.

24a adult (St. Helena Parish)

24b adult (St. Helena Parish)

24c adult, dorsal (western FL)

24d ventral (western FL)

24e metamorph (Walton Co., FL)

## Hurter's Spadefoot (*Scaphiopus hurterii*)

**Description**: Hurter's Spadefoots are squat-bodied, short-legged, and have **vertical pupils**. The parotoid glands are circular, and small warts are scattered on the back and sides. They are **brown or olive to dark gray**, with a yellow to dull white, **hourglass-shaped mark** running from behind the eyes, narrowing at the shoulders, widening along the sacral ridge, and joining on the tailbone. The face and sides of the body are yellow to dull white, often with dark mottling on the sides. The **dark patch beneath each eye may be vague or absent**. The underside is white under the throat, grading to pale yellow, yellow green, or pinkish gray on the abdomen. The young are colored like the adults.

**Size**: Maximum length 3.3 inches (83 mm); adults usually 2.1–2.6 inches (53–66 mm); metamorphs 0.3–0.5 inches (8–12 mm).

**Voice:** A disgorging bleat that lasts several seconds.

**Habitat:** Spadefoots occur from open pine woodland to upland mixed pine-hardwood forest, including pastures, and riverine forest bordering sandy streams and rivers. They are absent from bottomland hardwood forest.

**Natural history**: Spadefoots seem to be entirely nocturnal, and adults are rarely encountered, except during rainy nights. They are explosive breeders and usually only breed when at least 2.5 inches of rain have fallen in a 24-hour period and temperatures are at least 60° F. Breeding events may occur from February through July. Favored breeding sites are ephemeral ponds, but they also use ditches and overflow ponds along streams and rivers. Females deposit 1,900–4,900 eggs in strings, strands, and clusters attached to submerged plants and sticks. They feed on arthropods and worms. Spadefoots spend most of their lives in burrows that they construct by digging backward into the soil. Their skin secretions have a distinct odor and will cause burning if rubbed into one's eyes.

**Distribution and status**: Hurter's Spadefoots occur in northern Louisiana, except for the Mississippi River Delta and Red River Valley. They occur as far south as northeastern Rapides Parish and central Vernon Parish.

It is likely that they occur at least to Evangeline and Calcasieu Parishes. Because of a spotty distribution and the infrequency of observations, it is considered a Species of Conservation Concern.

25a adult (Bienville Parish)

25b venter (Natchitoches Parish)

25c juvenile (AR)

## Dwarf American Toad (*Bufo [Anaxyrus] charlesmithi*)
**Other names**: *Anaxyrus americanus, Bufo americanus charlesmithi*

**Description**: Dwarf American Toads bear paired, elongate parotoid glands and numerous warts over the upper body and limbs. The **cranial crests are moderate in height and slightly divergent, and there are one or two distinctly enlarged warts on the tibia.** They are brown above with a pale line down the middle of the back. At times the back may develop an orange or reddish tint. The sides of the body are brown, sometimes with lighter markings. The warts on the middle of the back may have dark brown or black borders. A dark bar runs from the lower back of the eye to the angle of the mouth, and there are a few irregular dark crossbands on the limbs. The underside is dirty white, with or without dark gray mottling on the chest. Juveniles are colored like the adults.

**Size**: Maximum length in Louisiana 3.1 inches (79 mm); adults usually 2.0–2.8 inches (51–72 mm); metamorphs 0.2–0.3 inches (6–8 mm).

**Voice**: A flat, melodious trill that lasts several seconds or longer.

**Habitat**: Dwarf American Toads occur in uplands with hardwood forest and marginally into mixed pine-hardwood forest.

**Natural history**: Dwarf American Toads may be active on the forest floor during the day but become crepuscular or nocturnal during hot weather. When not active, they can be found under logs. They breed in woodland pools and streams from February through May, and females lay 1,800–14,000 eggs in strings. They feed on earthworms and arthropods.

**Distribution and status**: Dwarf American Toads occur in the Tunica Hills district of West and East Feliciana Parishes, and in western St. Helena Parish. Their populations are considered secure.

26a adult (Wilkinson Co., MS)

26b adult (West Feliciana Parish)

26c adult (Wilkinson Co., MS)

26d venter (West Feliciana Parish)

26e venter (West Feliciana Parish)

## Southern Toad (*Bufo [Anaxyrus] terrestris*)

**Other names**: *Anaxyrus terrestris*

**Description**: Southern Toads bear paired, elongate parotoid glands and numerous warts over the upper body and limbs. The **cranial crests are moderate in height and slightly divergent, with a distinct rise at their posterior ends. There are several or more enlarged warts on the tibia.** They are brown or gray above, usually with a pale line down the middle of the back. At times the back may develop an orange or reddish tint. The sides of the body are brown or gray, often mottled with darker and lighter markings. The warts on the middle of the back may have dark brown or black borders, or the back and sides may have dark spots or blotches. A dark bar runs from the lower back of the eye to the angle of the mouth, and another may be present directly below the eye. There are a few irregular dark crossbands on the limbs. The underside is dirty white, with or without dark gray mottling on the chest and sides. Juveniles are colored like the adults.

**Size**: Maximum length in Louisiana 3.1 inches (78 mm), elsewhere to 4.4 inches (113 mm); adults usually 2.0–2.8 inches (51–71 mm); metamorphs 0.2–0.4 inches (6–10 mm).

**Voice:** A flat trill that lasts several seconds or longer.

**Habitat**: Southern Toads occur in pine flatwoods and mixed pine-hardwood forests.

**Natural history**: Southern Toads may be found active on the forest floor during the day but become crepuscular or nocturnal during hot weather. They breed in ephemeral wetlands, shallow ponds, ditches, and streams from mid-February to early August, and females lay approximately 1,700–16,500 eggs in strings. They feed on earthworms, snails, and arthropods.

**Distribution and status**: Southern Toads occur in the eastern and middle Florida Parishes, occurring as far west as the eastern portions of East Feliciana and East Baton Rouge Parishes. Observations since the 1980s indicate that their recent distribution is spotty, and population trends have yet to be determined.

27a adult (St. Tammany Parish)

27b adult (St. Tammany Parish)

27c adult (Apalachicola National Forest, FL)

27d adult (Hancock Co., MS)

27e venter (St. Tammany Parish)

27f juvenile (Hancock Co., MS)

## Fowler's Toad (*Bufo [Anaxyrus] fowleri*) and East Texas Toad (*Bufo [Anaxyrus] velatus*)

**Other names**: *Anaxyrus fowleri, Bufo woodhousii fowleri*

**Description**: These toads bear paired, elongate parotoid glands and numerous warts over the upper body and limbs. The **cranial crests are low to moderate in height and scarcely divergent, and there are no distinctly enlarged warts on the tibia**. They are brown or gray brown above with a pale line down the middle of the back. At times individuals may have an overall rust or orange tint. A dark band runs from the shoulder, down and back to the groin area, and is usually bordered above by an irregular pale band on the upper sides. Groups of several warts on the middle of the back are surrounded by dark spots and/or blotches. The **color pattern of old adults may darken to such an extent that the dark blotches are obliterated**. In western Louisiana, the back tends to be darker than the upper sides of the body, and there are often pale patches over the sacral humps. A dark bar runs from the lower back of the eye to the angle of the mouth, and another dark patch is located below the eye. There are a few irregular dark crossbands on the limbs. The underside is dirty white, with or without dark gray mottling on the chest. Juveniles are colored like young adults.

**Size**: Maximum length 3.7 inches (95 mm); adults usually 1.9–3.3 inches (47–83 mm); metamorphs 0.3–0.5 inches (8–12 mm).

**Voice:** An explosive, flat vibration that lasts several seconds or longer.

**Habitat**: These toads occur in nearly all habitats, except for extensive areas of marsh and swamp, and many urban and suburban areas. They seem to be most plentiful in hardwood or mixed pine-hardwood forest in the vicinity of sandy rivers and streams.

**Natural history**: These toads may be active on the forest floor during the day but become crepuscular or nocturnal during hot weather. They breed in woodland pools, shallow ponds, ditches, and stream and river shallows from March to mid-July. Females lay 2,000–15,600 eggs in strings. They feed on arthropods.

**Distribution and status**: These toads occur throughout Louisiana, except for extensive areas of marsh. The area of contact between Fowler's Toad and the East Texas Toad is undefined but may be the Atchafalaya Basin. The two species are difficult to distinguish from one another, differentiated only by subtleties in color pattern and by genetic differences with an imprecisely known geographic boundary. Fowler's Toad seems to have disappeared from some urban areas, but it and the East Texas Toad remain fairly abundant over much of their historic range.

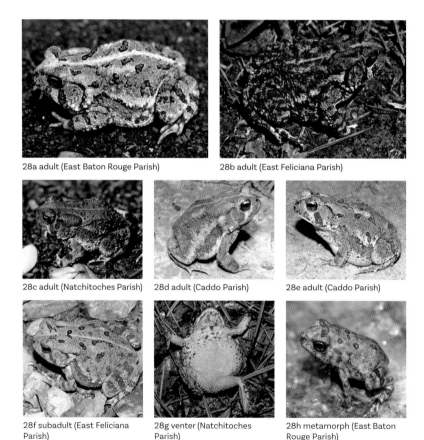

28a adult (East Baton Rouge Parish)

28b adult (East Feliciana Parish)

28c adult (Natchitoches Parish)

28d adult (Caddo Parish)

28e adult (Caddo Parish)

28f subadult (East Feliciana Parish)

28g venter (Natchitoches Parish)

28h metamorph (East Baton Rouge Parish)

## Oak Toad (*Bufo [Anaxyrus] quercicus*)
**Other names:** *Anaxyrus quercicus*

**Description**: Oak Toads are dwarfed in comparison to other Louisiana toads. They possess a pair of somewhat elongate parotoid glands behind the head, and small warts are present on the upper surface of the body and limbs. The **cranial crests are low and slightly divergent**. Oak Toads are gray with a dull white to yellow stripe down the middle of the back from the snout to the tailbone. **On either side of the stripe are three pairs of irregular dark gray to nearly black blotches**. A pale band runs from the back of the parotoid gland to the groin area, and a broader dark gray to nearly black band borders it below on the middle to lower sides. A dark patch is present on the side of the head between the eye and parotoid gland. The underside is dull white to pale gray and may be mottled with small, dark markings on the chin, chest, and sides. Juveniles are colored like the adults.

**Size**: Maximum length 1.3 inches (33 mm); adults usually 0.9–1.1 inches (22–29 mm); metamorphs 0.3 inches (7–9 mm).

**Voice:** A flat, repeated peep, each lasting about a second.

**Habitat**: Oak Toads occur primarily in pine flatwoods and coastal live-oak hammocks. They also occur in mixed pine-hardwood forests in flatwoods and marginally into uplands.

**Natural history**: Oak Toads may be active on the forest floor during the day and evening, and will breed from the late afternoon, into the night. They breed in ephemeral wetlands, ruts, and roadside ditches from mid-April to mid-August, and females deposit 300–500 eggs in short strands. They feed on insects and spiders, favoring ants.

**Distribution and status**: Oak Toads occur in the eastern and middle Florida Parishes, ranging west to near the Amite River in East Baton Rouge and East Feliciana Parishes. Their populations appear to be stable, at least around the north shore of Lake Pontchartrain.

29a adult (St. Tammany Parish)

29b adult (Hancock Co., MS)

29c adult (Hancock Co., MS)

29d venter (Hancock Co., MS)

29e juvenile (Collier Co., FL)

## Gulf Coast Toad (*Bufo [Incilius] nebulifer*)

**Other names**: *Incilius nebulifer, Ollotis nebulifer, Bufo valliceps*

**Description**: Gulf Coast Toads bear paired, somewhat triangular parotoid glands and numerous warts over the upper body and limbs. The **cranial crests are high and widely divergent, producing a concave trough between them on the top of the head.** The middle of the back is brown to very dark brown, often with irregular dark spots or blotches. A dull yellow band runs down the middle of the back, and another **broad, pale band runs from the back of the head at the parotoid glands, back and down the sides to the groin area**. The lower sides below the pale band are dark brown to nearly black, breaking into spots and mottling on the sides of the belly. There are a few irregular dark crossbands on the limbs. The underside is dirty white with dark gray or black patches and mottling on the chest and belly. Juveniles are less boldly colored than the adults and have a dark gray belly.

**Size**: Maximum length in Louisiana 3.7 inches (95 mm), elsewhere to 5.1 inches (130 mm); adults usually 2.2–3.5 inches (57–89 mm); metamorphs 0.3–0.5 inches (8–12 mm).

**Voice**: A long, flat, grating trill.

**Habitat**: Gulf Coast Toads favor bottomland hardwoods, mixed pine-hardwood flatwoods, and marsh margins. They extend marginally into uplands with mixed forest and longleaf pine woodland. They are also adapted to urban and suburban environments.

**Natural history**: Gulf Coast Toads may be found abroad during the day but become crepuscular or nocturnal during hot weather. When not active they can be found in shallow shelters and under logs and litter. They breed from April to mid-September in marshes (including brackish), swamp margins, woodland pools, ditches, and puddles, and females lay strings of up to 20,000 eggs. They are known to feed on arthropods and smaller toads. Gulf Coast Toads are the common yard toad of urban areas in southern Louisiana and seem capable of breeding in potentially polluted waters, such as ditches filled with runoff from industrial sites.

**Distribution and status:** Gulf Coast Toads occur in the southern half of Louisiana, being recorded as far north as Fort Polk and the Alexandria area. They remain common to abundant over most of their range, and their populations are considered to be stable.

30a adult (St. Martin Parish)

30b adult (East Baton Rouge Parish)

30c adult (East Feliciana Parish)

30d venter, adult (St. Tammany Parish)

30e venter, juvenile (East Baton Rouge Parish)

30f juvenile (East Baton Rouge Parish)

## Blanchard's Cricket Frog (*Acris blanchardi*) and Eastern Cricket Frog (*Acris crepitans*)
**Other names**: Northern Cricket Frog

**Description**: Cricket Frogs are small, with relatively long hind limbs and warts on the upper body and hind limbs. Their **color pattern is extremely variable.** The upper surface may be plain brown, gray, or olive green, with or without darker bars along the sides and shoulders and extending upward to the sacral hump. There are usually dark

bars along the mouth, crossbands on the limbs, a dark patch around the back of the tympanum, and a dark triangular mark from atop each eyelid, extending in a point to the back of the head. Some cricket frogs possess a reddish, tan, or bright green **broad band down the middle of the back** that contrasts with the basic dorsal color. An **irregular dark band runs along the rear of each thigh.** The **webbing of the hind foot extends to near or onto the base of the first segment of the longest toe.** The underside of the body is white and that of the limbs is gray. Juveniles are colored like the adults.

**Size**: Maximum length 1.6 inches (41 mm); adults usually 0.7–1.1 inches (18–29 mm); metamorphs 0.5–0.6 inches (12–14 mm).

**Voice:** Rapid, repetitious clicks.

**Habitat:** Blanchard's Cricket Frogs occur in nearly all habitats, from intermediate marsh to forested uplands. In the Florida Parishes, they are relatively uncommon in pinelands where the Southern Cricket Frog is abundant. They are absent from most urban areas and saline marshes.

**Natural history:** Cricket Frogs are most often seen on the ground in forests and poorly drained areas of grass, and along streams, swamps, and other breeding sites. Due to their small size, they easily rest upon and hop across floating plants and may be found far from shore in lakes and marshes covered in such vegetation. They breed from March to October during warm weather (over 60° F) in shallow ditches, ruts, ponds, swamp and marsh margins, and ephemeral wetlands. Females lay 125–430 eggs, singly or in small clumps of 2–7 eggs, and these are not attached to objects.

They feed on aquatic and terrestrial insects, and spiders. Cricket Frogs can jump many times their body length, often changing direction with each successive jump. This behavior serves to disorient potential predators.

**Distribution and status**: Cricket Frogs occur statewide, except in areas of brackish and salt marsh. The Blanchard's and Eastern Cricket Frogs are distinguished on the basis of genetic differences. Due to sparse genetic sampling in Louisiana, the boundary between the ranges of the two species is unknown. Further sampling may demonstrate that only the Blanchard's Cricket Frog occurs in Louisiana. Cricket Frogs have declined in a few areas, such as urban zones, but remain common to abundant elsewhere. Thus, their statewide population status is considered stable.

31a adult (East Baton Rouge Parish)

31b adult (Iberville Parish)

31c adult (Lafayette Parish)

31d adult (Atchafalaya Basin)

31e adult (East Baton Rouge Parish)

31f adult (Hardin Co., TX)

31g venter (St. Martin Parish)

31h juvenile (St. Martin Parish)

## Southern Cricket Frog (*Acris gryllus*)

**Subspecies**: Coastal Plain Cricket Frog (*A. g. gryllus*)

**Description**: Cricket Frogs are small, with relatively long hind limbs and warts on the upper body and hind limbs. Their **color pattern is extremely variable**. The upper surface may be tan, brown, or gray. A dark bar extends upward and forward from the groin to the middle of the back, and another runs along the lower sides of the body, then upward and forward to the base of each arm. There are vertical dark and light bars along the mouth, with a white streak that runs from the lower rear of the eye to the angle of the mouth. There are crossbands on the limbs, a dark bar behind the eye, and a dark triangular mark from atop each eyelid, extending in a point to the back of the head. There is a **thin stripe down the middle of the back, usually less than the diameter between the eyes**, which may be reddish, tan, or bright green. A **straight-edged dark band runs along the rear of each thigh**. The **webbing of the hind foot extends to the base or middle of the second segment of the longest toe**. The underside of the body is white to pale yellow, and that of the limbs is gray. Juveniles are colored like the adults.

**Size**: Maximum length 1.3 inches (32 mm); adults usually 0.7–1.1 inches (19–28 mm); metamorphs 0.3–0.6 inches (9–15 mm).

**Voice:** Rapid, repetitious clicks.

**Habitat**: Southern Cricket Frogs reach their greatest abundance in pine flatwoods, bayheads, and mixed pine-hardwood flats. They also occur in uplands of pine or pine-hardwood and in freshwater marsh.

**Natural history**: Cricket Frogs are most often seen on the ground in forests and poorly drained areas of grass, and along streams, bayheads, and other breeding sites. They breed from March to October during warm weather in shallow ditches, ponds, swamp and marsh margins, and ephemeral wetlands. Females lay up to 340 eggs in small clumps of 7–10 eggs, and these are not attached to objects. They feed on insects and spiders. Cricket Frogs can jump many times their body length, often changing direction with each successive jump. This behavior serves to disorient potential predators.

**Distribution and status**: Southern Cricket Frogs occur in the Florida Parishes. They seem to have disappeared from southern East Baton Rouge Parish but are abundant elsewhere. Their population status is considered secure.

32a adult (St. Tammany Parish)

32b adult (Tishomingo Co., MS)

32c adult (St. Tammany Parish)

32d adult (St. Tammany Parish)

32e adult (Apalachicola National Forest, FL)

32f adult (Washington Parish)

32g venter (St. Tammany Parish)

32h juvenile (St. Tammany Parish)

## Spring Peeper (*Pseudacris crucifer*)

**Description**: Spring Peepers are small frogs of average build with slightly expanded toe tips. Above they are pale tan or pale gray to reddish tan with a **darker X-shaped mark across the back,** from behind the eyes to the rear of the sides of the body, though it may be irregular or broken. There is a triangular, boomerang-shaped mark between the eyes and a similar, irregular or broken bar across the rear of the back. The **face bears a dark band extending from the snout past the eye and tympanum that usually continues back over the arm to the lower sides.** The **upper lip lacks a white stripe**, and there are dark cross-bars on the limbs. The underside of the body is dull white, usually with dark dots, and that of the limbs pale yellow to pinkish purple. Juveniles are colored like the adults.

**Size**: Maximum length 1.6 inches (41 mm); adults usually 1.0–1.4 inches (26–36 mm); metamorphs 0.3–0.6 inches (9–14 mm).

**Voice**: Short, repetitious peeps with a slightly ascending pitch.

**Habitat**: Spring Peepers occur in forested areas, except in coastal cheniers and river batture.

**Natural history**: When not at breeding sites, Spring Peepers are usually found on the forest floor. They breed in ephemeral ponds, ditches, and flooded fields from mid-November to April. Females produce about 240–1,650 eggs, which are attached singly to vegetation or leaves in shallow water. They feed on insects and other small arthropods. Rarely seen outside of the breeding season, Spring Peepers are usually only encountered by chance in the forest.

**Distribution and status**: Spring Peepers occur statewide in forested areas but are absent from the marshlands of the coastal zone and prairie in southwest Louisiana. They remain common in many areas, and their populations are considered secure.

33a adult (St. Tammany Parish)

33b adult (Caldwell Parish)

33c adult (Ascension Parish)

33d venter (East Baton Rouge Parish)

33e juvenile (Scott Co., AR)

## Cajun Chorus Frog (*Pseudacris fouquettei*)
**Other names:** previously Upland Chorus Frog (*Pseudacris feriarum*)

**Description:** Chorus Frogs are small frogs of average build without expanded toe tips. Above they are pale to medium gray or tan with **three stripes or spot rows down the back** that are vaguely darker than the ground color to nearly black. The median stripe originates on the top of the snout, proceeds backward to the sacral hump,  and then forks around the tailbone. On either side, another stripe originates behind the eye and passes back to the groin. Some Chorus Frogs lack the dorsal markings. All Chorus Frogs possess a **dark brown to black band that starts at the tip of the snout, passes through each eye, back over the arm, and onto the lower sides of the body. An unbroken cream stripe borders the upper lip above the dark mouth margin**, and dark crossbars are present on the limbs. The underside of the body is white, that of the hind limbs purple gray. Juveniles are colored like the adults.

**Size:** Maximum length 1.4 inches (36 mm); adults usually 1.0–1.3 inches (25–33 mm); metamorphs 0.3–0.6 inches (8–14 mm).

**Voice:** An ascending, slow grating, as made by running a thumb along the teeth of a stiff comb, with each call lasting one or two seconds.

**Habitat:** Cajun Chorus Frogs occur in nearly all natural habitats in Louisiana other than brackish marshes, salt marshes, and extensive regions of swamp.

**Natural history:** Outside of the breeding season, Chorus Frogs are very rarely seen and seemingly vanish into the surrounding woodlands to live in the ground litter or perhaps beneath the surface. They breed in ephemeral wetlands, ditches, and swamp margins, especially sites with emergent grasses, from November to April. Females deposit 450–1,460 eggs in small clumps of 20–100 eggs each that are attached to submerged grass stems and sticks. They feed on spiders, snails, and insects.

**Distribution and status:** Cajun Chorus Frogs occur throughout Louisiana, except in extensive tracts of coastal marshes and swamp. They are widespread and commonly heard, so their populations are considered secure.

34a adult (Ouachita Parish)

34b adult (St. Martin Parish)

34c adult (Iberville Parish)

34d venter (Natchitoches Parish)

34e juvenile (Iberville Parish)

## Ornate Chorus Frog (*Pseudacris ornata*)

**Description**: Ornate Chorus Frogs are small, somewhat compact frogs that lack expanded toe tips. They are gray, brown, reddish brown, or green, with or without darker markings on the back. When present, the markings include a dark triangular mark between the eyes that points backward, a **dark band on either side of the middle of the back** running from behind the eye to the groin, and crossbars on the limbs. Another dark bar runs from the groin, upward and forward on the rear sides. All Ornate Chorus Frogs have a **black mask that originates on the snout tip, passes back through the eye and over the arm. There is a break behind the arm, and the black bar continues downward and rearward on the lower sides of the body** or breaks into one or more spots. The **upper mouth area is white**, and there is **no spot below the eye**. The underside is whitish. Juveniles are colored like the adults but with a less distinct pattern.

**Size**: Maximum length 1.4 inches (37 mm); adults usually 1.0–1.4 inches (25–35 mm); metamorphs 0.5–0.6 inches (14–16 mm).

**Voice**: Quick, repetitious plinks.

**Habitat**: Ornate Chorus Frogs occur in pine flatwoods and mixed hardwood-pine flatwoods in the vicinity of breeding sites.

**Natural history**: Ornate Chorus Frogs are secretive ground dwellers that construct burrows in loose soil among the roots of plants and are rarely seen when not breeding. They breed in ephemeral ponds such as gum and grassy flatwoods ponds from December to March. Females lay eggs in clumps of about 10–100, attached beneath the surface on grass stalks and sticks. They feed on insects and other arthropods.

**Distribution and status**: Ornate Chorus Frogs occurred in tableland bordering the Pearl River floodplain in eastern St. Tammany and Washington Parishes. In Louisiana, they were last seen in 1954 near the town of Pearl River. Unsuccessful searches of known sites in subsequent decades indicate that they are extirpated from Louisiana. The reasons for their disappearance are unknown.

35a adult (Okaloosa Co., FL)

35b adults (Okaloosa Co., FL)

## Strecker's Chorus Frog (*Pseudacris streckeri*)

**Description**: Strecker's Chorus Frogs are small, somewhat compact frogs that lack expanded toe tips. They are pale gray or gray brown with darker markings on the back. Markings include a dark triangular mark between the eyes that points backward; an **irregular, often broken dark band on either side of the middle of the back,** each running from behind the eye to the groin; and crossbars on the limbs. Another dark bar runs from the groin, upward and forward on the rear sides of the body. There is a **black mask that originates on the snout tip and passes back through the eye and over the arm. There is a break behind the arm, and the black bar continues downward and rearward on the lower sides of the body** or breaks into one or more spots. There is **usually a dark spot on the upper lip below the eye**. The underside of the body is white, and that of the hind limbs pink or pinkish gray. Juveniles are colored like the adults.

**Size**: Maximum length 1.9 inches (48 mm); adults usually 1.0–1.8 inches (25–45 mm); metamorphs 0.5–1.0 (12–25 mm).

**Voice**: A short, repeated plink-plink.

**Habitat**: In Louisiana, Strecker's Chorus Frogs have been found in pastures and woodlands of mixed pine-hardwoods.

**Natural history**: When not breeding, Strecker's Chorus Frogs are very rarely seen, spending their time in or near self-constructed burrows. They breed in ditches, flooded pastures, and shallow woodland pools from late December to early March. Females lay 150–1,000 eggs in an average of 40 clumps attached to grass and sticks just below the water surface. They feed on insects and spiders.

**Distribution and status**: Strecker's Chorus Frogs have been found in southern Caddo and northern De Soto Parishes. There is also an unverified report from Calcasieu Parish. The most recent record is from 1982, but little effort has been made to determine its current population status. It is a Species of Conservation Concern.

36a adult (Johnson Co., AR)

36b adult (Johnson Co., AR)

36c venter (Johnson Co., AR)

## Eastern Gray Tree Frog (*Hyla versicolor*)

**Description**: Eastern Gray Tree Frogs are of
moderate build with a grainy skin and enlarged,
circular toe pads. They are pale to medium gray
or brown above with darker, lichenlike patches
with black margins. The patches are irregularly
shaped and are on the middle of the back, connect
across the eyelids, and extend upward from the

groin toward the sacral hump. Another, irregular dark marking extends
from the back of the eye around the tympanum onto the shoulder and
lower sides of the body. There are crossbands on the limbs and a **white
patch beneath each eye**. The **rear of each thigh has deep yellow to orange
yellow circles that are outlined by dark brown**. At times the dorsal surface may be bright green, with or without darker markings. The underside
of the body is white to pale yellow and that of the groin and hind limbs is
orange yellow. Juveniles are colored like the adults.

**Size**: Maximum length 2.4 inches (60 mm); adults usually 1.3–2.0 inches
(32–51 mm); metamorphs 0.5–0.8 inches (13–20 mm).

**Voice**: A vibrating blast, like that of Cope's Gray Tree Frog, but only of
about one second duration and with a higher pitch.

**Habitat**: In Louisiana, Eastern Gray Tree Frogs have been found in upland
pine woodland and bottomland hardwood forest.

**Natural history**: When not breeding, Eastern Gray Tree Frogs spend
most of their time in trees and shrubs. During warm weather, they are
nocturnal, and during the day they pull their limbs close to their bodies
in tree cavities or on trunks or limbs, using their camouflaged pattern
for protection. They breed from late March at least to June in ephemeral
ponds and wetlands, ditches, and swamp margins. Females lay up to 2,600
eggs, deposited in packets of 30–40 eggs that remain as a film on the water
surface. They feed on insects. Whereas the Cope's Gray Tree Frog is diploid,
with the typical number of chromosomes (24), Eastern Gray Tree Frogs
are tetraploid, having twice as many chromosomes (48). The two species
cannot be externally distinguished, though their calls are different.

**Distribution and status**: Based on their unique call, Eastern Gray Tree Frogs occur in southwestern Louisiana in the lower Sabine River drainage. Microscopic tissue studies indicate that they also occur in scattered sites in Allen, Evangeline, Iberville, and Lafourche Parishes. Numbers of chorusing males at known sites indicate that their populations are stable.

37a adult (Vernon Parish)

37b adult (Elkhart Co., IN)

37d venter (Benton Co., AR)

37c adult (Calcasieu Parish)

37e metamorph (Benton Co., AR)

## Cope's Gray Tree Frog (*Hyla chrysoscelis*)

**Description**: Cope's Gray Tree Frogs are of moderate build with a grainy skin and enlarged, circular toe pads. They are pale to medium gray or brown gray, sometimes greenish, above with darker, lichenlike patches with or without black margins. The patches are irregularly shaped and are on the middle of the back, connect across the  eyelids, and extend upward from the groin toward the sacral hump. Another, irregular dark marking extends from the back of the eye, over the tympanum onto the shoulder and onto the lower sides of the body. There are crossbands on the limbs and a **white or pale green patch beneath each eye**. The **rear of the thighs has deep yellow to orange yellow circles that are outlined by dark brown**. The underside of the body is white, except that of the groin and hind limbs is orange yellow. Juveniles are colored like the adults.

**Size**: Maximum length 2.4 inches (60 mm); adults usually 1.4–2.0 inches (35–51 mm); metamorphs 0.6–0.7 inches (15–17 mm).

**Voice**: A grating bleat, lasting about 1.5 to 2.5 seconds.

**Habitat**: Cope's Gray Tree Frogs inhabit forested and wooded areas, from swamp margins and bottomland forest to pine savannahs and upland mixed pine-hardwood forest.

**Natural history**: When not breeding, Cope's Gray Tree Frogs spend most of their time in trees and shrubs. During warm weather, they are nocturnal, and during the day they pull their limbs close to their bodies in tree cavities or on trunks or limbs, using their camouflaged pattern for protection. They breed from late March to early September in ephemeral ponds and wetlands, ditches, and swamp margins. Females lay 830–4,800 eggs, deposited in packets of 30–40 eggs that remain as a film on the water surface. They feed on insects. Cope's Gray Tree Frog is diploid, having the normal complement of chromosomes (24). It and the Eastern Gray Tree Frog, which is tetraploid (with 48 chromosomes), cannot be distinguished from each other based on external morphology, though their calls are different.

**Distribution and status**: Cope's Gray Tree Frogs occur statewide in forested and wooded areas, except for the cheniers. Their statewide population is considered stable.

38a adult (Caldwell Parish)

38b adult (St. Martin Parish)

38c adult (Atchafalaya Basin)

38d adult (St. Mary Parish)

38e venter (Pointe Coupée Parish)

38f juvenile (East Baton Rouge Parish)

## Bird-voiced Tree Frog (*Hyla avivoca*)

**Subspecies**: Western Bird-voiced Tree Frog (*H. a. avivoca*)

**Description**: Bird-voiced Tree Frogs are of medium build with a fine, grainy texture to the skin and enlarged, circular toe pads. The upper surface is pale gray, brown, or green, or green above and gray or brown on the sides. There are slightly darker, highly irregular markings that tend to be in the middle of the back, on the rear sides of the body, on the anterior flanks, and between the eyes. Markings on the flanks continue forward over the shoulder to the rear margin of the eye. There are darker bars on the limbs and **a white to pale green patch below each eye**. The groin usually has black markings and a pale green tinge, and the **rear of the thighs have a dark band that is covered with very pale greenish yellow spots**. The underside of the body is white to dull yellow, that of the hind limbs purple gray. Juveniles are colored like the adults.

**Size**: Maximum length 2.0 inches (52 mm); adults usually 1.1–1.9 inches (28–49 mm); metamorphs 0.4–0.6 inches (9–13 mm).

**Voice**: A whirring trill.

**Habitat**: Bird-voiced Tree Frogs occur primarily in swamps, swamp margins, and riverine forests.

**Natural history**: When not breeding, Bird-voiced Tree Frogs spend most of their time in trees and shrubs. During warm weather, they are nocturnal, and during the day they pull their limbs close to their bodies in tree cavities or on trunks or limbs, using their camouflaged pattern for protection. They breed from early April to mid-August in ephemeral wetlands and swamps. Females lay 400–800 eggs, which drift to the bottom. They feed on arboreal arthropods. Bird-voiced Tree Frogs are rarely encountered due to their arboreal habits.

**Distribution and status**: Bird-voiced Tree Frogs occur in forested portions of southeastern Louisiana as far south as the New Orleans and Lafitte areas. They have also been found in scattered parishes west of the Mississippi

River: Bossier, Evangeline, Grant, Lincoln, Ouachita, Rapides, Tensas, Terrebonne, Union, and Webster. Their populations are considered stable.

39a adult (Ouachita Parish)

39b adult (Ouachita Parish)

39c adult (Hancock Co., MS)

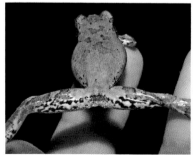

39d rear of thigh (St. Tammany Parish)

39e venter (Nevada Co., AR)

## Pine Woods Tree Frog (*Hyla femoralis*)

**Description**: Pine Woods Tree Frogs are of medium build with finely granular skin and enlarged, circular toe pads. They are gray or brown with very irregular darker patches on the back, the largest of which lies between the shoulders and has projections extending rearward and downward. Other marks are on the rear of the body, with another dark patch on the crown between the eyes. A **dark line originates on each nostril and extends backward at the level of the eyes, over the tympanum, and along the middle of the side of the body**. The area below the line is usually a little darker than the ground color above it. There are usually dark crossbars on the limbs. The **rear of the thighs are dark purple with yellow or orange spots**. The underside of the body is white, that of the limbs dull pink to lavender. Juveniles are colored like the adults.

**Size**: Maximum length 1.7 inches (44 mm); adults usually 1.0–1.5 inches (25–38 mm); metamorphs 0.4–0.6 inches (11–15 mm).

**Voice**: A rapid series of "tickety-tickety-tickety-tickety" sounds that last several seconds or longer.

**Habitat**: Pine Woods Tree Frogs occur in pine woodlands and forests or mixed forests dominated by pine, primarily stands of longleaf or slash pines, preferably in flatwoods.

**Natural history**: When not breeding, Pine Woods Tree Frogs spend much of their time in trees, shrubs, and stumps. During the day, they pull their limbs close to their bodies as they rest on limbs, trunks, or under the loose bark of pine snags, using their camouflage pattern as protection against predators. They breed in ephemeral wetlands, small shallow ponds, and ditches from April to August. Females lay a total of 700–2,100 eggs in clumps of about 100 each. They feed on insects and spiders.

**Distribution and status**: Pine Woods Tree Frogs occur in the Florida Parishes from eastern East Feliciana and northeastern East Baton Rouge Parishes eastward. They are absent from regions of extensive swamps and marshes. Since the 1990s, Pine Woods Tree Frogs have been newly found in three parishes, and their populations elsewhere seem to be stable.

40a adult (St. Tammany Parish)

40b adult (Washington Parish)

40c ventral (St. Tammany Parish)

## Green Tree Frog (*Hyla cinerea*)

**Description**: Green Tree Frogs are of moderate build with finely granular skin and enlarged, circular toe pads. They are **pale green above and on the sides, with a bold white stripe that follows the upper lip, under the tympanum, over the top of the arm, and along the sides of the body variable distances toward the groin.** The groin  often has a lavender wash. The white **stripe may be outlined in black,** and on the side of the body there is **green coloration above and below the stripe.** There are no markings on the limbs. Some individuals may have small yellow or white spots on the back, and rare individuals are pale tan or brown rather than green. There is **no hint of a dark mask or dark marks behind the eyes,** except that the tympanum is sometimes partially or completely brown rather than green. The **rear of the thighs are unmarked.** The underside of the body is white, that of the hind limbs is dull white grading to pink or lavender. Juveniles are colored like the adults.

**Size**: Maximum length 2.8 inches (71 mm); adults usually 1.5–2.3 inches (37–59 mm); metamorphs 0.5–0.7 (12–17 mm).

**Voice**: A rapid series of slightly nasal "hey, hey, hey, hey" calls.

**Habitat**: Green Tree Frogs occur in nearly all habitats from brackish marsh to upland forests. They prefer the vicinity of shallow wetlands with an abundance of herbaceous vegetation or an area with a lot of shrubs, vines, and palmettos.

**Natural history**: When not breeding, Green Tree Frogs tend to be nocturnal and during the day will rest on limbs, palmetto fronds, stalks, and sides of buildings with their limbs tucked close to their bodies. They breed in ephemeral wetlands, ditches, and shallow lakes, ponds, and swamp margins from mid-March to late August. Females lay 275–3,975 eggs in small clumps that float in filmy masses on the surface. They feed on insects and spiders, primarily those that occur on leafy plants.

**Distribution and status**: Green Tree Frogs occur statewide, except in salt marshes. They remain abundant through most of their range.

41a adult (Reelfoot Lake, TN)

41b adult (Atchafalaya Basin)

41c adult (Hardin Co., TX)

41d adult (Iberville Parish)

41e venter (St. Martin Parish)

41f metamorph (Lafayette Parish)

## Squirrel Tree Frog (*Hyla squirella*)

**Description**: Squirrel Tree Frogs are of moderate build with finely granular skin and enlarged, circular toe pads. Their color pattern is highly variable, and individuals are capable of color change. They may be overall pale green, gray, pale tan, or brown above, with **a yellow or white line on the upper lip that continues back over the arm and onto the side of the body a varying distance**. On the sides of the body, the stripe may become wider or diffuse and usually has a jagged edge. The lower sides are pink or pale to medium gray, **usually not green both above and below the pale stripe**. There may be circular dark spots on the back, a dark bar between the eyes, a dark mask through the eyes, and/or dark crossbars on the limbs. If a mask is not present, there is **usually a dark patch or mark behind the eyes and/or tympanum that is usually brown**. The **rear of the thighs are pink or lavender and are unmarked**. The underside of the body is white and that of the hind limbs pinkish. Juveniles are colored like the adults.

**Size**: Maximum length 1.9 inches (49 mm); adults usually 0.9–1.4 inches (23–37 mm); metamorphs 0.4–0.5 inches (11–13 mm).

**Voice**: Short, pulsing, creaky notes.

**Habitat**: Squirrel Tree Frogs occur in nearly all habitats in southern Louisiana, aside from brackish and salt marshes. They favor bottomland hardwoods and other flatwood habitats, and follow river bottoms into the interior of upland regions.

**Natural history**: When not breeding, Squirrel Tree Frogs tend to be nocturnal and during the day will rest on limbs, stalks, knotholes, and sides of buildings with their limbs tucked close to their bodies. They breed in ephemeral wetlands, ditches, ponds, and swamp margins from mid-March to early October. Females lay 390–2,080 eggs, which drop to the bottom when deposited. They feed on insects and spiders.

**Distribution and status**: Squirrel Tree Frogs occur throughout the southern half of Louisiana and range northward to the headwaters of the Calcasieu River, the Red River Valley at least to Alexandria, along the Little

River, and from scattered sites in the upper Mississippi Delta to near Arkansas. Squirrel Tree Frogs are abundant at many sites, and their populations are considered stable. In fact, their populations are expanding into portions of the upper Mississippi River Delta.

42a adult (East Carroll Parish)

42b adult (Atchafalaya Basin)

42c adult (Lafayette Parish)

42d adult (Rapides Parish)

42e venter (Lafayette Parish)

42f juvenile (East Baton Rouge Parish)

## Barking Tree Frog (*Hyla gratiosa*)

**Description**: Barking Tree Frogs are somewhat robust in build with granular skin and large, circular pads on the finger and toe tips. Above they are bright to olive green, gray or brown, and **covered with brown or black spots that are intermingled with white or yellow dots**. Rarely, the spots are lacking. A **pale stripe usually runs from the upper lip over the arm and along the sides of the body, below which is an area that is dark brown or mottled dark and white**. The stripe may be indistinct or broken into spots and dashes. The limbs possess crossbars that are slightly darker than the ground color. The underside of the body is white, that of the hind limbs purple gray. Markings in metamorphs are poorly developed but begin to appear during the first few postmetamorphic months.

**Size**: Maximum length 2.8 inches (70 mm); adults usually 1.9–2.6 inches (49–67 mm); metamorphs 0.7–0.9 inches (18–23 mm).

**Voice**: "Toonk toonk," repeated in series of twos or threes.

**Habitat**: Barking Tree Frogs favor pine woodlands or mixed pine-hardwood forests.

**Natural history**: When not breeding, Barking Tree Frogs tend to be nocturnal and during the day will rest in cavities on loose substrate, on tree limbs and trunks, or in knotholes and tree hollows, with their limbs tucked close to their bodies. They breed in ephemeral wetlands, ditches, and ponds from late March to mid-August. Females lay 1,000–4,000 eggs, which drop to the bottom in shallow water. They feed on insects and other arthropods. Barking Tree Frogs are more selective about breeding conditions than other tree frog species and are very difficult to locate when not in or travelling to breeding sites.

**Distribution and status**: Barking Tree Frogs occur in the Florida Parishes, except in the Mississippi River floodplain and regions of extensive swamp. They occur in widely scattered sites, several of which are in protected areas, and their status is considered secure.

43a adult (St. Tammany Parish)

43b adult (St. Helena Parish)

43c adult (Hancock Co., MS)

43d juvenile (Hancock Co., MS)

## Cuban Tree Frog (*Osteopilus septentrionalis*)

**Description**: Cuban Tree Frogs are of medium build with granular skin and **large, circular pads on the finger and toe tips. The skin on top of the head is fused with the skull so that it does not shift when rubbed**. They are gray, brown, or green above, with a pattern of irregular darker markings on the head and back, and dark crossbands on the limbs. The markings may be faded to a point that they are difficult to see, and at night the frogs may appear pale and patternless. A dark line may be present from the upper edge of the nostril to the eye, and the area around the tympanum is typically darker than the surrounding skin. The underside of the body is white, that of the limbs pale, dull pink. Metamorphs are similar in color to adults but may have a pale line on the sides.

**Size**: Maximum length 5.5 inches (140 mm); adult males usually 1.5–3.5 inches (39–89 mm), females 2.1–5.0 inches (53–127 mm); metamorphs 0.6–0.7 inches (15–17 mm).

**Voice:** A series of quick, squeaky, snorelike rasps.

**Habitat:** In Louisiana, Cuban Tree Frogs occur in landscaped urban areas.

**Natural history:** Cuban Tree Frogs are active only at temperatures above 60°F. They are usually nocturnal and have been found on buildings and plants in urban areas. In Florida, they breed in ditches and ponds from March to October. Females lay up to 16,000 eggs in clumps of several hundred each that form a thin film on the water surface. They feed on insects and other arthropods, as well as lizards and other frogs. When agitated, they produce a milky secretion from the skin that is very irritating to human mucous membranes.

**Distribution and status:** Cuban Tree Frogs are native to Cuba and the Bahamas. They have been introduced into Florida and are now widespread there. In recent years, individuals have been found in the New Orleans area and in 2015 were located there with some frequency. There is no evidence that they are reproducing in Louisiana yet, but they seem to be regularly transported here in nursery plants from Florida.

43.1a adult (southern FL)

43.1b adult (Orleans Parish)

43.1c adult (southern FL)

43.1d venter (Orleans Parish)

43.1e juvenile (Orleans Parish)

## Greenhouse Frog (*Eleutherodactylus planirostris*)

**Description**: Greenhouse Frogs are small frogs with slightly expanded finger and toe tips, and no webs between the toes. There are two color morphs: striped and spotted. Striped frogs are brown or gray on the back and sides of the body, with a tan, orange, or pale gray stripe on the upper side of the body. The stripe extends forward to the top of each eye and over the top of the snout. A distinct dark line extends between the eyes to separate the back color from the paler snout color. The sides tend to be paler than the back, and both sides and the back often have very small dark markings. Spotted frogs are tan, brown, or gray with irregular dark brown or black markings over the back and sides. Like the striped frogs, the snout is distinctly paler. In all Greenhouse Frogs, a **black line passes from the snout tip, through the eye, around the tympanum, to just above the arm. The face usually has dark markings, and the lips are dark with white spots over the mouth**. The limbs have dark crossbars. The underside is pale pink or dull white, somewhat translucent, with a dark line up the middle of the belly. Hatchlings are colored like the adults.

**Size**: Maximum length 1.3 inches (32 mm); adults usually 0.6–1.1 inches (16–28 mm); hatchlings 0.1–0.3 inches (4–6 mm).

**Voice**: One or more faint, high-pitched chirps, each lasting less than a second.

**Habitat**: Greenhouse Frogs occur in landscaped yards in urban and suburban areas, and in the vicinity of nurseries.

**Natural history**: Greenhouse Frogs are active in warm, humid weather. They are secretive, dwelling in leaf litter and ground cover. In summer, females lay a clutch of 3–26 eggs in humus, loose soil, or under cover objects, and the eggs hatch directly into tiny juveniles. They feed primarily on ants but also eat other small insects, mites, and spiders.

**Distribution and status**: Greenhouse Frogs are native to the West Indies but have been introduced by way of the nursery plant trade to parts of the southeastern United States. In Louisiana, they have been found in ten parishes in the southern one-third of the state. Their populations are considered to be expanding, though severe winters may periodically eliminate some populations.

44a adult (Lafayette Parish)

44b adult (Lafayette Parish)

44c adult (St. Bernard Parish)

44d venter (Orleans Parish)

## Rio Grande Chirping Frog (*Eleutherodactylus cystignathoides*)
**Other names**: *Syrrhophus cystignathoides*

**Subspecies**: Camp's Chirping Frog (*E. c. campi*)

**Description**: Chirping Frogs are small frogs with expanded finger and toe tips, and no webs between the toes. The back is golden tan with small, irregular dark markings. There is a somewhat irregular pale bar between the eyes with a dark rear border. A **black mask passes from the snout tip, across the face and tympanum, back to above the arm.** The **mouth area is dark and unmarked, or it may have a few pale dots.** The dark markings fade out along the sides of the body, which are otherwise tan or lavender with white dots. The limbs are golden tan with dark crossbars. The underside is dull white to pale gray or lavender, with a dark line down the middle of the belly. Hatchlings are dark brown.

**Size**: Maximum length 1 inch (26 mm); adults usually 0.6–0.9 inches (15–24 mm); hatchlings 0.2–0.3 inches (5–8 mm).

**Voice**: One or more faint, high-pitched chirps, each lasting less than a second.

**Habitat**: In Louisiana, Chirping Frogs are usually found in landscaped urban and suburban areas but have been found in nearby woodlands, mixed pine-hardwood forest, and swamp margins.

**Natural history**: Chirping Frogs are active in warm, humid weather. They are secretive, dwelling in leaf litter and ground cover. Females lay a clutch of 5–13 eggs in humus and loose soil, and the eggs hatch directly into tiny juveniles. Known prey includes small insects and spiders.

**Distribution and status**: Chirping Frogs are native to the southern tip of Texas and adjacent Mexico. The first Louisiana population was discovered by Dr. Laurence Hardy of Louisiana State University Shreveport in 1998. As of 2015, they had been found in Caddo, Calcasieu, East Baton Rouge, East Feliciana, Lafayette, Rapides, and St. Martin Parishes. They have been introduced into Louisiana and other parts of Texas via nursery plant soil in which either adults or eggs are concealed. Their populations are considered to be expanding.

45a adult (Lafayette Parish)

45b adult (Lafayette Parish)

45c venter (East Baton Rouge Parish)

## Eastern Narrow-mouthed Toad (*Gastrophryne carolinensis*)

**Description**: Eastern Narrow-mouthed Toads are small, chunky frogs with a **small, pointed head and a fold of skin at the back behind the eyes.** The **mouth is tiny, and there is no webbing between the toes.** The back and top of the head are tan, brown, gray, or dull orange, sharply offset from the sides of the head and body, which are  dark gray to nearly black, overlain by numerous silver flecks. There is often an irregular dark line on the back from above the groin on each side, meeting at the back of the head; this line often encloses an area slightly or much darker in color than the rest of the back. The top of the snout is usually paler than the rest of the dorsum. The limbs are dark, with the entire upper surfaces colored like the back, or with patches of the paler dorsal color. The underside is gray, darkest on the throat, and covered with many pale gray spots and dots. Metamorphs tend to be overall dark above.

**Size:** Maximum length 1.5 inches (38 mm); adults usually 0.8–1.4 inches (20–36 mm); metamorphs 0.4–0.5 inches (10–13 mm).

**Voice:** A nasal buzz lasting two to four seconds.

**Habitat:** Narrow-mouthed Toads occupy nearly any habitat in Louisiana, from brackish marsh to upland pine-hardwood forests, including suburban settings.

**Natural history:** Narrow-mouthed Toads are ground dwellers that are usually concealed in grass clumps, leaf litter, or under logs. They breed from April to September, usually in very shallow water, such as gum ponds, grassy ditches, and rain-filled depressions, tire ruts, and margins of small ponds and swamps. Females lay 150–1,450 eggs in a surface film or in a number of small surface packets. They feed on small snails and arthropods, especially ants, termites, and small beetles. Narrow-mouthed Toads tend to scramble for cover, rather than hop, when disturbed.

**Distribution and status:** Narrow-mouthed Toads occur statewide, except in extensive areas of trackless marsh, and their populations are considered stable.

46a adult (Stone Co., MS)

46b adult (Atchafalaya Basin)

46c adult (Atchafalaya Basin)

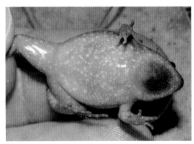

46d venter (St. Tammany Parish)

46e metamorph (Atchafalaya Basin)

## Crawfish Frog (*Rana [Lithobates] areolata*)
**Other names**: *Lithobates areolatus*

**Subspecies**: Southern Crawfish Frog (*R. [L.] a. areolata*)

**Description**: Crawfish Frogs are somewhat robust frogs with a **dorsolateral fold along each
side of the back** and **numerous smooth warts
on the back and sides of the body**. They are **dirty
white to gray or pale brown**, darkest between the
dorsolateral folds, and covered with **circular dark
brown spots**. The area between the spots contains

smaller dark markings. There are irregular dark markings on the face and
mouth, and there are dark crossbands on the limbs. The tympanum bears
a large white spot, and the raised dorsolateral folds may be dull yellow or
tan. The **underside is white to pale yellow, yellow under the hind limbs,
and unmarked** or with a few dark dots in the groin. Juveniles are colored
like the adults, except that the dark spots are smaller.

**Size**: Maximum length 3.6 inches (92 mm); adults usually 2.5–3.5 inches
(62–88 mm); metamorphs 0.8–1.2 inches (20–30 mm).

**Voice**: A vibrating snore that lasts for one to two seconds.

**Habitat**: Crawfish Frogs occur in open prairie, pastures, and open woodland in both upland areas and the upper Mississippi River Delta.

**Natural history**: When not breeding, Crawfish Frogs live in abandoned
crawfish burrows and those made by other animals, moving only short
distances from their shelters to feed. They breed during winter in shallow,
ephemeral ponds, usually after heavy rain events. Females lay 2,000–7,000
eggs in a single mass, usually attached near the surface of the water. They
feed on insects, crawfish, and other arthropods.

**Distribution and status**: Crawfish Frogs are confirmed for only 15 widely
separated sites in nine parishes in Louisiana: Acadia, Allen, Beauregard,
Caddo, Ouachita, Rapides, Richland, Vernon, and Webster. Most records
are from the 1920s through 1970s, with a confirmed call record for 1996
and a photograph from 2010. Due to the scarcity of recent reports, it is
considered a Species of Conservation Concern.

47a adult (Benton Co., AR)

47b adult (Van Buren Co., AR)

47c venter (Van Buren Co., AR)

47d juvenile (Bryan Co., OK)

## Dusky Gopher Frog (*Rana [Lithobates] sevosa*)

Other names: *Lithobates sevosus, Rana capito sevosa,* Mississippi Gopher Frog

**Description:** Dusky Gopher Frogs are somewhat robust frogs with a relatively large head, **dorso-lateral folds**, and **numerous smooth warts on the back and sides of the body.** The back and sides are **gray or brown, covered with numerous black spots and flecks.** The raised ridges and warts are usually brown. The limbs have dark crossbars.  The **underside is dull white, yellowish under the hind limbs and groin, and covered in black dots, though the abdomen of females is often un-marked.** Juveniles are paler than the adults, and the spots are smaller.

**Size:** Maximum length 4.1 inches (105 mm); adults usually 2.8–3.7 inches (71–93 mm); metamorphs 1.0–1.6 inches (25–42 mm).

**Voice:** A snorelike, vibrating call that lasts two to three seconds.

**Habitat:** Dusky Gopher Frogs occurred in pine flatwoods and mixed pine-hardwood woodland in the vicinity of ephemeral wetlands.

**Natural history:** When not breeding, Dusky Gopher Frogs live in abandoned animal burrows and stump holes, moving only short distances from their shelters to feed. They breed during winter in shallow, ephemeral ponds, usually after heavy rain events. Females lay 500–2,800 eggs in a single mass, usually attached near the surface of the water. They are known to feed on beetles and probably also feed on other arthropods and small frogs.

**Distribution and status:** Dusky Gopher Frogs were known from the flatwoods areas north of Lake Pontchartrain, from near Ponchatoula to Slidell, and north on the tableland west of the Pearl River to near Bush. They were last found in Louisiana in 1967 near Hickory, St. Tammany Parish, by graduate students from the University of Louisiana at Lafayette. That site and others have been heavily monitored through the early 2000s without detecting any Gopher Frogs, and the species is considered extirpated from Louisiana. The Gopher Frog is listed as Endangered under the Endangered Species Act and is one of the rarest amphibian species in North America, now only known from two or three ponds in Mississippi.

48a adult (Harrison Co., MS)

48b venter (Harrison Co., MS)

48c juvenile (Harrison Co., MS)

## Pickerel Frog (*Rana [Lithobates] palustris*)
**Other names:** *Lithobates palustris*

**Description:** Pickerel Frogs are of medium build, with smooth skin and a **smooth dorsolateral fold along each side of the back.** They are very pale tan or beige with **two rows of large, dark brown, rounded or squared blotches between the dorsolateral folds, which occupy much more space than the ground color.** The dark blotches tend to have black outer margins. A similar row of large spots is found on the upper sides of the body, and there are usually smaller dark spots on the lower sides. There is also a circular dark spot on each eyelid. The dorsolateral folds are often bright gold to dull orange. The limbs are pale tan or beige with very distinct dark brown crossbars. There is a **pale streak along the upper lip** and a dark patch behind the eye and tympanum. The **tympanum is metallic gold, usually with a dark central spot.** The underside and lower sides are white except for the **limbs and groin, which are bright yellow.** Metamorphs are colored like the adults.

**Size:** Maximum length 3.4 inches (87 mm); adults usually 1.7–3.0 inches (44–75 mm); metamorphs 0.7–1.1 inches (19–27 mm).

**Voice:** A soft, snorelike vibration lasting two or three seconds.

**Habitat:** Pickerel Frogs occur in upland forests—hardwoods, pine, or combinations of both—as well as infrequently flooded bottomland hardwood forest.

**Natural history:** Outside of the breeding season, Pickerel Frogs appear to disperse widely from breeding areas, foraging at night on the forest floor and near small streams. Breeding takes place from December to March in ephemeral wetlands, such as depressions and ponds. Females lay clusters of 960–3,000 eggs, which drift to the shallows or attach to submerged sticks. They are thought to feed on arthropods, such as insects and spiders.

**Distribution and status:** Pickerel Frogs occur in areas of northern and central Louisiana as far south as northeastern Rapides Parish and Beauregard Parish. They also occur in the northern margin of the Florida

Parishes from the Tunica Hills to northern Washington Parish. No data are available on population trends.

49a adult (Natchitoches Parish)

49b adult (Hinds Co., MS)

49c adult (Vernon Parish)

49d venter (Natchitoches Parish)

49e juvenile (West Feliciana Parish)

## Southern Leopard Frog (*Rana [Lithobates] sphenocephala*)
**Other names**: *Lithobates sphenocephalus, Rana utricularia*

**Subspecies**: Coastal Plain Leopard Frog (*R. [L.] s. utricularia*)

**Description**: Leopard Frogs are of medium build, with smooth skin and smooth, **cream or pale yellow dorsolateral folds**. There may also be smaller and shorter ridges down the middle of the back. They are tan to medium brown or pale gray, occasionally green on the head and back. There are **scattered round or oval dark brown spots on the back and sides that occupy less space than the ground color**. The dark blotches may or may not have dark outer margins. Rarely, the dark spots are lacking. There may be circular dark spots on each eyelid and between the eyes but not on the snout. The limbs are colored like the back, with very distinct dark brown crossbars. There is a **pale stripe along the upper lip** and a dark patch behind the eye and tympanum. The **tympanum is brown with a whitish central spot**. The **underside and lower sides of the body are white**. Metamorphs are colored like the adults but have fewer spots.

**Size**: Maximum length 5.0 inches (127 mm); adults usually 2.1–3.5 inches (53–89 mm); metamorphs 0.8–1.3 inches (20–33 mm).

**Voice**: A combined series of growls and chuckles, variously described as quacking ducks and rubbed wet balloons.

**Habitat**: Leopard frogs occur in nearly all Louisiana habitats, except for salt marsh.

**Natural history**: Leopard frogs tend to be nocturnal in warm or hot weather and may occur in wooded areas and grasslands, using leaf litter, ditches, streams, puddles, ponds, and marsh areas as daytime retreats. They breed opportunistically at almost any time of the year after heavy rains, but the core of their reproductive activity is fall and winter. They breed in ponds, ditches, sloughs, swamp margins, shallow marshes, and other shallow, slack waters. Females lay 900–5,000 eggs in globular masses in shallow water. They feed on insects and other arthropods. Leopard frogs will often jump into dense vegetation rather than water when approached.

**Distribution and status:** Leopard frogs occur statewide, except in salt marshes. They remain common to abundant in many areas, and their populations are considered stable.

50a adult (St. Tammany Parish)

50b adult, non-spotted (East Baton Rouge Parish)

50c adult (St. Martin Parish)

50d adult (St. Martin Parish)

50c venter (Livingston Parish)

50f metamorph (East Baton Rouge Parish)

**Bronze Frog** (*Rana [Lithobates] clamitans*)
**Other names:** *Lithobates clamitans,* Green Frog

**Subspecies:** Bronze Frog (*R. [L.] c. clamitans*)

**Description:** Bronze Frogs are of medium build with a **dorsolateral fold along each side of the back that breaks into sections toward the groin.** The back and sides are **bronze or medium brown with or without a few dark spots.** The limbs are also brown and may or may not have darker crossbars. A dark mark extends from the shoulder, down the front of the forearms. The mid or lower sides of the body are often white with black mottling. The **face and top of the snout may be green, or there may only be a green to whitish line along the upper lip** back to the upper arm. The **margins of the mouth are gray with white bars.** The tympanum is about the same color as the back. The underside is white with varying amounts of gray or black mottling, especially on the chest, groin, and under the legs. Juveniles are colored like the adults but lack the green face.

**Size:** Maximum length 3.5 inches (88 mm); adults usually 1.9–3.3 inches (50–83 mm); metamorphs 0.7–1.2 inches (19–30 mm).

**Voice:** A flat cluck, cluck-cluck, or cluck-cluck-cluck.

**Habitat:** Bronze Frogs occur in forested and wooded areas, preferably those with a closed canopy. They favor small woodland ponds, small streams, batture sloughs, and swamps.

**Natural history:** Bronze Frogs spend most of their time near water. By day they rest on embankments and near shoreline vegetation, usually only one leap away from water. They breed in streams, ponds, and swamps from late March to late August. Females produce 1,000–5,700 eggs in a filmy surface mass. They feed on worms, snails, and arthropods, including insects, centipedes, and crawfish.

**Distribution and status:** Bronze Frogs occur statewide, except in extensive areas of marsh. They remain abundant in many areas of Louisiana, and their populations are considered secure.

51a adult (Natchitoches Parish)

51b adult (Vermilion Parish)

51c adult (Evangeline Parish)

51d adult (St. Mary Parish)

51e venter (St. Tammany Parish)

51f juvenile (Lafayette Parish)

## Pig Frog (*Rana [Lithobates] grylio*)

**Other names:** *Lithobates grylio,* lagoon frog, grunter

**Description:** Pig Frogs are large, robust frogs with **smooth skin and no dorsolateral folds.** The **webbing of the hind feet extends to near the toe tips.** The head is relatively narrow and pointed. They are **greenish to tan or brown, with the green often limited to the head and shoulder region,** occasionally only to the face. The limbs are usually brown with few dark markings on the hind limbs. **Circular black spots may be present on the back.** The underside is white, often with yellow on the throat and groin area. A **network of gray markings is present under the hind limbs and often onto the abdomen.** The **rear of the thigh is mostly dark gray or brown, with a white, lengthwise stripe through the middle.** Juveniles are colored like the adults but tend to **lack dark spots and have distinct, pale tan dorsolateral bands.**

**Size:** Maximum length 6.4 inches (162 mm); adults usually 3.2–6.0 inches (82–152 mm); metamorphs 1.3–1.9 inches (32–49 mm).

**Voice:** A series of two or three rapid piglike grunts.

**Habitat:** Pig Frogs occur in permanent, freshwater habitats such as freshwater marsh, cypress-lined rivers and bayous, cypress lakes, and flatwood ponds. They prefer open, vegetated conditions, such as lagoons with a covering of water lilies.

**Natural history:** Pig Frogs may be active day or night and tend to stay in water, either at the shoreline or resting atop floating vegetation. They breed from March to August. Females deposit 8,000–15,000 eggs in a filmy surface mass. They feed primarily on arthropods, including crawfish, but also eat leeches, minnows, other frogs, and small snakes. The Pig Frog's habit of staying on offshore, floating vegetation makes them difficult to observe except by boat.

**Distribution and status:** Pig Frogs occur in the southern one-third of the state, into the Florida Parishes in the east, and north to the Lake Charles area in the west. They remain common in some areas, and their populations are considered secure.

52a adult (Assumption Parish)

52b adult (St. Martin Parish)

52c adult (St. Martin Parish)

52d venter (St. Martin Parish)

52e juvenile (St. Tammany Parish)

### Bullfrog (*Rana [Lithobates] catesbeiana*)
**Other names:** *Lithobates catesbeianus,* ouaouaron

**Description:** Bullfrogs are large, robust frogs, often with **small bumps on the skin and no dorso-lateral folds**. The **webbing of the hind feet does not reach the ends of the toes.** The head is relatively broad with a blunt snout. The back and upper sides are **olive green to medium brown or black and are often densely covered with irreg-**  **ular brown or black markings, blotches, or mottling.** The **snout and sides of the head are green.** The limbs are brown with dark crossbands. The **belly is whitish with irregular gray markings, especially under the legs, along the sides, and on the throat.** The **rear of the thighs are heavily mottled dark and light, and there is no longitudinal white line.** The throat of males is yellow. Juveniles are colored like the adults, except that the **only markings on the back are scattered black dots.**

**Size:** Maximum length 8.7 inches (220 mm); adults usually 3.4–7.1 inches (85–180 mm); metamorphs 1.2–2.3 inches (31–59 mm).

**Voice:** A deep, single groan with a distinct inflection at midpoint, lasting about 1.5 seconds.

**Habitat:** Bullfrogs occur in most habitats in Louisiana that have sufficiently large, permanent water bodies, from marshes and lakes, to bayous and farm ponds. They are absent from brackish and salt marshes.

**Natural history:** Bullfrogs favor areas of large, slack water bodies and often sit on the shoreline or on logs in full sun, in shallow water near shore, or among emergent vegetation. They breed from March to August. Females lay 10,000–43,000 eggs in a filmy mass among vegetation on the surface. They feed on nearly any animal that can be swallowed: insects, leeches, worms, crawfish, and other frogs, and occasionally fish, small turtles, snakes, birds, and rodents. When startled, Bullfrogs usually emit a screech or yelp as they jump into the water.

**Distribution and status:** Bullfrogs occur statewide, except in brackish and salt marsh. Their populations are considered stable.

53a adult (Livingston Parish)

53b adult (East Baton Rouge Parish)

53c adult (St. John the Baptist Parish)

53d venter (Lafayette Parish)

53e venter (Monterey Co., CA)

53f metamorph (Iberia Parish)

# Crocodilians

# ALLIGATORIDAE

## American Alligator (*Alligator mississippiensis*)
**Other names**: gator, cocodrie

**Description**: Alligators are dark gray to nearly black above and dull white or pale yellow beneath. The sides of the body and tail are dark gray, alternating with paler, irregular vertical bars that become less distinct in large adults. The sides of the neck and jaw area are dull white. Hatchlings and juveniles are black above with six to nine narrow yellow crossbands down the middle of the back between the neck and base of the tail, and with yellow vertical bars on the sides of the body and tail.

**Size:** Maximum length 19 feet 2 inches (5.8 m); adult females usually to 9 feet (2.7 m), males to 14 feet (4.2 m); hatchlings usually 8.1–10.4 inches (205–264 mm).

**Habitat:** Alligators usually occur in permanent wetlands, but juveniles may inhabit ephemeral wetlands, such as ditches and temporarily flooded depressions. They tolerate but do not favor salt marshes.

**Natural history:** Alligators are primarily aquatic, leaving the water to bask or, occasionally, to travel overland between water bodies. They court and mate in April to early June, during which time they will bellow and establish territories. In June, females construct nests by dragging, pushing, and pulling vegetation into a mound about four to eight feet wide and two to four feet tall. At that time they deposit about 20–60 (average 35–40) oblong eggs in a chamber in the vegetation, and these hatch in about 65–70 days. The female sometimes guards the nest, then the hatchlings, through the year. Alligators feed on a wide range of animals, but prey is often size specific. Young alligators feed on aquatic insects, crawfish, small fish, and frogs, whereas adults may feed on fish, frogs, turtles, waterfowl, wading birds, and small mammals. As of 2015, there have been no recorded human fatalities from alligators in Louisiana, although there have been several attacks that have led to severe injury.

**Distribution and status**: Alligators occur statewide in suitable habitat. By the 1960s, they were largely limited to the coastal zone due to overhunting.

By the late 1970s, they had become reestablished in all Louisiana parishes, and their statewide population is estimated at a little over 1.5 million.

54a adult (Vermilion Parish)

54b adult (Cameron Parish)

54c subadult (Atchafalaya Basin)

54e juvenile (Cameron Parish)

54d venter (captive)

# Turtles

## IDENTIFICATION

All turtles lay eggs on land, and the hatchlings may or may not resemble the adults. In species with a hard shell, the carapace tends to become smoother with age, and keels and ridges on hatchlings become less defined (Common Snapping, Mud, Musk, and Map Turtles), or the shell may become taller in adults (Box Turtles). Old female Softshells develop a mottled or patchy appearance to the carapace that conceals the unique color pattern of the different species and subspecies. Male Red-eared Sliders often lose most of their color pattern with age, resulting in a dark turtle with a uniformly dark gray skin.

Key characters: Aside from color pattern, turtle species are differentiated by the shell scute arrangements, shape of the carapace, form of the limbs and tail, and shape of the front of the upper jaw.

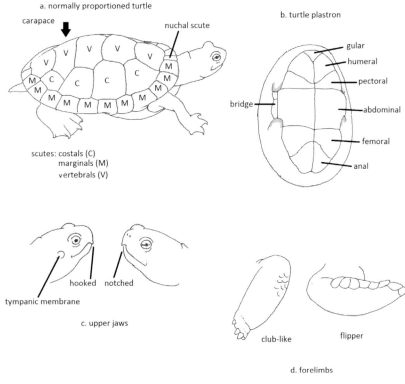

a. normally proportioned turtle

carapace

nuchal scute

V V V V

M
C C C M
M M
M M M M M M

scutes: costals (C)
marginals (M)
vertebrals (V)

b. turtle plastron

gular
humeral
pectoral
bridge
abdominal
femoral
anal

hooked notched

tympanic membrane

c. upper jaws

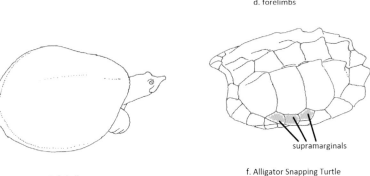

club-like

flipper

d. forelimbs

e. Softshell

supramarginals

f. Alligator Snapping Turtle

# KEY TO TURTLE GENERA

**1a** Forelimbs are of normal form (fig. a) . . . . . **2**

**1b** Forelimbs are clublike, with claws but no visible toes (fig. d) . . . . . *Gopherus,* pp. 198–199

**1c** Forelimbs are flipperlike (fig. d) . . . . . **12**

**2a** Carapace is flat and soft, lacking scutes (fig. e) . . . . . *Apalone,* pp. 159–165

**2b** Carapace is hard, with scutes (fig. a) . . . . . **3**

**3a** Plastron is "+" shaped, much smaller than the carapace, and the tail is nearly as long as the carapace . . . . . **4**

**3b** Plastron is oblong, covering most of the underside of the turtle (fig. b), and the tail is less than one-fourth the length of the carapace . . . . . **5**

**4a** Carapace has three slightly raised ridges, or none, and lacks supramarginal scutes . . . . . *Chelydra,* pp. 210–211

**4b** Carapace has three high ridges and has supramarginal scutes (fig. f) . . . . . *Macrochelys,* pp. 212–214

**5a** Plastron has five pairs of scutes, with or without a single gular scute (fig. b), and the pectoral scutes are separated from the carapace marginals by one or more other scutes of the bridge . . . . . **6**

**5b** Plastron has six pairs of scutes, and the pectoral scutes contact the carapace marginals . . . . . **7**

**6a** Plastron lacks interstitial skin between the seams . . . . . *Kinosternon,* pp. 215–217

**6b** Plastron has interstitial skin between the seams . . . . . *Sternotherus,* pp. 218–223

**7a** Shell is high and lacks a bridge, the plastron has a hinge, and the upper jaw is hooked in front (fig. c) . . . . . *Terrapene,* pp. 190–197

**7b** Shell is not unusually high, it has a bridge, and the upper jaw is not hooked in front . . . . . **8**

**8a** Carapace has a ridge down the middle with two or more raised, black points or knobs . . . . . **9**

**8b** Carapace lacks a ridge but has a red stripe down the middle . . . . . *Chrysemys,* pp. 182–183

**8c** Carapace lacks a ridge, and there is no red stripe down the middle . . . . . **10**

**9a** Skin of the head is gray with black spots . . . . . *Malaclemys,* pp. 180–181

**9b** Skin of head is dark with numerous white, yellow, or orange stripes . . . . . *Graptemys,* pp. 168–179

**10a** Head is oblong, and forelimbs have a broad yellow band in front that is about half the width of the limb . . . . . *Deirochelys,* pp. 166–167

**10b** Head is of normal proportions, and forelimbs have thin, pale stripes . . . . . **11**

**11a** No red stripe behind the eye, the skin is never black overall, and the front of the upper jaw lacks a notch . . . . . *Pseudemys,* pp. 184–186

**11b** Red stripe present behind the eye unless the skin is black, and the front of the jaw has a shallow notch (fig. c) . . . . . *Trachemys,* pp. 187–189

**12a** Carapace lacks scutes and has five raised, white ridges . . . . . *Dermochelys,* pp. 208–209

**12b** Carapace has scutes and lacks raised, white ridges . . . . . **13**

**13a** Carapace has four costal scutes on each side . . . . . **14**

**13b** Carapace has five, rarely six, costal scutes on each side . . . . . **15**

**14a** Front of upper jaw has a round profile, and scutes of the carapace do not overlap . . . . . *Chelonia,* pp. 200–201

**14b** Front of upper jaw has a projecting profile, and scutes of the carapace overlap those behind . . . . . *Eretmochelys,* pp. 202–203

**15a** Carapace and top of head and neck are reddish brown, and there are five enlarged scutes on the bridge . . . . . *Caretta,* pp. 204–205

**15b** Carapace and top of head and neck are gray, and there are four enlarged scutes on the bridge . . . . . *Lepidochelys,* pp. 206–207

## Spiny Softshell (*Apalone spinifera*)

**Other names**: caille-molle, leatherback, *Trionyx spinifer*

**Subspecies**: Eastern Spiny Softshell (*A. s. spinifera*), Gulf Coast Spiny Softshell (*A. s. aspera*), Pallid Spiny Softshell (*A. s. pallida*)

**Description**: Spiny Softshells have flat, skin-covered, leathery shells that lack scutes, and they have a **row of prominent spines on the anterior margin of the carapace, as well as other patches of shorter spines**. The feet are extensively webbed, the nostrils are located at the tip of a snorkel-like proboscis, and the margins of the mouth have flaps of skin that appear like fleshy lips.  The carapace and skin of the upper surfaces of the soft parts have a similar basic coloration that is pale to dark brown, tan, olive brown, or olive green. The carapace of males and juveniles usually has scattered black spots or ocelli over the majority of it, and the carapace is bordered by a narrow, pale rim from the sides around the back, set off by one or more black lines. Female carapace coloration is an irregular patchwork of indistinct dark blotches over the basic coloration, and the pale rim is less distinct. The underside of the carapace, plastron, limbs, and neck are usually dull white, but may be mottled gray or black. The forelimbs are usually speckled with irregular black markings and may have a yellow stripe on the outer edge. A bright to dull yellow stripe, usually with a black border, starts on the side of the snout and passes through the eye and onto the side of the head and neck, where it may or may not connect with a similar stripe that originates near the corner of the mouth. The head stripes may disappear with age in adult females. **Hatchlings are sand-colored, tan, or olive, and the pale rim on the carapace is distinct**. Geographic variation in carapace color pattern is as follows: Gulf Coast Spiny Softshell in the Florida parishes exhibits ocelli and two to three black marginal lines on the carapace, Eastern Spiny Softshell in the Ouachita and Mississippi River drainages has variable-sized black spots and/or large ocelli with one black marginal line, and Pallid Spiny Softshell from the Red and Atchafalaya Rivers and west has only small white spots on the posterior carapace, along with one black marginal line.

**Size**: Maximum CL 21.2 inches (540 mm); adult males usually 4.9–8.0 inches (125–203 mm), females usually 9.8–18.0 inches (250–457 mm); hatchlings 1.2–1.7 inches (30–44 mm).

**Habitat**: Spiny Softshells occur in rivers, streams, ditches, canals, ponds, lakes, impoundments, and oxbows—nearly any permanent aquatic habitat in Louisiana, except for extensive coastal marsh areas.

**Natural history**: Spiny Softshells are highly aquatic but frequently bask on logs or a bank no more than a few feet from water. They are most often seen when foraging in shallow water or basking at the surface of the water. When inactive, they will burrow into the sand or muck in shallow water, extending their long necks to breathe at the surface. Females lay clutches of 11–25 eggs two or three times each year. They feed on aquatic worms, small mussels, crawfish, aquatic insects, carrion, and fish.

**Distribution and status**: Spiny Softshells occur throughout Louisiana, except in extensive coastal marsh zones. Recent nest and trapping surveys indicate that they remain common, and their populations are considered stable.

56a old adult female (Catahoula Parish)

56b adult male aspera (East Baton Rouge Parish)    56c adult male spinifera (Reelfoot Lake, TN)

56d adult pallida (Lafayette Parish)    56e adult male (Caldwell Parish)

56g plastron (Caldwell Parish)

56f anterior (Caldwell Parish)    56h plastron (Natchitoches Parish)

56i hatchling spinifera (Ouachita Parish)    56j juvenile aspera (East Baton Rouge Parish)

## Florida Softshell (*Apalone ferox*)

**Description**: Florida Softshells have a flat, skin-covered, leathery shell that lacks scutes. The **middle of the carapace has a pebbly surface, with an area of numerous raised bumps at the front**. The carapace is medium to dark brown, with or without vague darker patches. The carapace has a very thin, pale margin, and the plastron is pale dull yellow or dirty white. The feet are extensively webbed, and the nostrils are located on the end of a snorkel-like proboscis. The skin of the soft parts is gray or brown, paler on the underside, and is unmarked in adults. The **carapace of hatchlings is nearly black with a yellow-orange rim**. It has a network pattern of olive or tan that widens during the first two years of life to isolate the black coloration into dark brown oval spots. The plastron is dark gray, and the skin is black, mottled with olive spots and bands. There are orange spots around the mouth, a long orange or yellow stripe behind the eye and on the neck, and a bright yellow Y-shaped mark on top of the snout, forking toward the eyes.

**Size**: Maximum CL 29.0 inches (736 mm); males usually 7.7–12.8 inches (195–324 mm), females usually 12.4–18.0 inches (312–457 mm); hatchlings 1.4–1.7 inches (36–44 mm).

**Habitat**: In Louisiana, the Florida Softshell is known from canals and impoundments in fresh, intermediate, and brackish marsh.

**Natural history**: Florida Softshells are highly aquatic, coming onto land to bask or to cross levees. Females lay clutches of 7–38 (average about 20) eggs up to five to seven times each year. They feed on aquatic insects, snails, fish, and carrion. Florida Softshells were first noticed at the Rockefeller Wildlife Refuge in 2001, and since that time at least a half-dozen adults of both sexes have been found, plus nests and hatchlings indicative of reproduction. The origin of the population is believed to be based on the incidental release of turtles used in culture studies that were brought from Florida in the 1970s.

**Distribution and status**: An introduced, reproducing population of Florida Softshells occurs in the vicinity of the headquarters for the Rockefeller Wildlife Refuge in southeastern Cameron Parish.

55a adult female (Cameron Parish)

55b adult female (Cameron Parish)

55c adult, anterior (Cameron Parish)

55d hatchling (Cameron Parish)

## Smooth Softshell (*Apalone mutica*)

**Other names**: *Trionyx muticus, Apalone calvata*

**Subspecies**: Midland Smooth Softshell (*A. m. mutica*), Gulf Coast Smooth Softshell (*A. m. calvata*)

**Description**: Smooth Softshells have a flat, skin-covered, leathery **shell that lacks scutes, spines, and bumps; the surface and anterior margin of the carapace are smooth**. The feet are extensively webbed, and the nostrils are located on the end of a snorkel-like proboscis. Basic carapace coloration is some shade of brown over most of the surface—pale to medium dark brown or brownish gray—and with a narrow, pale rim. Coloration of the skin of the upper surface of the soft parts is similar to the basic carapace color. Adult males and juveniles have scattered distinct dark marks, spots, or ocelli on the carapace, whereas females develop a scattered patchwork of dark blotches over the basic coloration, and the pale rim is less distinct. The underside of the carapace, plastron, limbs, and neck are dull white. The forelimbs may be finely stippled with black and have a yellow stripe on the outer edge. A bright to dull white or yellow stripe, usually bordered by black lines, passes from the side of the snout through the eye and onto the sides of the head and neck. **Hatchling carapace color is sand brown, tan, or pale orange brown, with a vague or no color difference on the rim**. Geographic variation in coloration of the carapace is as follows: the Midland Smooth Softshell, from the Mississippi River and west, has a carapace with scattered dark spots and dashes, and the Gulf Coast Smooth Softshell in the Florida Parishes has large ocelli or dark oval or round spots scattered evenly over the carapace.

**Size**: Maximum CL 14 inches (356 mm); adult males usually 4.7–7.0 (120–178 mm), females usually 7.9–10.4 inches (200–265 mm); hatchlings 1.2–1.5 inches (30–37 mm).

**Habitat**: Smooth Softshells inhabit rivers and large streams, usually with abundant sand and relatively clear water.

**Natural history**: Smooth Softshells frequently bask on shore just a quick dash from the water and are easily spooked. They may also warm themselves by burying themselves in sand in shallow water. Females produce two or three clutches of 4–17 eggs each year, often on east-facing beaches. They feed on aquatic worms, small mussels, crawfish, aquatic insects (mostly), and fish. Most feeding is done on the bottom.

**Distribution and status**: Smooth Softshells occur in the Sabine, Calcasieu, Red, and Ouachita Rivers in western Louisiana and sparingly in the Mississippi River. They also occur in most rivers and large streams in the Florida Parishes. Recent trapping and nest surveys indicate that Smooth Softshells are fairly common in their favored habitat, and their populations are considered stable.

57a old adult female (Richland Parish)

57b adult mutica (Red River Parish)

57c plastron (East Baton Rouge Parish)

57d anterior (Red River Parish)

57e hatchling mutica (Ouachita Parish)

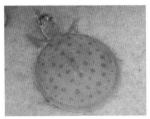

57f juvenile calvata (Hancock Co., MS)

## Chicken Turtle (*Deirochelys reticularia*)

**Subspecies**: Eastern Chicken Turtle (*D. r. reticularia*): distinct stripes on chin and throat, no dark markings on plastron. Western Chicken Turtle (*D. r. miaria*): indistinct stripes on chin and throat, dark markings present on plastron.

**Description**: Chicken Turtles have an oblong, slightly domed shell. There is a median notch in the upper jaw, and the **head and neck are long** relative to other water turtles. The basic carapace coloration is olive brown to dark gray. There is a narrow yellow or light-colored stripe down the midline of the carapace, which also has a narrow  yellow rim. In addition, there may be a network of pale yellow markings forming polygonal shapes on the carapace, or it may be marked with a patchwork of black blotches. The plastron and underside of the carapace are yellow and may have a variable amount of gray to black markings along some seams of the plastral scutes, bridge, and carapace. The skin of the soft parts is pale olive or gray. There are three primary, black-edged, pale yellow or white stripes on each side of the head and a dorsal median stripe starting on the snout. Thinner stripes may occur between the wider ones. There is a **broad, yellow band on the front of each forelimb, and there are vertical white or yellow stripes on each side of the tail, extending onto the back of the thigh**. Hatchlings have a more distinctly green carapace with indistinct carapace markings.

**Size**: Maximum CL 10.0 inches (254 mm); adults usually 4.5–6.0 inches (115–152 mm); hatchlings 1.1–1.3 inches (28–34 mm).

**Habitat**: Chicken turtles favor open, vegetated shallow water, including freshwater marshes, beaver and farm ponds, sloughs, brakes, broad ditches, and ephemeral wetlands, usually in lowlands.

**Natural history**: Chicken Turtles forage in shallow water. If their water body dries up, they travel overland in search of another water source or simply excavate a shallow depression underneath vegetation or leaf litter and estivate for weeks or months at a time. They spend the winter buried on land rather than in the water. Females may lay two clutches of up to

12 eggs each year. Chicken Turtles feed primarily on crawfish but also eat aquatic insects, tadpoles, and some vegetation.

**Distribution and status**: Chicken Turtles occur nearly statewide, except for regions of coastal marshes with any salinity and in extensive swamps. There are many gaps in their known distribution. Due to their rarity and the apparent decline of populations of the Chicken Turtle over much of the range (though the reasons are not known), it is considered a Species of Conservation Concern.

58a adult reticularia
(Apalachicola region, FL)

58b adult miaria
(Vernon Parish)

58c adult miaria
(Ouachita Parish)

58d adult miaria (Acadia Parish)

58e plastron (Calcasieu Parish)

58f anterior (Calcasieu Parish)

58g posterior (Ouachita Parish)

58h hatchling (Ouachita Parish)

58i plastron, hatchling
(Ouachita Parish)

## Ringed Sawback (*Graptemys oculifera*)
**Other names**: Ringed Map Turtle

**Description**: The carapace of the Ringed Sawback has a pronounced keel and serrated posterior margin. The **keel includes four raised knoblike projections that are black—the second and third are very prominent and spinelike.** The carapace is olive or olive brown, and there is a **single, large, dull orange or yellowish ring or partial ring on each scute** of the carapace. The plastron is primarily dull pale yellow with some orange highlights and with dark markings or smudges along the seams. The bridge has dark, curving bars, and the undersides of the marginal scutes have a dark circular blotch centered on the seams, with a dull orange or yellowish blotch in between. The skin of the soft parts is black, and there are numerous yellow stripes on the head, neck, and limbs. The stripes on the side of the head and neck are yellow, and there is a **yellow oval or comma-shaped spot behind the eye**. Stripes on top of the head and on the upper eyelids are blue green. Hatchlings and juveniles have a color pattern similar to adults, but the colors are brighter, and the black projections of the carapace keel are more pronounced. In addition, the plastron is marked by dark markings along the seams. Females do not develop oversized heads.

**Size**: Maximum CL 8.5 inches (216 mm); adult males usually 2.3–4.2 inches (58–108 mm), females usually 5.1–7.8 inches (130–198 mm); hatchlings 1.0–1.6 inches (24–40 mm).

**Habitat**: Ringed Sawbacks inhabit rivers and large streams with forested margins, and they nest on sandbars.

**Natural history**: Ringed Sawbacks are highly aquatic, leaving the water only to nest or bask. They are most often seen basking on logs and branches sticking out of the water and may be observed feeding from submerged portions of these structures. Females lay clutches of one to ten (average about four) eggs twice or sometimes three times each year. They feed on aquatic insects. The Ringed Sawback was "discovered" in the 1880s in a New Orleans fish market, but its true source was not located until 1950, when Fred Cagle of Tulane University found them living in the Pearl River.

**Distribution and status**: Sawbacks inhabit the Pearl and Bogue Chitto Rivers. Surveys conducted from the 1980s to 2010 indicate that it is the most frequently observed basking turtle in its Louisiana range. Due to a potential reservoir project that could have impacted much of the Pearl River, the Ringed Sawback was listed as Threatened under the Endangered Species Act.

59a adult female (Washington Parish)

59b adult male (Simpson Co., MS)

59c adult female (Simpson Co., MS)

59d plastron (St. Tammany Parish)

59e hatchling (Simpson Co., MS)

59f hatchling plastron (Simpson Co., MS)

## Pearl River Map Turtle (*Graptemys pearlensis*)

**Other names**: previously included within Pascagoula Map Turtle (*Graptemys gibbonsi*) and Alabama Map Turtle (*G. pulchra*)

**Description**: The carapace of a Pearl River Map Turtle has a pronounced keel and a serrated posterior margin. The keel has projecting knobs and is surrounded by a middorsal black stripe that is nearly continuous. The carapace is olive or olive brown. There are large, dull orange polygonal markings on the outer edge of the costal scutes, and **each marginal scute has a dull orange or yellow vertical bar or incomplete ring and a yellow rim**. The plastron is dull pale yellow and unmarked, but there are dark markings along the seams of the bridge and underside of the carapace. The skin of the soft parts is dark with numerous yellow stripes on the head, neck and limbs. The **top of the head is marked by a large, pale green to yellow blotch between the eyes that connects to a large, irregular blotch behind each eye**. Hatchlings and juveniles have a color pattern similar to adults, but with more distinct but paler colors, and with the black projections of the median keel more pronounced. Females develop oversized heads.

**Size**: Maximum CL 11.5 inches (292 mm); adult males usually 2.5–4.2 inches (64–108 mm), females usually 7.3–9.3 inches (185–236 mm); hatchlings 0.9–1.5 inches (23–38 mm).

**Habitat**: Pearl Map Turtles inhabit rivers and large streams with forested margins, and sandbars for nesting.

**Natural history**: Pearl Map Turtles are highly aquatic, leaving the water only to nest or bask. They are most often seen basking on logs and branches sticking out of the water. At night they sleep a few inches below the surface on these structures. Females lay an average of 6–8 eggs in each of several clutches per year. They feed on aquatic insects, snails and fish, and large females can crush and eat mussels.

**Distribution and status**: Pearl Map Turtles inhabit the Pearl and Bogue Chitto Rivers, and lower parts of tributaries such as Pushepatapa Creek. Surveys conducted from the 1980s to 2010 indicate a slight decline in

Pearl Map Turtle numbers. Due to the species' limited range and habitat requirements, it is considered a Species of Conservation Concern.

60a adult male (Simpson Co., MS)

60b young adult female (Simpson Co., MS)

60c old adult female (Simpson Co., MS)

60d plastron, female top, male bottom (Copiah/Simpson Co., MS)

60e juvenile (Lawrence Co., MS)

### Northern Map Turtle (*Graptemys geographica*)
**Other names**: Common Map Turtle

**Description**: Northern Map Turtles have a gently arched carapace with a serrated posterior margin and traces of a black, median keel on the posterior portion of each vertebral scute. The carapace is olive or olive brown with an interconnected network of pale circular and polygonal markings. There may also be one or two dark brown to black  blotches on each scute. The underside of the carapace is pale yellow, with a dark circular or semicircular ring or ocellus straddling the seams. The plastron is dull pale yellow, usually with thin dark margins along the seams. The skin of the soft parts is dark gray or olive green, with numerous yellow stripes on the head, neck, and limbs. There is **a small, somewhat circular yellow spot behind each eye, usually no larger than the eye**, and **a yellow bar on each side of the throat that extends upward to form a "thumbs-up" shaped mark at the angle of the jaw**. The carapace of hatchlings and juveniles has a distinct median keel and is brownish gray; it may exhibit one or more dark brown spots on each scute, in addition to the network of linear markings. Females may develop enlarged heads.

**Size**: Maximum CL 10.7 inches (273 mm); adult males usually 3.0–5.0 inches (77–128 mm), females usually 7.3–10.2 inches (185–260 mm); hatchlings 1.0–1.3 inches (25–33 mm).

**Habitat**: Northern Map Turtles inhabit rivers, large streams, lakes, and oxbows with sandbars for nesting.

**Natural history**: Northern Map Turtles are highly aquatic, leaving the water only to nest and bask. They are most often seen basking on logs and branches sticking out of the water. Females lay two or three clutches of 6–17 eggs each year. They feed on aquatic insects, snails, and crawfish, and large females can crush and eat mussels.

**Distribution and status**: The Northern Map Turtle has positively been recorded only once in Louisiana, in the Ouachita River. Recently, published records indicate that the species is widely distributed in all regions of

Arkansas, including in several rivers and bayous that flow into northern Louisiana. It has yet to be determined if there is a native population of this species in Louisiana.

61a adult male (Oregon Co., MO)

61b adult female (Carroll Co., AR)

61c plastron (Rutherford Co., TN)

61d hatchling (Madison Co., AR)

## False Map Turtle (*Graptemys pseudogeographica*)
**Other names**: *Graptemys kohnii,* grayback turtle

**Subspecies**: Mississippi Map Turtle (*G. p. kohnii*)

**Description**: The carapace of a False Map Turtle is olive gray, brownish gray, or dark gray with a pronounced keel and serrated posterior margin. The keel has at least two projecting knobs that are black, part of a nearly continuous black middorsal stripe. The carapace has an interconnected network of pale yellow polygonal markings, outlined in black, that fade with age. There may also be one or two dark brown or black blotches on each scute. The bridge has pale yellow, dark-outlined longitudinal bars, and the underside of the carapace is pale yellow with dark, concentric ocelli, semicircles, or blocky rings straddling or following the seams. The plastron is often dull pale yellow with or without faded dark smudges, rather than the extensive pattern of concentric dark lines found in younger individuals. The skin of the soft parts is medium gray to black, and there are numerous light-colored stripes on the head, neck, and limbs. There is a short, longitudinal stripe between the eyes that is usually yellow but may be orange. Dorsal neck stripes may change from yellow to orange on the back of the head. There is **a distinct yellow or orange crescent behind the eye on the side of the head, which prevents stripes on the neck and side of the head from reaching the eye margin.** Hatchlings and juveniles have a color pattern similar to that of adults, with more distinct but paler markings. The plastron is dull pale yellow with a central, intricate design of concentric dark lines expanding outward in a kaleidoscopic pattern. Also, the middorsal keel, its knobby projections, and the carapace serration are much more pronounced. Females may develop enlarged heads.

**Size**: Maximum CL 10.3 inches (262 mm); adult males usually 3.5–4.8 inches (88–121 mm), females usually 6.6–8.3 inches (168–210 mm); hatchlings 1.2–1.5 inches (31–38 mm).

**Habitat**: False Map Turtles inhabit permanent water bodies such as rivers, large streams, impoundments, lakes, and oxbows.

**Natural history**: False Map Turtles are highly aquatic, usually only leaving the water to nest and bask, though juveniles may feed on land. They are most often seen basking on logs and branches sticking out of the water. Females lay two to four clutches of 4–13 eggs each year. They feed on aquatic insects, sponges, bryozoans, snails, fish, algae, and aquatic vegetation, and large females can crush and eat mussels.

**Distribution and status**: False Map Turtles occur across most of Louisiana in and around large rivers (Sabine, Calcasieu, Mermentau, Red, Ouachita, Atchafalaya, and Mississippi) and far up some tributaries, but they do not extend downstream into the coastal marsh zone. Their populations are considered stable.

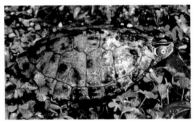

62a adult male (Caldwell Parish)

62b adult female (Ouachita Parish)

62c old female (Sabine Parish)

62d plastron (West Baton Rouge Parish)

62e hatchling (Ouachita Parish)

62f hatchling plastron (Ouachita Parish)

## Ouachita Map Turtle (*Graptemys ouachitensis*)
**Other names**: Southern Map Turtle, *Graptemys pseudogeographica ouachitensis,* brownback turtle

**Description**: The carapace of the Ouachita Map Turtle is pale brown or gray brown with a pronounced keel and serrated posterior margin. The keel has at least two projecting knobs that are black, part of an incomplete or continuous black middorsal stripe. The carapace has an interconnected network of pale orange to yellow polygonal

markings outlined in black that fade with age. There may also be one or two dark brown or black blotches on each scute. The bridge has pale yellow to orange, dark-outlined longitudinal bars, and the underside of the carapace is pale yellow to orange with dark, concentric ocelli, semicircles, or blocky rings straddling or following the seams. The plastron is dull pale yellow with an extensive pattern of concentric pairs of lines forming loops and swirls, expanding outward in a kaleidoscopic pattern along the seams. This pattern fades to dark smudges with age but usually never disappears completely. The skin of the soft parts is medium to dark gray or brown, and there are numerous light-colored stripes on the head, neck, and limbs. Stripes on top of the head and on the upper eyelids are blue green, including a short middorsal stripe between the eyes. Dorsal neck stripes usually change from yellow to orange on the back of the head. There is **a yellow square or rectangular spot behind each eye, usually with at least three light-colored stripes below it (on the side of the head) that reach the margin of the eye.** In addition, there is **a large yellow spot below the eye on the upper jaw and below that on the lower jaw, and a similar spot in the midline on the lower jaw.** Hatchlings and juveniles have a color pattern similar to that of adults, but the markings are distinct and pale. Also, the middorsal keel, its knobby projections, and the carapace serration are much more pronounced. Females do not develop enlarged heads.

**Size**: Maximum carapace length 8.0 inches (203 mm); adult males usually 3.3–4.5 inches (85–115 mm), females usually 5.9–7.9 inches (150–200 mm); hatchlings 1.1–1.4 inches (27–35 mm).

**Habitat**: Ouachita Map Turtles inhabit rivers and adjacent borrow pits and oxbows.

**Natural history**: Ouachita Map Turtles are highly aquatic, leaving the water only to nest and bask. They are most often seen basking on logs and branches sticking out of the water. Females lay two to three clutches of three to ten eggs each year. They feed on aquatic insects, sponges, bryozoans, snails, carrion, algae, and aquatic vegetation.

**Distribution and status**: Ouachita Map Turtles occur in the vicinity of large rivers (Red, Ouachita, Atchafalaya, and Mississippi), but do not extend downstream into the coastal marsh zone. Though populations are thought stable, the species is considered a Species of Conservation Concern due to its limited habitat requirements.

63a adult male (Crawford/Franklin Co., AR)

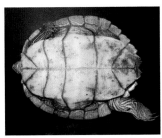

63c plastron (West Baton Rouge Parish)

63b adult female (Red River Parish)

63d hatchling (Ouachita Parish)

63e juvenile plastron (Arkansas River, AR)

## Sabine Map Turtle (*Graptemys sabinensis*)
**Other names**: *Graptemys ouachitensis sabinensis*

**Description**: The carapace of the Sabine Map Turtle is dull olive gray to pale brown or gray, with a pronounced keel and serrated posterior margin. The keel has projecting knobs that are black, part of a nearly complete black middorsal stripe. The carapace has numerous, concentric and interconnected pale ocelli and rounded polyg-

onal markings that may fade with age. There may also be one or two dark brown or black blotches on each costal scute. The bridge has pale yellow, dark-outlined longitudinal bars, and the underside of the carapace is pale yellow with a dark, concentric ocellus or semicircular ring straddling the seams. The plastron is pale yellow with an extensive pattern of concentric pairs of lines forming loops and swirls, expanding outward in a kaleido-scopic pattern along the seams. This pattern fades to dark smudges in older adults. The skin of the soft parts is medium to dark gray, and there are numerous yellow stripes on the head, neck, and limbs. There is **a small yellow or white oval to circular spot behind each eye, combined with three or more light stripes below it (on the side of the head) that reach the margin of the eye.** There is usually a short middorsal yellow stripe on top of the head between the eyes, and there are usually **three yellow bars like "chin straps" below the lower jaw.** Hatchlings and juveniles have a color pattern similar to that of adults, but with pale, distinct markings. Also, the middorsal keel, its knobby projections, and the carapace serra-tion are much more pronounced. Females do not develop enlarged heads.

**Size**: Maximum length 8.0 inches (202 mm); adult males usually 3.0–4.1 inches (75–104 mm), females usually 3.5–6.2 inches (89–158 mm); hatch-lings 1.1–1.3 inches (29–34 mm).

**Habitat:** Sabine Map Turtles inhabit rivers and large streams in forested areas.

**Natural history**: Sabine Map Turtles are highly aquatic, leaving the wa-ter only to nest and bask. They are most often seen basking on logs and branches sticking out of the water. Females lay two to three clutches of one to seven (usually one to four) eggs each year. They feed on aquatic insects, algae, and, sparingly, mussels.

**Distribution and status**: Sabine Map Turtles occur in the Mermentau, Calcasieu, and Sabine Rivers but do not extend downstream into the open coastal marsh zone. The upstream range follows tributaries into Vernon and southwestern St. Landry and Rapides Parishes. Surveys in the early 2010s, compared with observations in the 1980s, indicate that their populations are relatively stable.

64a adult male (Jefferson Co., TX)

64b plastron (Hardin Co., TX)

64c juvenile (Allen Parish)

64d hatchling plastron
(Newton Co., TX)

## Diamondback Terrapin (*Malaclemys terrapin*)

**Subspecies**: Mississippi Diamondback Terrapin (*M. t. pileata*)

**Description**: Terrapins have slightly peaked shells with three or four low projections along the midline of the carapace. The upper jaw is notched, and females may develop oversized heads. The carapace is dark gray to nearly black, sometimes dark brown and gray, often with a brown center in each scute. **Each carapace scute bears distinct, concentric ridges, each of which may be highlighted by brown and black margins.** The rim of the carapace is slightly upturned, showing pale coloration from the underside. The plastron and underside of the carapace are dull orange or yellow, usually overlain by black smudges, which are more extensive in adult males and older females, such that the yellow or orange may only remain on the plastron margin. The **skin is pale to dark gray and covered with black spots**, which on the limbs occupy scales. The spots of the limbs and neck are smaller and denser than the larger, scattered spots on the head and chin. Adults may or may not possess a black "mustache" on the upper jaw, and the top of the head is usually black. Hatchlings and juveniles have a brownish gray carapace and dull yellow plastron with dark, concentric lines on each scute. The dark knobs on the carapace are black.

**Size:** Maximum CL 9.4 inches (238 mm); adult males usually 3.9–5.5 inches (100–140 mm), females usually 5.7–8.0 inches (145–203); hatchlings 1.0–1.3 inches (25–34 mm).

**Habitat**: Terrapins occur in brackish and salt water, in marshes, estuaries, nearshore shallow bays, and barrier islands.

**Natural history**: Terrapins favor shallow estuaries and tidal zones of open water up to five or six feet deep. Little is known of their daily activities, but they appear to operate singly or in small pods, and when needing to warm themselves they bask at the surface or burrow into tidal wrack during low tides. In winter, they nestle into the surface layer of bottom muck in shallow estuaries. Each year, females produce two or three clutches of 4–12 eggs, which are laid in the vegetation line above beaches and in elevated shell mounds. For the first two or three years of life, young terrapins disappear into the marshes, apparently living in the dense grass and wrack. They feed on snails, crabs, and clams.

**Distribution and status**: Terrapins range coastwide in shallow zones of mucky, vegetated waters and seem capable of travelling, at least sparingly, offshore along beaches. They also occasionally enter low salinity zones, such as Calcasieu Lake and the eastern portion of Lake Pontchartrain. Due to the species' restrictive habitat preference and our lack of knowledge of its populations, it is considered a Species of Conservation Concern.

65a adult male (Vermilion Parish)

65b adult female (Vermilion Parish)

65c old adult female (Barataria Bay)

65d plastron male
(Vermilion Parish)

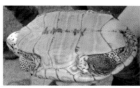

65e plastron female
(Vermilion Parish)

65f juvenile
(Terrebonne Parish)

## Southern Painted Turtle (*Chrysemys dorsalis*)
**Other names**: *Chrysemys picta dorsalis*

**Description**: Southern Painted Turtles have a low, smooth shell, with **no keel or marginal serration**. The **front of the upper jaw bears a notch**. The **carapace is dark olive or gray to nearly black with an orange or red stripe down the middle**. The larger scutes may have tan, yellow, or dull orange margins. The plastron is pale yellow  and is often stained a rusty color in adults. The underside of the marginal scutes are marked with an orange to red central mark, with intervening gray or olive and pale yellow markings. The skin is dark olive or gray. The **head has an elongate yellow bar behind the eye apart from a yellow stripe that runs down the upper side of the neck**. Another large yellow stripe originates below the eye and runs down and back along the side of the throat. Other small, yellow lines and spots are present on the snout and on the sides of the head and neck, including one around the top of the snout. Some of these stripes turn orange or red toward the base of the neck. Each limb also possesses two or three red or orange stripes. Hatchling and juvenile coloration is like that of adults, though the plastron may be bright orange.

**Size**: Maximum CL 6.1 inches (156 mm); adults usually 3.5–5.0 inches (90–127 mm); hatchlings 0.7–1.0 inches (18–26 mm).

**Habitat**: Southern Painted Turtles occur in swamps, batture sloughs, oxbows, shallow cypress lakes, and slack, shallow bayous bounded by forest.

**Natural history**: Southern Painted Turtles favor shallow backwaters and may often be seen basking on logs in light patches filtered by the tree canopy. Females may travel some distance from water to lay one to seven eggs in each of two to five clutches per year. They feed on algae, duckweed, small crawfish, and aquatic insects.

**Distribution and status**: Southern Painted Turtles occur in the Red, Ouachita, Mississippi, and Atchafalaya River basins. Their populations appear to be stable.

66a adult (West Baton Rouge Parish)

66b adult (Union Parish)

66c plastron (Union Parish)

66d juvenile (Reelfoot Lake, TN)

66e hatchling plastron (Union Parish)

## River Cooter (*Pseudemys concinna*)

**Other names**: Eastern River Cooter (P. c. concinna), yellowbelly turtle, king turtle, ventre jaune, mobilien

**Description**: The River Cooter has a gently arched carapace that may be somewhat domed, moreso toward the front of the carapace, and the posterior margin is slightly serrated. The **front of the upper jaw is smooth, nearly straight, and lacks a notch.** The carapace is olive brown, dark brown, or black, usually with a single dominant

tan, yellow, or somewhat orange irregular vertical bar on each costal scute that may curve or have anterior and/or posterior projections toward other scutes, forming a C-shape, with complete or partial concentric rings in between that are usually less distinct. Each marginal scute has a vertical yellow or dull orange bar near the middle, often expanding to follow the edge and form a pale rim around the shell. The plastron and underside of the carapace is pale to bright yellow, sometimes with orange highlights. The plastron may be unmarked or have diffuse, irregular gray markings that are symmetrical around the midline. The underside of the carapace has a large, dark ocellus straddling each seam. The skin of the soft parts is olive gray to black, and there are yellow primary stripes bounded by less prominent, pale secondary stripes on the head and neck. **The most distinctive yellow stripes originate below the eye and beneath the lower jaw, and the two join behind the corner of the mouth to continue onto the lower side of the neck; another may follow the side of the head behind the eye, and it never contains red.** The upper and lower jaw margins are serrated, but it is more obvious when the mouth is open. Hatchlings and juveniles have more distinctive and somewhat greenish concentric swirls or rings on the carapace around the principal network of pale, interconnected yellowish lines, giving them an overall dark green appearance. They also have a prominent median keel that often results in them being mistaken for map turtles. The plastron is either unmarked, or has symmetric dark spots, ocelli, or blotches.

**Size**: Maximum CL 14.8 inches (375 mm); adult males usually 6.3–9.3 inches (160–235 mm), females usually 9.3–13.8 inches (236–352 mm); hatchlings 1.1–1.5 inches (27–39 mm).

**Habitat**: River Cooters occur in permanent freshwater of marshes, lakes, ponds, oxbows, sloughs, bayous, rivers, and streams.

**Natural history**: River Cooters are highly aquatic, rarely travelling over-land except to nest. They are most often seen basking on logs in the water or foraging in shallows. Females lay one to three clutches of 7–18 eggs each year. Adults feed primarily on aquatic vegetation, but adults and juveniles may also eat bryozoans, snails, mussels, aquatic insects, and tadpoles.

**Distribution and status**: Cooters occur statewide, except in brackish and salt marshes. They remain common to abundant in many areas, and their populations are considered stable.

67a adult (East Baton Rouge Parish)

67b adult (Reelfoot Lake, TN)

67c adult (Ouachita Parish)

67d adult (Hardin Co., TX)

67e adult (Ouachita Parish)

67f plastron (Ouachita Parish)

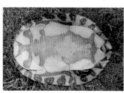

67g plastron (Ouachita Parish)

67h hatchling
(St. Bernard Parish)

67i hatchling plastron
(Ouachita Parish)

## Pond Slider (*Trachemys scripta*)

**Other names**: streak-head, tête verte, green turtle, greenhead

**Subspecies**: Red-eared Slider (*T. s. elegans*)

**Description**: The Pond Slider has a gently arched carapace with a serrated posterior margin. The **front of the upper jaw bears a shallow notch**. The carapace ground color is a dull greenish or brownish that grows increasingly dark with age. There is usually a dull yellow, straight transverse bar outlined in black found near the center of each costal scute; in addition, there may be less prominent pale yellow and black bars in between that may be wavy or curved. On the vertebral scutes appear a prominent pair of yellow stripes outlined in black that appear on opposite sides of the midline like parentheses. The plastron and underside of the carapace are pale to bright yellow. The plastron has a central black blotch on each scute, and the bridge usually has separate blotches that may join lengthwise into a stripe. The underside of the carapace has a dark ocellus straddling each seam and may blacken with age. The dorsal skin is dark olive green to black, with numerous yellow stripes on the head, neck, and limbs. An **elongate red stripe is present on the side of the head behind the eye**. A **prominent yellow stripe originates below the eye and another beneath the lower jaw, and the two join behind the corner of the mouth to continue under the neck**. **Old males often lose their original pattern** primarily by darkening; the stripes vanish, leaving the skin uniformly black or with a reticulate pattern, and the shell becomes either completely black or dull gray brown to yellowish with black along the seams of the carapace and plastron. Hatchlings and juveniles have a green carapace with alternating concentric bars around the central yellow one. The plastron has a symmetric pattern of olive green ocelli or irregular blotches with a pale center.

**Size**: Maximum CL 11.4 inches (290 mm); adult males usually 4.1–8.6 inches (105–220 mm), females usually 7.4–10.6 inches (187–270 mm); hatchlings 0.9–1.4 inches (23–35 mm).

**Habitat**: Pond Sliders occur in nearly any permanent and semipermanent aquatic habitat in Louisiana that has ample sunlight, except salt marshes.

**Natural history**: Pond Sliders are primarily aquatic but may wander overland to find suitable water bodies if their habitat dries up. They can be seen basking on logs or floating at the surface in all manner of water bodies during any month of the year when the weather is warm enough. Individuals are often encountered on roadways near water during the nesting season, primarily in May and June. They readily populate newly constructed water bodies, such as farm ponds and subdivision lakes. Females lay up to 19 (usually 4–11) eggs per clutch, two to five times per year. They are omnivorous, eating a wide variety of aquatic plants, leaves, grass, aquatic insects, crawfish, snails, tadpoles, and carrion, such as dead fish.

**Distribution and status**: Sliders occur throughout Louisiana, except in regions of salt and some brackish marshes. They are the most abundant turtle species in samples from all but major rivers. Recent surveys indicate that their populations are stable.

68a adult female (Lafayette Parish)

68b adult male (Catahoula Parish)

68c adult female (Louisiana)

68d old male (Union Parish)

68e old male (Ouachita Parish)

68f plastron (Ouachita Parish)

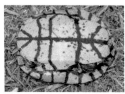

68g plastron old male
(Cameron Parish)

68h hatchling (Ouachita Parish)

68i hatchling plastron
(Caddo Parish)

## Gulf Coast Box Turtle (*Terrapene carolina major*)

**Other names**: Woodland Box Turtle, caouane de rosée

**Description:** Gulf Coast Box Turtles have high-
domed shells, with a transverse hinge on the
plastron that allows them to close the shell, although not so tightly as in the Three-toed Box
Turtle. The **rear, and often front, of the carapace
margin is flared**, and **at least in males the central carapace is relatively flat topped** rather than

forming a smooth arc. The upper jaw is slightly hooked in front, and there
are **four claws on each hind foot**. The carapace may be medium brown to
black. Paler-shelled turtles are often unmarked, but those with dark shells
often possess **numerous, small yellow or orange streaks and spots** in a
radiating pattern on each carapace scute. The plastron and underside of
the carapace is dull yellow with dark margins to the scute seams or may
be mostly dark brown with paler markings or patches. Adult males have
a pronounced concavity in the posterior lobe of the plastron. The skin of
the soft parts is also very dark, and the head and forelimbs may or may
not be covered with yellow or orange spots. Juveniles have a relatively
lower shell than the adults and the plastral hinge is nonfunctional during
the first few years of life. There is a central keel on the carapace, which is
pale to dark gray, with a central yellow or orange spot on each scute.

**Size**: Maximum CL 7.5 inches (191 mm); adults usually 5.6–7.3 inches
(142–185 mm); adult males average 6.6 inches (167 mm), females average
6.1 inches (156 mm); hatchlings 1.3–1.6 inches (32–40 mm).

**Habitat**: Gulf Coast Box Turtles favor wooded or forested areas from
swamp margins to upland hardwood forests, preferring bottomland hardwoods with palmettos. In coastal Mississippi, they enter brackish marsh,
but such habitat use has not been observed in Louisiana.

**Natural history**: Gulf Coast Box Turtles are partially aquatic, freely entering
swamps, shallow streams, and sloughs. They are active during the day and
may be found buried in mud up to the tops of their shells. It is also not unusual to find algae growing on the shell or leeches on the soft parts, additional indications of their propensity to enter and spend time in the water.

Females typically lay six to eight eggs in one to six clutches each year. They feed on mushrooms, certain flowering plants and berries, slugs, worms, insects and other arthropods, carrion, and small vertebrates such as frogs. Juvenile Gulf Coast Box Turtles remain effectively hidden in surface litter for the first four to five years of life.

**Distribution and status**: Gulf Coast Box Turtles occur in Coastal Plain areas of southeastern Louisiana, at least as far west as the Atchafalaya Basin, and in the Mississippi alluvial plain at least as far north as remnant forest in Tensas Parish. In the Florida Parishes, they are found into the Tunica Hills and along the north shore of Lake Pontchartrain. Their overall distribution and relative abundance indicates that the Louisiana population is secure. The taxonomic status of this box turtle has been questioned recently, based primarily on genetic evidence, but in Louisiana it appears to be morphologically and ecologically distinct from the Three-toed Box Turtle.

69a adult (Atchafalaya Basin)

69b adult (East Baton Rouge Parish)

69c adult (Jefferson Parish)

69d adult (Jefferson Parish)

69e adult (Concordia Parish)

69f plastron (Concordia Parish)

69g juvenile (East Baton Rouge Parish)

## Three-toed Box Turtle (*Terrapene carolina triunguis*)

**Other names**: *T. mexicana triunguis*, *T. triunguis*, caouane de rosée

**Description:** Three-toed Box Turtles have high-domed shells, with a transverse hinge of the plastron that allows them to close the shell completely. The **carapace is relatively smoothly arched in profile, with a low median keel and little flaring of the carapace margin**. The posterior plastral lobe is nearly flat in both sexes, and there are usually **three claws on each hind foot**. The carapace may be a uniform yellow or horn brown to medium brown, and the plastron somewhat lighter in color. Some have a **radiating pattern of small, darkly colored or light yellow or orange streaks on each scute**, and some may have a radiating dark pattern on the pale plastral scutes. The skin is usually medium to dark brown, and on males the side of the head and neck may have white patches and/or red or orange markings, and the front of the forelimb scales usually have bright orange or yellow spots. Juveniles have a relatively lower shell than the adults, with a central keel on the carapace. The carapace is pale to dark gray or yellow brown, with a central yellow or orange spot on each scute.

**Size**: Maximum CL 6.5 inches (165 mm); adults usually 4.1–5.8 inches (104–147 mm); hatchlings 1.1–1.4 inches (27–35 mm).

**Habitat:** Three-toed Box Turtles favor forest in upland areas. They prefer hardwood forests over pure pine stands and occur sparingly into grasslands in southwestern Louisiana.

**Natural history:** Three-toed Box Turtles are primarily terrestrial and active during the day. They are most often encountered on warm or hot, overcast days when they are moving through their individual territories or foraging. At night they typically dig into leaf litter enough to cover the head and anterior shell. During hot, dry weather they may seek moister or deeper locations in leaf litter and may wander to small bodies of water to drink or soak. A typical clutch contains two to four eggs, and a female may lay multiple clutches each year. They feed on mushrooms, fungi, certain flowering plants and berries, slugs, earthworms, insects and other arthropods, carrion, and small vertebrates such as frogs. Juvenile Three-toed Box Turtles remain effectively hidden in surface litter for the first four to five years of life.

**Distribution and status:** Three-toed Box Turtles occur nearly statewide, except for bottomland hardwood forests in the Mississippi Alluvial Valley and coastal marshes. There is observational evidence of population declines in a few areas of the state, but their overall distribution and relative abundance indicates that Louisiana populations are secure. There has been recent genetic research suggesting that the Three-toed Box Turtle should be considered a species distinct from *Terrapene carolina*. We have treated this conservatively and retained it as a subspecies of *T. carolina* but acknowledge its distinctiveness by treating it separately from the Gulf Coast Box Turtle, another subspecies of *T. carolina*.

70a adult female (East Feliciana Parish)

70b adult male (Ouachita Parish)

70c adult male (East Feliciana Parish)

70d adult (East Baton Rouge Parish)

70e plastron (Rapides Parish)

70f hatchling (Union Parish)

70g plastron, hatchling
(Union Parish)

## Ornate Box Turtle (*Terrapene ornata*)
**Other names**: Plains Box Turtle, Western Box Turtle

**Description**: Ornate Box Turtles have **domed shells that are flat on top** and have a transverse hinge on the plastron that allows them to close the shell. The **rear of the carapace is somewhat flared, and there are four claws on each hind foot**. The front of the upper jaw is slightly hooked. The **carapace is black or dark brown with three to six yellow streaks that radiate outward** from the core growth center of each carapace scute, and there is a **yellow stripe down the midline of the carapace**. The plastron is yellow, with a nearly symmetrical pattern of radiating black or dark brown lines and blotches on most scutes. The skin is gray to black above, and pale yellow to gray below. The forelimbs, neck, and head are marked with irregular yellow areas or spots. Juveniles have a relatively lower shell than the adults, with a central, yellow stripe down the middle. Otherwise, the carapace is dark gray or black with irregular pale yellow markings on each scute.

**Size**: Maximum CL 6.1 inches (154 mm); adults usually 3.9–5.0 (100–127 mm); hatchlings 1.1–1.3 inches (28–32 mm).

**Habitat**: Ornate Box Turtles occur in the relict Cajun Prairie or in areas converted to well-drained pastureland, including cheniers, in southwestern Louisiana.

**Natural history**: Ornate Box Turtles are terrestrial inhabitants of open grasslands or prairies but tend to remain concealed as they forage around vegetative ground cover. Warm rains and thundershowers stimulate surface activity, but at other times they occupy the bases of vegetation or hide beneath surface objects. Females deposit one, sometimes two, clutches of two to eight (usually four to six) eggs each year. They feed primarily on insects but also other arthropods, worms, carrion, and, rarely, plant material. Juvenile box turtles remain effectively hidden in surface vegetation such as grass clumps for the first few years of life.

**Distribution and status**: Ornate Box Turtles are known from open habitats in Cameron and Calcasieu Parishes. At one time they likely occurred eastward into other parts of Acadiana before the prairie was converted to agricultural use. Scattered, individual records from the Lafayette area and northward are considered to be released captives. No native Ornate Box Turtles have been found in Louisiana since the 1970s. For that reason, and due to the diminished habitat, it is considered a Species of Conservation Concern.

71a adult (southwest MO)

71b adult (Ellis Co., OK)

71c plastron (southwest MO)

71d hatchling (Lyon Co., KS)

## Gopher Tortoise (*Gopherus polyphemus*)
**Other names**: Florida Gopher Tortoise

**Description**: Tortoises have domed shells that are somewhat flat on top, and the **plastron bears a frontal prong that projects under the neck**. Growth rings are evident on the scutes of the carapace as little ridges, unless worn with age. The **forelimbs are somewhat flattened and clublike, and stubby claws are the only indication of the digits. The hind feet are cylindrical and elephantlike, with no trace of toes other than the claws.** The tail is very short. The carapace and skin is dark blackish brown or very dark gray, and the plastron is dull yellow. Hatchlings begin life being mostly yellow, with dark brown margins to all of the carapace scutes, As they age, the dark color encroaches further onto the scutes, as well as onto the skin, until the yellow or tan color vanishes from the core growth center of each scute.

**Size**: Maximum CL 15.2 inches (387 mm); adults usually 7.9–9.5 inches (200–240 mm); hatchlings 1.3–2.2 inches (32–55 mm).

**Habitat**: Tortoises occur in well-drained, open-canopy woodlands, typically those of longleaf pine. In areas in which forests have developed a closed canopy, tortoises may persist by occupying power-line rights-of-way and pasture margins.

**Natural history**: Tortoises construct home burrows, the openings of which are roughly the size and shape of the cross-section of the tortoise. The burrows are often 8–12 feet long and usually angle downward, ending four to five feet below the surface. The soil that is dug from the burrow is fanned out from the entrance into an "apron." Tortoises spend most of their lives in these burrows, leaving to mate or forage, usually only in warm or hot weather. Females lay 4–12 eggs each year in a single nest that is near the burrow entrance or on the apron. They feed on herbaceous plants, mostly grasses, and the type consumed depends on the season and on those that occur in the home range of each tortoise.

**Distribution and status**: Tortoises are found from central St. Tammany Parish, north through Washington Parish, and west into the northeastern part of Tangipahoa Parish east of the Tangipahoa River. Tortoises seem never to have been abundant in Louisiana, possibly due in part to undesirable soil types. The species now mostly occurs in disconnected population groups with low reproductive output, and it is considered a Species of Conservation Concern as well as threatened under the Endangered Species Act.

72a old adult (Tangipahoa Parish)

72b adult (Tangipahoa Parish)

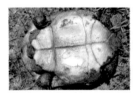

72c plastron (Washington Parish)

72d hatchling
(St. Tammany Parish)

## Green Sea Turtle (*Chelonia mydas*)
**Other names**: Green Turtle, Atlantic Green Turtle

**Description**: Green Turtles have a streamlined, bony, scute-covered carapace and forelimbs that are flipper shaped. There are **four costal scutes on each side of the carapace**. The **upper jaw is rounded in profile, and there is a single pair of enlarged scales atop the snout**. The carapace is brownish, gray brown, or olive gray, often with brown, radiating streaks on each scute. The plastron is dull to bright yellow. The skin is darkly colored above like the carapace and is white or yellow below. The shell and skin of hatchlings and juveniles are dark gray to black above and white below, with a white margin on the flippers and carapace.

**Size**: Maximum CL 60.2 inches (1,530 mm); adults usually 27.6–48.0 inches (700–1,220 mm); hatchlings 1.0–2.3 inches (25–59 mm).

**Habitat**: Green Turtles occur in the sea, usually over the continental shelf, and may also be found in shallow bays and marine estuaries in Louisiana.

**Natural history**: Green Turtles found near shore in Louisiana are usually immature individuals that enter shallow lagoons and estuaries to feed. They are not known to nest in Louisiana. In more tropical zones, females usually deposit 90–200 eggs in each clutch, nesting as many as eight times per year. However, each female may reproduce only every three years. Young turtles feed on marine invertebrates, such as sponges, jellyfish, mollusks, and polychaete worms, but adults are primarily herbivores, favoring algae and sea grasses.

**Distribution and status**: Green Turtles occur along the coast from the Biloxi Marsh in St. Bernard Parish, to estuaries in Cameron Parish, as well as near the barrier islands. They are considered transient in Louisiana waters and are listed as Threatened under the Endangered Species Act. Populations in the Atlantic Ocean basin were previously referred to as the subspecies *Chelonia mydas mydas* (Atlantic Green Turtle).

73a adult (Colombia)

73b young adult (captive)

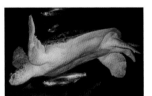

73c plastron (captive)

73d hatchling (Santa Rosa Co., FL)

## Hawksbill Sea Turtle (*Eretmochelys imbricata*)
**Other names**: Hawksbill, Atlantic Hawksbill

**Description**: Hawksbills have a streamlined, bony, scute-covered carapace, and forelimbs that are flipper shaped. There are **four costal scutes on each side of the carapace**. The **upper jaw is protruding and somewhat pointed in profile, and there are two pairs of enlarged scales atop the snout**. The carapace has a calico or mottled appearance of pale gray, orange and reddish, to dark brown patches, with the dark brown forming a feathered or radiating pattern over each scute. The plastron is dull white to yellowish, with a dark brown patch on each scute in young adults. The skin is dull white to dull yellow, and the skin and scutes on the head, neck, and top of the limbs is black or dark brown. The shell and skin of hatchlings and juveniles are dark brown or dark gray, slightly paler below. The carapace has a median keel, plus less prominent lateral keels that diminish with age.

**Size**: Maximum CL 44.5 inches (1,140 mm); adults usually 24.4–35.0 inches (620–890 mm); hatchlings 1.3–1.8 inches (32–46 mm).

**Habitat**: Hawksbills are found in the sea, usually over the continental shelf, occasionally coming to near-shore areas of Louisiana's coast.

**Natural history**: Outside of the open sea, Hawksbills tend to occur in coral reef and mangrove areas, and are rarely encountered in Louisiana. Females produce clutches of 25–250 eggs three to five times each year, although they usually reproduce about every third year. There is no evidence that they nest in Louisiana. They specialize in eating sponges, but also feed on corals, jellyfish, sea urchins, crabs, and other marine invertebrates, as well as some marine vegetation.

**Distribution and status**: Hawksbills are transient in our area and have been confirmed only a few times in Louisiana waters. The most recent capture was a few miles out of Southwest Pass, Plaquemines Parish, in 2010. They are considered Endangered under the Endangered Species Act. Populations in the Atlantic Ocean basin are sometimes referred to as the subspecies *Eretmochelys imbricata imbricata* (Atlantic Hawksbill).

74a adult (captive)

74b subadult (off Southwest Pass)

74c anterior (off Southwest Pass)

74d plastron (off Southwest Pass)

74e hatchling (Molokai, HI)

## Loggerhead Sea Turtle (*Caretta caretta*)
**Other names**: Loggerhead, Atlantic Loggerhead

**Description**: Loggerheads have shells with large scutes, forelimbs that are flipper shaped, and a **somewhat protruding, overhanging upper jaw.** There are **five, rarely six costal scutes on each side of the carapace and usually five enlarged scales on the shell bridge.** The **carapace is reddish brown to brown**, often overlain by blackish areas. The plastron is dull white to yellowish. The skin of the dorsal head, neck, and limbs is gray brown to reddish brown, while that of the underside and limb pockets is dull white to dull yellow. The shell and skin of hatchlings and juveniles are gray brown to dark brown, usually with a pale margin around the carapace, which has a median keel and pair of lateral keels.

**Size**: Maximum CL at least 57.8 inches (1,470 mm); adults usually 25.6–45.0 inches (650–1,143 mm); hatchlings 1.3–2.1 inches (33–53 mm).

**Habitat**: Loggerheads are found in the sea, usually over the continental shelf, and in the shallows near barrier islands.

**Natural history**: Loggerheads found near shore in Louisiana are usually adults traveling between feeding and nesting areas. They are known to nest in small numbers on beaches of barrier islands in Louisiana, but such events may not occur every year. Females deposit 45–170 (usually 110–130) eggs each in two or three nesting episodes per year, though females don't reproduce every year. They feed on marine invertebrates, such as sponges, jellyfish, cephalopods, gastropods, crabs, clams, and polychaete worms, as well as fish and some marine plants. The large-sized head of this species is related to the number of hard-bodied organisms in its diet and is also the source of the common name "loggerhead." The colloquial name "logger-head" is extensively used for the Alligator Snapping Turtle in Louisiana, but the name is used worldwide for this sea turtle.

**Distribution and status**: Loggerheads have been found near shore from St. Bernard to Cameron Parishes, as well as around the barrier islands. They are listed as Threatened under the Endangered Species Act. Populations in the Atlantic Ocean basin were previously referred to as the subspecies *Caretta caretta caretta* (Atlantic Loggerhead).

75a adult (LA coast)

75b subadult (captive)

75c plastron (captive)

75d hatchlings (Virginia Beach Co., VA)

## Kemp's Ridley Sea Turtle (*Lepidochelys kempii*)

**Other names**: Kemp's Ridley, Atlantic Ridley

**Description**: Ridleys are sea turtles with a bony shell that is covered by large scutes, forelimbs that are flipper shaped, and a **slightly protruding, slightly hooked upper jaw. There are five costal scutes on each side of the carapace and four enlarged scales on the shell bridge. The carapace is pale gray**, olive, or brown, and the plastron is dull white to yellowish. The skin is dull white to dull yellow, and the top of the head, neck, and flippers is gray or pale olive. The shell and skin of hatchlings and juveniles are dark gray to nearly black, and there is a median keel, plus a lateral keel on each side of the carapace, that disappear with age.

**Size**: Maximum CL 29.5 inches (749 mm); adults usually 23.2–27.5 inches (590–700 mm); hatchlings 1.5–1.9 inches (37–47 mm).

**Habitat**: Ridleys occur in the Gulf over the continental shelf, as well as in shallow bays and estuaries.

**Natural history**: Ridleys begin their lives on beaches along the western Gulf of Mexico. They remain in the Gulf or are carried into the open Atlantic by ocean currents, returning after many years to reproduce on beaches where they hatched. Nearly every female Ridley nests during daylight on a beach in Tamaulipas, Mexico, between April and July. They lay one to four clutches, usually of 90–110 eggs each, every year or two. They feed primarily on crabs, clams, and snails but also eat marine worms, jellyfish, and vegetation.

**Distribution and status**: Ridleys occur along the entire coast of Louisiana and occasionally enter coastal canals. During the 1940s, tens of thousands of female Ridleys nested each year, but the number dropped to only a few hundred by 1985. Due to protective measures on beaches, plus head-starting of eggs and juveniles, the number of annual nesters is now back into the low thousands in Mexico, and females have started nesting along the Texas coast, primarily on Padre Island. However, the Ridley remains listed as Endangered under the Endangered Species Act.

76a adult female (Rancho Nuevo, Mex.)

76b subadult (LA coast)

76d plastron (LA coast)

76c subadult (captive)

76e hatchling (Tamaulipas, Mex.)

## Leatherback Sea Turtle (*Dermochelys coriacea*)
**Other names:** Leatherback

**Description:** Leatherbacks have **elongate shells that lack scutes and have five distinct ridges down the carapace.** The forelimbs are long and flipper shaped, and the upper jaw is notched with a small cusp on each side of the notch. The **shell and skin are dark gray or blue black to black with numerous small, white spots and patches scattered over the upper surface.** The plastron is dark with four ridges that are edged with dirty white. The underside of the head, neck, and limbs is dirty white mottled with dark markings. Juveniles have numerous tiny, scalelike plates over the body and shell, and are dark gray black. The throat, rear margin of the front flippers, and rim of the carapace are white, as are the crests of the shell ridges.

**Size:** The world's largest living turtle: maximum CL 74.4 inches (1,890 mm); adults usually 48.0–70.0 inches (1,220–1,778 mm); hatchlings 2.0–2.7 inches (51–68 mm).

**Habitat:** Leatherbacks are creatures of the open ocean, rarely coming inshore.

**Natural history:** In Louisiana waters, Leatherbacks are usually only observed at the ocean surface, and there have been a few cases of them beaching but none of them nesting in the state. Elsewhere, females nest every two to four years, with up to ten clutches of 25–165 eggs in each nest. They feed primarily on jellyfish, which must be consumed in large quantities due to their low nutritive content.

**Distribution and status:** Leatherbacks occur, probably seasonally, along the length of the Louisiana coast. They are listed as Endangered under the Endangered Species Act. Populations in the Atlantic Ocean basin were previously referred to as the subspecies *Dermochelys coriacea coriacea* (Atlantic Leatherback).

77a adult (Trinidad)

77b hatchling (Panama)

## Common Snapping Turtle (*Chelydra serpentina*)
**Other names**: alligator turtle, cailleux

**Description**: Common Snapping Turtles have a relatively low shell with **three weak keels on the carapace that diminish with size and age, and lack supramarginal scutes**. The **upper jaw is slightly hooked, and the eyes are visible from above**. The tail is only a little shorter than the shell, with a serrate crest down the top. The cara-

pace is dark gray brown to black, and its underside and the plastron are dull pale yellow with brown smudges. The skin is black, brown, or gray, and paler underneath, with numerous knobby tubercles. The head of the young adult has two tan bands extending backward from the eye, the lower one angled down toward the rear of the mouth, then along the neck. Hatchlings and small juveniles have a rugose shell that is uniformly dark muddy brown to nearly black above, and dark with white markings below.

**Size**: Maximum CL 19.4 inches (494 mm), though rarely over 12 inches (30 cm) in Louisiana; adults usually 7.3–12.0 inches (185–303 mm); hatchlings are 1.0–1.5 inches (26–38 mm).

**Habitat**: Common Snapping Turtles occur in most wetlands in Louisiana, from intermediate marsh to impoundments, lakes, rivers, creeks, bayous, sloughs, swamps, and ditches. They appear to favor still rather than flowing water.

**Natural history**: Common Snapping Turtles are rarely seen unless they are in shallows (usually during spring) or crossing roads. Females lay one clutch of about 6–65 eggs each year, which may be deposited in a nest relatively far from water. Snapping Turtles eat aquatic invertebrates, such as leeches, worms, crawfish, and dragonfly larvae, as well as vertebrates such as fish, frogs, and small mammals. They also feed to some degree on aquatic vegetation and carrion.

**Distribution and status**: Common Snapping Turtles occur statewide, and recent observations and trapping surveys (1997–2013) suggest that their populations are stable.

78a adult (Lafayette Parish)

78b adult (Caldwell Parish)

78c subadult (St. Tammany Parish)

78d anterior (Lafourche Parish)

78e plastron (Reelfoot Lake, TN)

78f juvenile (East Baton Rouge Parish)

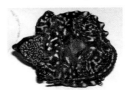

78g plastron, hatchling
(Ouachita Parish)

## Alligator Snapping Turtle (*Macrochelys temminckii*)

**Other names**: *Macroclemys temminckii,* loggerhead, trois rangs

**Description**: Alligator Snapping Turtles have a relatively low shell with **three tall ridges down the carapace**, and **three to five supramarginal scutes on each side**. The **upper jaw is strongly hooked at the tip of the narrow snout, and the eyes face to the side**. The tail is only a little shorter than the shell, with a serrate crest down  the top and on each side. The shell is brown to dark gray brown, paler beneath the rim. The plastron is also pale, though it may be water stained a rust red to black color. The skin is brown or gray, with the color the same or slightly paler underneath. A reddish, rust color often develops on the skin from natural chemicals in the water. The head of a young adult has a vague dark band extending backward from the eye onto the neck, bordered below by a paler band. The inside of the mouth is darkly colored like the skin on the outside of the head, except for the transparent, wormlike lure on the tongue that appears pink or red from the blood in the underlying blood vessels. The neck and throat often have dark irregular markings, with abundant fleshy projections from the skin. Hatchlings and small juveniles have a rugose shell that is uniformly muddy brown above with black flecks.

**Size**: Maximum carapace length 31.5 inches (800 mm); adult males usually 15.0–23.4 inches (380–595 mm), females usually 13.0–21.0 inches (330–533 mm); hatchlings 1.3–1.8 inches (34–46 mm). Maximum reported weight 268 pounds (122 kg).

**Habitat**: Alligator Snapping Turtles are wholly aquatic, occurring in permanent streams, bayous, rivers, oxbows, swamps, and lakes. They favor sites bounded by woodlands and forest, and range only marginally into open marsh habitats.

**Natural history**: Alligator Snapping Turtles rarely leave the water: young individuals may bask on logs, and females leave the water to nest. Nesting is usually done at night or in the early morning, and usually no more than 100–115 feet from the water. Females lay 10–44 eggs once per year.

Young turtles feed by luring and ambushing prey, which is accomplished by lying still on the bottom, mouth agape, exposing the wormlike lure that attracts fish. Adults tend to forage for food, which includes nearly anything digestible in the water: water hickory nuts, water tupelo fruits, acorns, muscadines, insects, leeches, mussels, crawfish, fish, amphibians, other turtles, birds, mammals, and carrion. Alligator Snapping Turtles have a reputation for being vicious biters when out of the security of water, but the same can be said of most aquatic turtle species.

**Distribution and status**: Alligator Snapping Turtles occur nearly state-wide, except in the open terrain of coastal marshes and prairie. They were heavily harvested during the 1970s and early 1980s. Commercial take was banned in 2004, and a number of trapping surveys have been conducted starting in the late 1990s to the time of writing (2015). Without baseline data on their abundance, it is difficult in that time span to determine population trends, although the turtles were found with regularity over most of Louisiana. Presently it is considered a Species of Conservation Concern.

79a adult male (Ouachita Parish)

79b adult female (Ouachita Parish)

79c juvenile (East Baton Rouge Parish)

79d anterior (Ouachita Parish)

79e plastron (Ouachita Parish)

79f juvenile (Ouachita Parish)

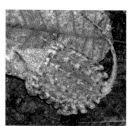

79g hatchling (Ouachita Parish)

## Common Mud Turtle (*Kinosternon subrubrum*)
**Other names**: box mud turtle

**Subspecies**: Eastern Mud Turtle (*K. s. subrubrum*), Mississippi Mud Turtle (*K. s. hippocrepis*)

**Description**: The Common Mud Turtle is a small species with a low-domed and rounded shell, and a slightly hooked upper jaw. The carapace is olive brown to dark brown, or dark brownish gray to near black. The plastron and underside of the marginal scutes are dull yellow brown to chestnut brown with darker coloration (black) following the **scute seams, which lack overlying interstitial skin**. The underside of the marginals may be entirely dark or black. The extensive plastron has two moveable hinges, and when the plastral lobes are closed, the soft parts are relatively well protected. The skin is medium brown to very dark gray, slightly paler beneath, and may be olive brown on the head. There are **two irregular, dull yellow to white stripes on the head and neck**: one may originate on the snout and pass across the upper eyelid onto the side of the head toward the neck, or it may only start at the back corner of the eye; the other stripe originates at the lower edge of the eye, crosses the corner of the mouth, and passes down across the lower jaw on the side of the head. The head stripes are irregular in that they usually vary in width, may have jagged edges, and may be broken into segments. The head may also have dark dots or other light-colored spots and streaks. Hatchlings are nearly black above except for the head stripes. Each plastral scute and underside of each marginal scute has a bright orange to dull yellow blotch surrounded by black. The carapace bears a weak keel on each side.

**Size**: Maximum CL 4.9 inches (124 mm); adults usually 3.0–4.0 inches (75–102 mm); hatchlings 0.7–1.1 inches (17–27 mm).

**Habitat:** Mud Turtles occur in most habitats in Louisiana that contain permanent or semipermanent shallow water, including fresh and intermediate marshes, sloughs, swamps, gum ponds, ditches, small streams, and bayous.

**Natural history**: Mud Turtles are aquatic and forage in shallows that are usually less than ten inches deep. The species is known to hibernate on land rather than in the water, and it may also leave the water to estivate on land if its habitat dries up. In fact, in spring Mud Turtles may be seen in very shallow pools from which their shells stick above the surface. Also, in early spring they frequently bask on logs in shallow water but rarely do so after April. Females deposit two or three clutches of two to five eggs each year, usually in shaded sites. They feed on small snails, crawfish, aquatic insects, and algae.

**Distribution and status:** Mud Turtles occur statewide, and they appear to be common in many areas. Their populations are considered stable.

80a adult (Atchafalaya Basin)

80d plastron (St. Tammany Parish)

80e plastron (Vermilion Parish)

80b adult (Atchafalaya Basin)

80c subadult (Tensas Parish)

80f hatchling (Vermilion Parish)

80g hatchling plastron
(Ouachita Parish)

## Razor-backed Musk Turtle (*Sternotherus carinatus*)
**Other names**: Keel-backed Musk Turtle, ridgeback, caouane de saule

**Description**: Razor-backed Musk Turtles have a **high, tentlike carapace with a distinct, angular ridge down the top.** The upper jaw is weakly hooked, and adults may have disproportionately large heads. The carapace is medium brown or gray brown, usually with dark flecks and streaks in a radiating pattern on each scute. The plastron is dull yellow, usually with brown smudges, and the **gular scute is usually absent**. The interstitial skin on the plastron is pale pinkish. The **skin is olive brown or pale to medium gray and covered with numerous dark dots.** Juvenile coloration is similar to that of adults, except that juveniles tend to be paler and have fewer dark markings on the shell.

**Size**: Maximum CL 6.9 inches (176 mm); adults usually 3.7–5.0 inches (95–127 mm); hatchlings 0.9–1.2 inches (23–31 mm).

**Habitat**: Razor-backed Musk Turtles are highly aquatic and usually inhabit forest-bounded rivers and streams, preferably those with some flow and some visibility in the water. They also inhabit lakes connected to flowing streams, as well as oxbows and impounded streams.

**Natural history**: Razor-backed Musk Turtles forage on the bottom, usually at depths up to two to six feet, and are often seen basking on logs and narrow tree trunks. They may also be encountered when they forage in the shallows of clear water. Females lay two clutches of one to seven eggs each year. They feed on freshwater clams, crawfish, snails, aquatic insects, and some aquatic vegetation.

**Distribution and status**: Razor-backed Musk Turtles occur over most of Louisiana, except for the southernmost portion. They are absent from the region south of Lakes Maurepas and Pontchartrain, the lower Atchafalaya Basin, and the nonforested portions of Acadiana and southwestern Louisiana. Trapping surveys conducted between 1996 and 2014 found Razor-backed Musk Turtles to be abundant at many sites, and their populations are considered stable.

81a adult (Natchitoches Parish)

81b adult (Atchafalaya Basin)

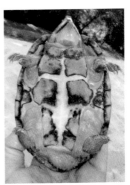

81c plastron (Natchitoches Parish)

81d juvenile (Atchafalaya Basin)

## Loggerhead Musk Turtle (*Sternotherus minor*)

**Subspecies**: Stripe-necked Musk Turtle (*S. m. peltifer*), *Sternotherus peltifer*

**Description**: Stripe-necked Musk Turtles have a carapace that is slightly domed in cross-section with a vague median peak in adults. In very old adults, the midline can become flattened, and in the very young the median peak is distinct, with a low secondary ridge on either side of the midline. The carapace is medium brown, with numerous small, dark brown spots or radiating lines and dashes on each scute. The plastron and underside of the marginals are pale yellow to brown. Pinkish interstitial skin intrudes into the seams between plastral scutes, and **a small gular scute is present**. The **skin is pale brown, and the head and neck are covered in dark brown, linear, wavy vermiculations**. The carapace of hatchlings is yellowish tan, and the plastral scutes are pale orange. The head of old adults may be extremely enlarged.

**Size**: Maximum CL 4.9 inches (124 mm); adult males usually 2.3–3.7 inches (60–95 mm), adult females usually 2.8–4.2 inches (70–107 mm); hatchlings 0.9–1.2 inches (22–30 mm).

**Habitat**: In Louisiana, the Stripe-necked Musk Turtle has been found only in the upper reaches of spring-fed streams that are surrounded by upland pine-hardwood forest.

**Natural history**: Stripe-necked Musk Turtles occupy relatively clear streams and are active in water that is 1.5–4 feet deep. There, they feed upon mollusks and other aquatic invertebrates, and occasionally on fish. Females lay one to five eggs per clutch and may lay three clutches per year.

**Distribution and status**: The half dozen Stripe-necked Musk Turtles that have been found in Louisiana were all taken in the upper tributaries of Pushepatapa Creek in Washington Parish. The species has received little study, especially in the western half of its range. Due to its limited distribution in Louisiana, apparent requirement of relatively clear water, and the lack of data on its natural history, it is considered a Species of Conservation Concern in the state.

82a adult (Washington Parish)

82b plastron (Washington Parish)

## Stinkpot (*Sternotherus odoratus*)

**Other names**: Common Musk Turtle, Eastern Musk Turtle

**Description**: Stinkpots have a **somewhat tent-like or domed shell**, and the upper jaw is slightly hooked. The carapace varies from pale brown to dark gray or black, often fading to gray brown or medium brown in old adults. In such individuals the shell may be marked with brown dots. The plastron and underside of the marginals are dull  yellow or tan, occasionally splotched with black. The **plastron bears a gular scute**, and pale interstitial skin overlays the seams. The skin is olive or gray to nearly black. There are **two nearly straight and evenly wide yellow stripes on each side of the head**: one starts on the snout and runs over the top of the eye onto the neck, and the other starts along the snout, then passes under the eye and back varying distances onto the sides of the neck. Hatchlings and juveniles have a color pattern similar to that of adults, but the carapace and skin are nearly black, and there is a pale spot on the underside of each marginal. The plastron is pale yellow with black blotches. Juveniles have a keel down the middle of the carapace, with another keel on either side, both of which disappear with age.

**Size**: Maximum CL 5.4 inches (137 mm); adults usually 2.6–4.5 inches (65–115 mm); hatchlings 0.7–1.0 inches (17–25 mm).

**Habitat**: Stinkpots inhabit most permanent water-body types in Louisiana, including swamps, lakes, ponds, rivers, bayous, and slow-moving streams. They are rare or absent in coastal marshes.

**Natural history**: Stinkpots are bottom foragers, favoring depths of up to five feet. During morning and evening, they may be seen foraging in the shallows along shorelines, and in early spring may bask on small trunks sticking out of the water. Females deposit one or more clutches of one to four eggs within 100 feet of water, but usually much closer. They feed on leeches, snails, small crawfish, aquatic insects, tadpoles, carrion, algae, and aquatic plants. Like all mud and musk turtles, Stinkpots often discharge a foul-smelling, volatile fluid from pores near the plastral bridge when captured, earning them their common name.

**Distribution and status:** Stinkpots occur statewide, except in much of the coastal marshes. Their populations are considered stable.

83a adult (St. Martin Parish)

83c adult (Lafayette Parish)

83b adult (Atchafalaya Basin)

83d plastron (Lafayette Parish)

83e subadult (St. Martin Parish)    83f subadult (Caldwell Parish)    83g hatchling (Reelfoot Lake, TN)

# Lizards

## IDENTIFICATION

All Louisiana lizards are egg layers. Most hatchlings resemble the adults, except for most skink species and Eastern Glass Lizards, in which the hatchling pattern may fade, disappear, or change completely during the first year or two of life. All Louisiana lizards have external ear openings. Most lizards are capable of losing, then regrowing their tails. Regenerated portions of tails usually do not achieve the length or color brightness of the original.

Key Characters: Lizard species are most easily recognized by characteristics of the eye, toe shape, and body scalation. Color pattern in skinks usually changes with age, and between the sexes, and there may be more variation in color pattern within than between species.

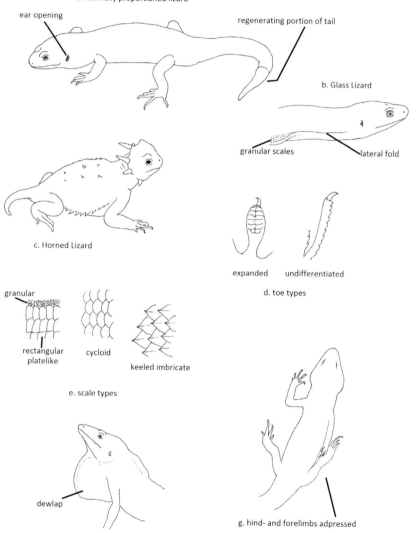

a. normally proportioned lizard

ear opening

regenerating portion of tail

b. Glass Lizard

granular scales

lateral fold

c. Horned Lizard

expanded     undifferentiated

d. toe types

granular

rectangular
platelike

cycloid

keeled imbricate

e. scale types

dewlap

g. hind- and forelimbs adpressed

f. Anole

# KEY TO LIZARD GENERA

**1a** Lacks limbs, and has a lateral fold (fig. b) . . . . . *Ophisaurus,* pp. 240–243

**1b** Limbs present, and lacks the lateral fold (fig. a) . . . . . **2**

**2a** Expanded fingers and toes (fig. d) . . . . . **3**

**2b** Fingers and toes are narrow (undifferentiated) and are rounded in cross-section (fig. d) . . . . . **4**

**3a** Eyes are large, lack lids, and have a vertical pupil, and tail is somewhat flattened and a little longer than the body . . . . . *Hemidactylus,* pp. 228–231

**3b** Eyes relatively small, with lids and a round pupil (fig. f), and a long narrow tail . . . . . *Anolis,* pp. 232–235

**4a** Flat body with spikes around the back of the head (fig. c) . . . . . *Phrynosoma,* pp. 236–237

**4b** Scales overlapping (imbricate), with a spine at the tip of those on the back and tail (fig. e) . . . . . *Sceloporus,* pp. 238–239

**4c** Scales fine and granular on the back but are in rows of platelike scales on the belly (fig. e) . . . . . *Aspidoscelis,* pp. 244–245

**4d** Smooth, cycloid scales on the body and tail (fig. e) . . . . . **5**

**5a** Toes are widely separated when the front and hind limbs are adpressed against the body . . . . . *Scincella,* pp. 246–247

**5b** Toes of the hind and front limbs touch or overlap when adpressed (fig. g) . . . . . *Plestiodon,* pp. 248–257

### Sri Lankan House Gecko (*Hemidactylus parvimaculatus*)
**Other names**: formerly within Brook's House Gecko (*Hemidactylus brookii*)

**Description**: House Geckos are of moderate build, with very large, **lidless eyes, vertical pupils,** and flared digits. The skin is covered with tiny, granular scales, which are interspersed with small, wartlike tubercles on the back and top of the head and tail. They are dull yellowish to gray with numerous brown to dark brown spots on the head and body. The **spots are somewhat rectangular and form several irregular, longitudinal rows**. A dark stripe passes from the snout back through each eye. The **tail bears brown crossbands that usually do not change to black near the tip.** The underside is whitish. Juveniles are colored like the adults. At night, under artificial light, Sri Lankan House Geckos appear pale pink and almost patternless.

**Size**: Maximum total length 4.6 inches (118 mm); maximum SVL 2.2 inches (56 mm); adults usually reach 2.0 inches (52 mm); hatchling length is unreported.

**Habitat**: House Geckos are associated with man-made structures, usually in urban settings.

**Natural history**: House Geckos were first found in Louisiana by David Heckard of the Audubon Zoo in 2012. The source of the introduced population is unknown, but they are native to Sri Lanka and the southern tip of India. They are known from four sites in Louisiana and are restricted to specific buildings at each. Their nocturnal behavior is like that of the Mediterranean Gecko. They are known to feed on insects and small frogs, and probably eat other arthropods. They lay two eggs per clutch, likely laying several clutches per year.

**Distribution and status**: House Geckos have been found in Kenner, at the Audubon Zoo in New Orleans, in Abita Springs, St. Tammany Parish, and at Galva on Pass Manchac in southern Tangipahoa Parish. They appear to be established at the zoo, but their persistence elsewhere is unknown.

84a adult (St. Tammany Parish)

84b adult (Orleans Parish)

84c venter (St. Tammany Parish)

84d hatchling (Orleans Parish)

## Mediterranean Gecko (*Hemidactylus turcicus*)

**Description**: Mediterranean Geckos are of moderate build, with large, **lidless eyes, vertical pupils**, and flared digits. The skin is covered with tiny, granular scales, which are interspersed by small, wartlike yellow tubercles on the back and top of the head and tail. They are yellowish to gray with numerous brown to dark brown spots on  the head and body. The **spots tend to be rounded and irregular or in a somewhat transverse series**. A dark stripe passes from the snout back through each eye. The upper surfaces of the limbs have irregular dark markings. The **tail bears brown crossbands that become black rings near the tip,** though these markings are usually lacking on regenerated tails. The underside is dull whitish to pale pinkish purple. Juveniles have a more strikingly crossbanded tail than adults. At night, under artificial light, Mediterranean Geckos appear pale pink and almost patternless.

**Size**: Maximum total length 5.0 inches (127 mm); maximum SVL 2.4 inches (60 mm); adults usually 1.8–2.2 inches (46–57 mm); hatchlings 0.8–1.2 inches (20–30 mm).

**Habitat**: Mediterranean Geckos are normally associated with man-made structures in urban and suburban settings. They may also be found among discarded demolition or construction debris that has been dumped in natural habitats.

**Natural history**: In their native habitat, Mediterranean Geckos are associated with rocks, rock faces, outcrops, and stone structures that offer shelter in crevices and gaps. In Louisiana, they are usually found on buildings and houses, living by day under siding, in roof gaps, or in weep holes and at night foraging across outside walls and windows. They can also be found in adjacent structures (fences, landscaping material, dead trees, sidewalk borders, etc.), and in discarded material dumped on the landscape. They are strictly nocturnal, usually not leaving shelter until dusk. They will gather in small groups near lights, feeding on insects attracted to the lights. Females lay two or three clutches of two eggs each per year. They feed on insects and spiders. Geckos bite when captured, and the tail readily breaks off.

**Distribution and status:** Mediterranean Geckos became established in New Orleans in the 1940s, likely via material shipped from the Mediterranean region. In 1988 they were in four Louisiana parishes, but by 2013 they were established in 34 parishes, and their populations are considered to be expanding.

85a adult (East Baton Rouge Parish)

85b adult, night (St. Tammany Parish)

85c ventral (Lafayette Parish)

85d hatchling (East Baton Rouge Parish)

## Carolina Green Anole (*Anolis carolinensis*)
**Other names**: Green Anole, chameleon

**Subspecies**: Northern Green Anole (*A. c. carolinensis*)

**Description**: Green Anoles are somewhat slim lizards with **flared digits** and a slender tail that is round in cross-section. The **body is covered by fine, granular scales,** and males possess an expandable dewlap. An individual's color can change relatively quickly between **bright green and medium or grayish brown.** There is often an **irregular white line down the middle of the back**. The border of the mouth and underside of the body are white. The **dewlap is bright pink or red** on the exposed skin, with the scales forming rows of white dots. In combat mode, adult males elevate a small crest on the nape and develop a black patch behind the eyes. Juveniles are colored like the adults.

**Size**: Maximum total length 9.1 inches (231 mm); maximum SVL 3.1 inches (80 mm); adult females usually 1.7–2.3 inches (44–58 mm), males often to 2.8 inches (72 mm); hatchlings 0.8–1.0 inches (20–26 mm).

**Habitat**: Green Anoles occur in shrubby areas and woodland habitats, including urban and suburban areas and their associated landscaping and structures.

**Natural history**: Green Anoles are usually found off the ground on logs, stumps, tree trunks, walls, and fences, and in vines, shrubs, and foliage of trees. When not active, especially in cool weather, they may retreat to leaf litter or the interior of logs and snags. They forage by hopping and crawling from one spot to another, periodically tasting the substrate for odors. Males are territorial and will fight other males for coveted space. To signal their territory, males bob their head and expand their dewlap. They feed on insects and spiders, and may eat flower petals. Females deposit one egg (rarely, two) at a time, at about two-week intervals from May through August. Anoles will bite and hang on if captured but are less likely to drop their tail than other lizard species.

**Distribution and status**: Green Anoles occur statewide, except in areas of trackless marsh. Their populations are considered stable.

86a adult (St. John the Baptist Parish)

86b adult (St. Martin Parish)

86c adult, dewlap (Evangeline Parish)

86d venter (West Feliciana Parish)

86e hatchling (East Baton Rouge Parish)

## Cuban Brown Anole (*Anolis sagrei*)
Other names: *Norops sagrei*

**Subspecies**: Cuban Brown Anole (*A. s. sagrei*)

**Description**: Brown Anoles are somewhat slim lizards with **flared digits** and a **low crest on the tail**. The **body is covered with tiny, granular scales**, and males possess an expandable dewlap. The dorsal surface is **pale gray or tan to brown gray**. The top of the head is reddish brown to gray, and there is a **pale stripe down the middle of the back, bordered on each side by a dark band or zone**. There **may be pale marks in the dark bands that break the area into a row of dark rectangular spots**. There are two pale stripes on the sides of the body between the back of the head to the base of the hind limbs. Large males may be dark gray or brown, with the row of black blotches along the upper sides separated from each other by pale vertical bars or rows of spots that extend down to the lower sides of the body. Darker markings on the head and tail may be present. The border of the mouth is pale and unmarked or has faint gray markings over it. The underside is dull white to very pale gray, and large males may have gray spotting on the chest and dark gray areas under the neck. The **dewlap of males is reddish orange with a yellow margin**. In combat mode, males elevate a crest on the neck and back. Hatchlings are pale gray to beige down the middle of the back and gray or reddish brown on the sides, with wavy crossbands or triangular projections from the neck to the tail base.

**Size**: Maximum total length 8.4 inches (213 mm); maximum SVL 2.5 inches (64 mm); adults usually 1.7–2.3 inches (43–59 mm); hatchlings 0.7–0.8 inches (17–19 mm).

**Habitat**: In Louisiana, Brown Anoles have only been found in urban areas.

**Natural history**: Brown Anoles tend to stay on or closer to the ground than Green Anoles. They can be found low on walls and fences, in shrubs, or on the ground near cover. They feed on insects, spiders, and other small lizards. Females lay one egg at weekly intervals through the breeding season from April to September. Brown Anoles are tropical and intolerant of cold winters. They are regularly transported via nursery plants originating from Florida to various places in the South, but the majority of these introductions seem to die out during most winters.

**Distribution and status**: Cuban Brown Anoles are native to Cuba but have spread through much of Florida, and they have appeared in nurseries in various places in southern Louisiana for several decades. By 2005 it was evident that they were established and expanding their range in the New Orleans area. Other groups of anoles have been found in Houma, Thibodaux, Lafayette, Baton Rouge, Lake Charles, and Slidell. In some cases, it is clear that populations had survived for one or more winters, but whether or not populations are permanently established in those places remains to be determined.

87a adult, dewlap (Collier Co., FL)

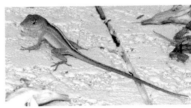

87b adult (Hancock Co., MS)

87c adult (Escambia Co., FL)

87d adult, dewlap (Escambia Co., FL)

87e venter (Orleans Parish)

87f hatchling (Orleans Parish)

## Texas Horned Lizard (*Phrynosoma cornutum*)
**Other names:** horned toad

**Description:** Horned lizards are **squat and somewhat flattened with a very short tail, a fringe of spinelike scales along the sides of the body and tail, and hornlike spikes on the rear of the head** and over each eye. The back is covered with fine, granular scales, interspersed with low spinelike scales. The scales of the belly are smooth, larger than those of the back. They are tan or brown above, with a whitish stripe down the middle of the back. A large dark brown patch occupies either side of this line on the back of the neck, and three more series of such spots occur across the back, each bordered behind by a whitish margin. A pale bar crosses between the eyes, bordered before and behind by a dark bar. Two other dark bars run below and behind each eye to the mouth. The underside of the body is white with dark gray dots on the belly. The middle of the belly and the shoulders may also be yellow. Juveniles are colored like the adults, but the spines on the head are much shorter.

**Size:** Maximum total length 7.1 inches (181 mm); adults usually 3.8–5.1 inches (97–130 mm); hatchlings 1.1–1.3 inches (29–32 mm).

**Habitat:** Over most of their range, Horned Lizards occur in open flatlands or on low hills with a sand or gravel substrate. Habitat at historical Louisiana sites was probably open pine on low, sandy hills.

**Natural history:** Horned Lizards actively forage in open or semi-open areas. They have a highly cryptic color pattern and are usually seen only when they scurry away when approached. They feed almost exclusively on harvester ants. Females produce an annual clutch of 13–49 eggs. Horned Lizards rarely attempt to bite when captured but wriggle vigorously and in so doing tend to jab their horns into one's hands and fingers. When stressed, they can spurt a small jet of blood from the corner of the eye to deter predators.

**Distribution and status:** There are at least a dozen records for Horned Lizards in Louisiana, but many are from urban areas and are probably based on released pets. There is a 1900 comment about them being common around Monroe, Ouachita Parish; there are two records from the 1920s in

Caddo Parish and another in 1965 near Quitman, Jackson Parish. It is not known whether these last records represent wild populations, extirpated introductions, or animals brought in from Texas or Oklahoma in oil field equipment. The Horned Lizard is tentatively considered an extirpated species for Louisiana.

88a adult (Grant Co., NM)

88b juvenile (Cleveland Co., OK)

## Prairie Fence Lizard (*Sceloporus consobrinus*)

**Other names:** Prairie Lizard, Northern Fence Lizard, Southern Fence Lizard, *Sceloporus undulatus,* pine swift, bluebelly

**Description:** Prairie Fence Lizards are of medium build. The body is covered by **moderate-sized scales that are smooth on the belly but more overlapping and with a spiny tip on each on the back and sides of the body**. They are brown or gray above, often with a rust-colored or dark brown band on each side of the body within which are  often small pale dots. Above the lateral band is another that is a little paler than the middle of the back. A **half-dozen dark, transverse bars cross the back in the form of paired chevrons that extend down to the lateral stripe.** The dark bars are obvious in females but often narrowed or somewhat obscured in males. Dark crossbands may be distinct or vague on the tail. There is usually a dark streak through or behind the eye. The underside is white to gray, and there is an **elongate medium blue patch on each side of the belly**, and a blue area on the throat. In males the blue bands may be dark blue, bordered on the inner side by black, and in older males the black may cover the middle of the belly, chest, and chin. Juveniles are colored like the females.

**Size:** Maximum length 7.7 inches (196 mm); maximum SVL 3.1 inches (80 mm); adults usually 2.1–2.8 inches (53–72 mm); hatchlings 0.8–1.1 inches (20–27 mm).

**Habitat:** Prairie Fence Lizards inhabit well-drained, open-canopy woodlands dominated by pine or of mixed pine-hardwoods.

**Natural history:** Prairie Fence Lizards occur in woodlands that have abundant sun exposure near ground level. They tend to be climbers, living around or on trees, walls, fences, logs, woodpiles, and rocks. If encountered on the ground, they usually dash for the nearest tree and run around and up the opposite side. In spring, the adults are often found in pairs. Females produce clutches of 4–12 eggs two to five times each year. They feed on insects and other arthropods. When defending territory or courting, males will laterally compress their bodies to expose their blue throats and bellies. They will bite when captured but are less likely to lose the tail than some other lizard species.

**Distribution and status**: Prairie Fence Lizards occur in the Florida Parishes, and in northern and central Louisiana they occur west of the Mississippi Delta and upper Atchafalaya region. Conversion of open woodlands to dense pine plantations has reduced their preferred habitat. Otherwise, their populations seem to be stable over much of their range.

89a adult (Natchitoches Parish)

89b adult (St. Tammany Parish)

89c adult (Natchitoches Parish)

89d adult female (Union Parish)

89e subadult (East Feliciana Parish)

89f venter, male top, female bottom
(Natchitoches Parish)

89g juvenile (West Feliciana Parish)

## Slender Glass Lizard (*Ophisaurus attenuatus*)

**Other names**: glass snake

**Subspecies**: Western Slender Glass Lizard (*O. a. attenuatus*)

**Description**: Slender Glass Lizards are **elongate and limbless with a lateral fold that produces a groove on each side of the body,** and with long tails. The scales of the back and underside are squared and form rows. The scales in the lateral fold are granular. They are dull yellow to pale tan above, with a black stripe running along the upper side of the body and tail, below which are one or two narrower black stripes alternating with white stripes. **One or two thin brown stripes run along the upper portion of the lateral fold**, and there is usually a **dark brown to black vertebral stripe**. There are vertical dark and light bars on the mouth and sides of the face and neck. Old adults develop white spots on the black lateral stripe, so that the sides appear black and white dotted. Also, short, white crossbars appear on the dorsal ground color, and the head may become speckled with white. The underside is white to yellow with vague dark lines between the rows of scales. Juveniles are pale gold with prominent dorsal and lateral stripes, as well as black lines under the body and tail.

**Size**: Maximum total length 42.0 inches (1,067 mm); maximum SVL 11.4 inches (289 mm); adults usually 5.9–10.6 inches (150–270 mm); hatchlings 2.0–2.5 inches (50–63 mm).

**Habitat**: Slender Glass Lizards occur in areas of tall grass in open woodlands such as pine savannas, grasslands, marsh margins, and cheniers.

**Natural history**: Slender Glass Lizards are diurnal predators that are most often observed in or along the margins of grassy swales. They are frequently observed along the coast of southwestern Louisiana and less often in remnant prairie and open woodlands. Females produce 4–16 eggs, which they guard by remaining coiled around the clutch. They feed on insects and other arthropods, small lizards, and snakes. Slender Glass Lizards give a pinching bite when captured and will often break, or seemingly throw, their tail off with little provocation.

**Distribution and status**: Slender Glass Lizards occur in the upper Florida Parishes, and in western Louisiana they occur in the prairies and cheniers of the southwest as far east as Lafayette Parish. From there they range northward in central and northern Louisiana west of the Mississippi River Delta but are absent from the Red River bottomland. The species is rarely encountered outside of a few areas in western Louisiana, and its habitat requirements are poorly known. It is a Species of Conservation Concern.

90a old adult (Vernon Parish)

90b young adult (Cameron Parish)

90c anterior (Vernon Parish)

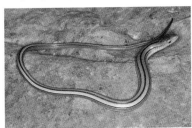
90d juvenile (Benton Co., AR)

## Eastern Glass Lizard (*Ophisaurus ventralis*)
**Other names**: glass snake

**Description**: Eastern Glass Lizards are **elongate and limbless with long tails and a lateral fold that forms a groove on each side of the body**. The scales of the back and underside are squared and form rows. The scales in the lateral fold are granular. As juveniles they have a broad tan or coppery band down the back and tail, **without a**

**continuous black stripe down the middle**, and each side is striped with three or four dark brown or black lines that alternate with dull white to pale olive lines. There are **no lines on the lateral fold**, and the face and neck are marked by vertical black and white bars. The underside is pale yellow. Within the first year, the pale lines on the sides acquire a black mark on each scale, and each row of brown scales on the back develops dark lines through their centers. As adults, each of the brown scales of the back, and the pale scales of the sides, takes on a yellow to pale green tint, and the overall effect is of tightly spaced rows of green dots over a dark head, body, and tail. The underside may be pale or deep yellow.

**Size**: Maximum total length 42.6 inches (1,083 mm); maximum SVL 12.0 inches (306 mm); adults usually 6.9–11.2 inches (174–285 mm); hatchlings 1.8–2.0 inches (46–50 mm).

**Habitat**: Eastern Glass Lizards occur in areas of tall grass in open pine flatwoods and savanna, forest clearings, marsh borders, and grassy areas of barrier islands.

**Natural history**: Eastern Glass Lizards are diurnal foragers usually found in and alongside grassy swales. They seem to be most common in pine-sawgrass flatwoods on the north shore of Lake Pontchartrain. They feed on insects and other arthropods, snails, small lizards and snakes, and the eggs of ground-nesting birds. Females produce a clutch of 4–15 (usually 7–10) eggs, which they guard by remaining coiled around the clutch. Glass lizards give a pinching bite when captured and will often break, or seemingly throw, their tail off with little provocation.

**Distribution and status**: The Eastern Glass Lizard occurs in the Florida Parishes, except for the Mississippi River floodplain and Tunica Hills. It also occurs on Grande Isle off the coast of southern Jefferson Parish. Two specimens were collected in the mid-1900s in Terrebonne and Lafourche Parishes. In general, glass lizards seem to be declining in the South, and it is considered a Species of Conservation Concern.

91a old adult (St. Tammany Parish)

91b adult (Glynn Co., GA)

91c venter (St. Tammany Parish)

91d anterior (Tangipahoa Parish)

91e juvenile (St. Tammany Parish)

## Six-lined Racerunner (*Aspidoscelis sexlineata*)

**Other names**: *Cnemidophorus sexlineatus*

**Subspecies**: Eastern Six-lined Racerunner (*A. s. sexlineatus*)

**Description**: Racerunners are of medium build, with a relatively long tail. The **scales of the back and throat are tiny and granular, those of the chest and belly are large and squared,** and those of the tail are also squared and are arrayed in rings. They are **black or very dark brown above, with six cream to yellow stripes** running from the back of the eye and nape onto the tail. The paravertebral stripes extend only a short way onto the tail and enclose a brown vertebral band. The lateral stripes extend halfway onto the tail, which is otherwise brown or gray. The underside and lower sides of the body are white or very pale blue. During the breeding season, adult males have a neon green wash over the face and sides of the body, and the throat and chest are bright blue. Juveniles are colored like the adults, except that they have blue tails.

**Size**: Maximum total length 9.5 inches (242 mm), maximum SVL 3.0 inches (76 mm); adults usually 2.2–2.8 inches (56–71 mm); hatchlings 1.1–1.4 inches (28–35 mm).

**Habitat**: Racerunners occur in dry, open, or semi-open habitats, preferably with sandy soil. They occur in open pine or mixed pine-hardwoods, scrublands, remnant prairie, riparian sand banks, liveoak ridges, cheniers, and sand dunes.

**Natural history**: Racerunners are terrestrial, active foragers that make rapid dashes interspersed with nervous movements during searches for prey. They are most active during the heat of the day and have an oddly short season of activity from mid-April to early September. Females produce one or two clutches of one to six (usually three) eggs, which are deposited in burrows they construct in the soil. They feed on insects and other arthropods. Racerunners are difficult to capture or photograph, due to their erratic stop-and-dash movements, rarely holding still for more than a moment.

**Distribution and status:** Racerunners occur in the upper Florida Parishes, north shore area of Lake Pontchartrain, and coastal beach and chenier zone of southwestern Louisiana. The bulk of their range is in northern and central Louisiana on either side of the Red River bottoms as far south as Beauregard, Evangeline, and northeastern Rapides Parishes. Their distribution is widely scattered in many areas, but their populations appear to be stable where they still exist.

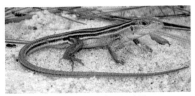

92a adult male (Natchitoches Parish)

92b adult male (Bienville Parish)

92c adult female (Catahoula Parish)

92d venter (Bienville Parish)

92e juvenile (Caddo Parish)

### Little Brown Skink (*Scincella lateralis*)
**Other names**: Ground Skink, soudée, chien de terre

**Description**: Little Brown Skinks are somewhat slender with relatively **short limbs that are widely separated from each other when addressed** along the sides of the body. All scales on the body and tail are small and cycloid, making the surface appear smooth and shiny. The **dorsum is occupied by a broad band that is coppery to**  **medium brown or gray,** which may break into pale spots on the top of the tail. There are usually small black spots in the band that may form vague rows. A dark brown or black upper lateral band runs from the snout, through the eye, to about the middle of the tail, where it grades into the dark gray of the posterior part of the tail. The lower sides bear several alternating dark and pale stripes or lines. The chin and throat are usually white, the belly yellow, and underside of the tail is blue gray. Hatchlings and juveniles have dull blue or bluish gray tails.

**Size**: Maximum total length 5.7 inches (146 mm); maximum SVL 2.3 inches (59 mm); adults usually 1.3–2.2 inches (30–55 mm); hatchlings 0.7–0.8 inches (18–21 mm).

**Habitat**: Little Brown Skinks occupy nearly all Louisiana habitats, from urban gardens and marshes to forests with a mostly closed canopy. The least favorable habitat is open grasslands; hardwood forests with an abundance of leaf litter are preferred.

**Natural history**: Being small in size, Little Brown Skinks are often the first lizards of the day to be observed, usually nervously foraging through leaf litter. Despite their localized abundance, their constant movement and quick dives into leaf litter make them difficult to photograph or capture. They occupy small territories, and populations have been estimated at up to 260 individuals per acre. Individuals near small streams and in marshes have been observed to take shelter under water. Females lay up to four clutches per year, with one to five eggs in each. They feed on small insects, spiders, and worms.

**Distribution and status**: The Little Brown Skink occurs statewide, except in coastal zones of extensive marsh. Their ubiquity and abundance indicate secure populations.

93a adult (Evangeline Parish)

93b adult (Vermilion Parish)

93c adult (St. Tammany Parish)

93d adult (Lafayette Parish)

93e venter (St. John the Baptist Parish)

93f juvenile (East Baton Rouge Parish)

## Coal Skink (*Plestiodon anthracinus*)
**Other names**: *Eumeces anthracinus*

**Subspecies**: Southern Coal Skink (*P. a. pluvialis*)

**Description**: Coal Skinks are of medium build, with smooth, cycloid scales covering the body and tail. They are **brown or grayish brown on the top of the back, with a broad black or dark brown band on the sides** that runs from the side of the head to partway onto the tail. The dark band is bordered above and below by a pale line. Some individuals have a vague, pale line down the middle of the back, and they usually have **white spots and/or dark marks on the upper labial scales**. During the breeding season adult males have orange faces and chins. Below, they are brownish gray with a fine dark margin to each scale. **Juveniles are black with orange and white spots on the face and upper labials**, and the tail is dark blue. There are **four upper labials and an undivided postmental scale** (the second broad scale back from the margin of the front of the lower jaw).

**Size**: Maximum total length 7.0 inches (178 mm); maximum SVL 2.8 inches (70 mm); adults usually 1.9–2.4 inches (48–61 mm); hatchlings 0.7–0.9 inches (19–23 mm).

**Habitat**: Coal Skinks inhabit wooded uplands, especially those dominated by pines, as well as pine flatwoods.

**Natural history**: Coal Skinks may be either terrestrial or arboreal, occurring around rocks and logs, or ascending trees, snags, and stumps. They are strictly diurnal. Females produce a clutch of 5–13 (usually 7 or 8) eggs, which they guard in cavities under rocks and other secluded spots. They feed on insects and other arthropods.

**Distribution and status**: Coal Skinks occur in the Florida Parishes and in wooded uplands of northern and central Louisiana as far south as the Camp Livingston area, Rapides Parish, northern Evangeline Parish, and the vicinity of DeRidder, Beauregard Parish. The species' natural history is poorly known in Louisiana, and most recent records are from a few sites in central Louisiana. For those reasons, it is considered a Species of Conservation Concern.

94a adult (Natchitoches Parish)

94b adult (southern MO)

94c subadult (Benton Co., AR)

94d venter (Nevada Co., AR)

94e juvenile (Muskogee Co., OK)

## Southern Prairie Skink (*Plestiodon obtusirostris*)

**Other names**: *Eumeces septentrionalis obtusirostris*

**Subspecies**: Southern Prairie Skink (*P. o. obtusirostris*)

**Description**: Prairie Skinks are of medium build, with smooth, cycloid scales covering the body and tail. They are **brown or grayish brown on the top of the back, with a black or dark brown band on each side** that runs from the side of the head to partway onto the tail. The dark band is bordered above, and usually below, by a pale line. Some individuals have a vague, pale line down the middle of the back, and the **upper labial scales are pale and unmarked.** During the breeding season adult males have orange faces and chins. Below, they are gray with a fine dark margin to each scale. **Juveniles are striped** and have blue tails. There are **four upper labials and a transversely divided postmental scale** (the second broad scale back from the margin of the front of the lower jaw, in which the dividing seam contacts the first lower labial scale on each side).

**Size**: Maximum total length 7.9 inches (201 mm); maximum SVL 2.9 inches (75 mm); adults usually 2.2–2.8 inches (55–70 mm); hatchlings 0.9–1.0 inches (24–26 mm).

**Habitat**: In Louisiana, Prairie Skinks have been found in well-drained woodland.

**Natural history**: In Louisiana, Prairie Skinks have been found under logs in mixed forest, and two were found on the ground in a yard adjacent to pine woodland. Females produce a clutch of six to ten eggs, which they guard. They are known to feed on arthropods.

**Distribution and status**: The Southern Prairie Skink has been found at several upland localities in Caddo and northern De Soto Parishes, and near Hico in Lincoln Parish. Because of its small range in Louisiana and a paucity of data on its biology in the state, it is considered a Species of Conservation Concern.

95a adult (Sebastian Co., AR)

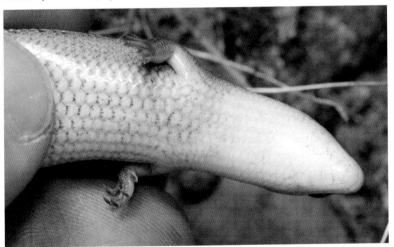

95b venter (Sebastian Co., AR)

## Common Five-lined Skink (*Plestiodon fasciatus*)
Other names: *Eumeces fasciatus*

**Description**: Common Five-lined Skinks are of medium build, with smooth, cycloid scales over the body and tail. **Juveniles are black above with five cream-colored stripes**: one down the middle of the back originates from a **cream hairpin-shaped mark on the snout and crown**, one on each upper side (dorsolateral) originates  from just above the eye, and one on each lower side of the body originates from the upper lip. The area just below the lower stripe is also black. The **dorsolateral stripe is almost one scale in width, covering a fourth to a half of the adjoining scale rows**. The dark ground color and pale stripes fade a short distance onto the **tail, which is otherwise slightly pale to medium blue**. The underside is whitish to very pale gray. As the skink ages, the blue of the tail becomes gray, the stripes become dull white to tan, and the top of the head and center of dark areas on the upper back become brown. In adult males, stripes fade even more, especially the vertebral stripe, which may fade almost completely. During breeding season, the snouts and faces of adult males become bright orange. There are **four or five upper labial scales** and a **row of enlarged scales under the tail**.

**Size**: Maximum total length 8.7 inches (222 mm); maximum SVL 3.4 inches (86 mm); adults usually 2.1–3.2 inches (54–81 mm); hatchlings 0.9–1.1 inches (23–27 mm).

**Habitat**: Five-lined Skinks are found in most forest and woodland habitats in Louisiana, though they occur sparsely in open pine savannah.

**Natural history**: Five-lined Skinks are good climbers and are often observed on the trunks of trees and on stumps, logs, fences, and railings. Strictly diurnal, they are active foragers. In hot weather, they tend to bask briefly early in the morning, otherwise remaining close to vegetative cover. Females produce a clutch of 5–14 (usually 6–8) eggs, which they guard in cavities, usually beneath or inside decaying wood. They feed on insects and other arthropods. Five-lined Skinks bite when captured and readily drop their tails.

**Distribution and status**: The Common Five-lined Skink occurs statewide in wooded habitats. Their populations are considered stable.

96a adult (St. Martin Parish)

96b adult (Atchafalaya Basin)

96c adult (East Carroll Parish)

96d adult (Wilkinson Co., MS)

96e adult (Natchitoches Parish)

96f venter (Grant Parish)

96g hatchling (AL)

## Southeastern Five-lined Skink (*Plestiodon inexpectatus*)

**Other names**: *Eumeces inexpectatus*

**Description**: Southeastern Five-lined Skinks are of medium build, with smooth, cycloid scales over the body and tail. **Juveniles are black above with five cream or yellow stripes**: one down the middle of the back originates from an **orange hairpin-shaped mark on the snout and crown**, one on each upper side (dorsolateral) originates

from just above the eye, and one on each lower side originates from the upper lip. The area just below the lower stripe is also black. The **dorsolateral stripe is less than one scale in width, often present only on part of one scale row or the edges of adjoining scale rows**. The dark ground color and pale stripes fade a short distance onto the **tail, which is otherwise medium to dark blue**. The underside is dull white to pale gray, paler on the chin and throat. As the skink ages, the blue of the tail becomes gray or brown, the stripes become dull white to tan, and the top of the head and center of dark areas on the upper back become brown. The stripes retain black borders. In adult males, stripes fade even more so, especially the vertebral stripe, which may fade completely. During the breeding season, the snouts and faces of adult males becomes bright orange. There are **usually four upper labial scales** and **no enlarged row of scales under the tail**.

**Size**: Maximum total length 8.5 inches (216 mm), maximum SVL 3.5 inches (89 mm); adults usually 2.2–3.2 inches (57–82 mm); hatchlings 1.0–1.1 inches (25–27 mm).

**Habitat**: Southeastern Five-lined Skinks occur in pine and mixed pine-hardwood forests. They are most abundant in open longleaf or slash pine woodlands.

**Natural history**: Southeastern Five-lined Skinks spend much of their time off the ground, usually on and around logs, stumps, and dead trees. They are strictly diurnal and actively forage for prey. They feed on insects, spiders, and other arthropods. Females produce a clutch of 5–13 eggs, which they guard in cavities in decaying logs or under surface objects. Five-lined Skinks bite when captured and readily drop their tails.

**Distribution and status:** The Southeastern Five-lined Skink is restricted to the Florida Parishes but is absent from the Tunica Hills and Mississippi River bottomland. They remain fairly common at a number of sites, and their populations are considered stable.

97a adult female (Washington Parish)

97b adult male (Tangipahoa Parish)

97c venter (Tangipahoa Parish)

97d juvenile (Hancock Co., MS)

## Broad-headed Skink (*Plestiodon laticeps*)
Other names: *Eumeces laticeps,* scorpion

Description: Broad-headed Skinks are of medium build, with smooth, cycloid scales over
the body and tail. **Juveniles are black above,
with five yellow stripes**: one down the middle
of the back originates from a **yellow or orange
hairpin-shaped mark on the snout and crown,**
one on each upper side (dorsolateral) originates

from just above the eye, and one on each lower side originates from the
upper lip. The area just below the lower stripe is also black, which may in
turn be bordered below by another pale line. The **dorsolateral stripe is
less than to nearly one scale in width and occupies the middle of a scale
row or portions of adjoining scale rows.** The dark ground color and pale
stripes fade a short distance onto the **tail, which is otherwise medium to
dark blue.** The underside is pale gray, except the chin and throat, which
are white. As the skink ages, the blue of the tail becomes gray or brown,
the stripes become dull white to tan, and the top of the head and center
of dark areas on the upper back become brown. The stripes retain black
borders if they do not fade completely. In **adult males, the stripes fade
and vanish so that the upper body and tail are plain coppery tan.** The
rear of the head of adult males widens to such an extent that the head is
triangular in dorsal profile, and during the breeding season, the entire
head becomes bright orange. There are **five upper labial scales** and **a row
of enlarged scales under the tail.**

Size: Maximum total length 12.8 inches (324 mm), maximum SVL 5.6
inches (143 mm); adults usually 3.2–5.1 inches (81–129 mm); hatchlings
1.2–1.4 inches (30–35 mm).

Habitat: Broad-headed Skinks occur primarily in hardwood forests or in
mixed pine-hardwood forests, from swamp margins to uplands.

Natural history: Broad-headed Skinks spend much of their lives in trees,
preferring large hardwoods, such as oaks and sweetgums, that have hollow
cavities and crevices for shelter, or around hollow logs, brush, and wood
piles. Pairs may spend the season together by sharing the same shelter
and foraging area. Females lay a clutch of 6–27 (usually 15–22) eggs, which

they guard in cavities in trees, logs, or humus piles. They feed on insects and other invertebrates, smaller lizards, and some fruits, such as blackberries. They can provide a painful, pinching bite when captured. Male Broad-headed Skinks are sometimes called "scorpions" and are mistakenly thought to be venomous or capable of stinging with their tails.

**Distribution and status**: Broad-headed Skinks occur statewide in forested areas, except in the chenier woodlands near the southwest coast, river batture, and swamp forest. Their population status appears to be secure.

98a adult male (Ouachita Parish)

98b adult female (Wilkinson Co., MS)

98c adult female (East Baton Rouge Parish)

98d adult (Jefferson Co., TX)

98e venter (St. Tammany Parish)

98f hatchling (Ouachita Parish)

# Snakes

## IDENTIFICATION

Snakes are limbless, with bodies that are longer than the tails, and lack eyelids and external ear openings. The underside of the body bears a series of transverse plates (ventrals). They either lay eggs or produce living young. The neonates possess the form and structure of the adults, differing, if at all, by color pattern (Racer, Yellow-bellied Water Snake, Cottonmouth). In most species, color pattern does not change as adults.

Key characters: Snake genera are differentiated from each other by forms of scalation (counts, keeling of scales, division of the anal shield) and other external features, such as presence or absence of loreal pits and rattles. Dorsal scales are counted midway along the body, from the first scale bordering a ventral plate (scale), in an alternating fashion over the top, to the last scale bordering a ventral plate on the other side (fig. f).

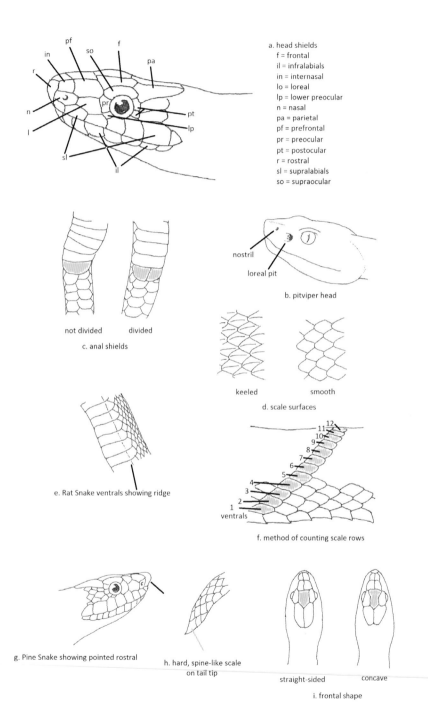

a. head shields
  f = frontal
  il = infralabials
  in = internasal
  lo = loreal
  lp = lower preocular
  n = nasal
  pa = parietal
  pf = prefrontal
  pr = preocular
  pt = postocular
  r = rostral
  sl = supralabials
  so = supraocular

nostril

loreal pit

b. pitviper head

not divided    divided

c. anal shields

keeled    smooth

d. scale surfaces

e. Rat Snake ventrals showing ridge

12
11
10
9
8
7
6
5
4
3
2
1
ventrals

f. method of counting scale rows

g. Pine Snake showing pointed rostral

h. hard, spine-like scale
on tail tip

straight-sided    concave

i. frontal shape

# KEY TO SNAKE GENERA

**1a**  Loreal pits are present, and the pupil is vertical (fig. b) . . . . . **17**

**1b**  Loreal pits are absent, and the pupil is round (fig. a) . . . . . **2**

**1c**  Loreal pits are absent, eye is visible only as a dark dot under a shield, tail and head are bluntly rounded, and all scales are cycloid . . . . . *Indotyphlops,* pp. 264–265

**2a**  Dorsal scales are keeled (fig. d), and the anal shield is not divided (fig. c) . . . . . **3**

**2b**  Dorsal scales are keeled (fig. d), at least on the upper back, and the anal shield is divided (fig. c) . . . . . **4**

**2c**  Dorsal scales are smooth throughout (fig. d), and the anal shield is not divided (fig. c) . . . . . **9**

**2d**  Dorsal scales are smooth throughout (fig. d), and the anal shield is divided (fig. c) . . . . . **10**

**3a**  Nineteen scale rows, rostral scale not pointed, and belly without large dark markings . . . . . *Thamnophis,* pp. 304–310

**3b**  Twenty-nine or 31 scale rows, rostral scale pointed (fig. g), and belly with large dark markings . . . . . *Pituophis,* pp. 332–335

**4a**  At least 21 scale rows . . . . . **5**

**4b**  Nineteen or fewer scale rows . . . . . **6**

**5a**  Scales on the middle sides are keeled, and rostral is pointed and upturned . . . . . *Heterodon,* pp. 276–277

**5b**  Scales on the middle sides are keeled, rostral is normal, and belly is smooth from side to side . . . . . *Nerodia,* pp. 292–303

**5c**  Scales on the middle sides are smooth, rostral is normal, and belly has a slight "edge" on each side (fig. e) . . . . . *Pantherophis,* pp. 322–331

**6a**  Nineteen scale rows . . . . . **7**

**6b**  Fifteen or 17 scale rows . . . . . **8**

**7a**  Two black stripes down the belly, and pale ventral color only goes up to the first scale row . . . . . *Liodytes,* pp. 288–289

**7b**  One black stripe down the middle of the belly, and pale ventral color goes three scales up the sides . . . . . *Regina,* pp. 290–291

**8a**  Five supralabial scales on each side, and the tail is short . . . . . *Haldea,* pp. 284–285

**8b**  Six or seven supralabial scales on each side, tail of moderate length, and back marked by stripes and/or black dots . . . . . *Storeria,* pp. 280–283

**8c** Seven supralabial scales on each side, tail long and slender, and back plain green . . . . . *Opheodrys,* pp. 316–317

**9a** Rostral pointed, usually six supralabial scales, and belly entirely white and unmarked . . . . . *Cemophora,* pp. 336–337

**9b** Rostral normal, seven or eight supralabial scales, and belly with obvious dark and pale markings . . . . . *Lampropeltis,* pp. 338–349

**10a** Thirteen or 19 scale rows, and tail with a hard, spinelike scale on the end (fig. h) . . . . . **11**

**10b** Fifteen or 17 scale rows and tail with a normal tip . . . . . **12**

**11a** Thirteen midbody scale rows, five or six supralabials, and belly pink and not marked . . . . . *Carphophis,* pp. 268–271

**11b** Nineteen midbody scale rows, seven or eight supralabials, and belly red with black blotches or rows of black spots . . . . . *Farancia,* pp. 272–275

**12a** Fifteen scale rows . . . . . **13**

**12b** Seventeen scale rows . . . . . **14**

**13a** Dorsum dark gray, belly and neck ring bright yellow, and has a loreal scale (fig. a) . . . . . *Diadophis,* pp. 266–267

**13b** Dorsum tan, belly pink, and lacks a loreal scale . . . . . *Tantilla,* pp. 318–321

**13c** Black, red, and yellow rings along entire body, dorsal and ventral, and lacks a loreal scale . . . . . *Micrurus,* pp. 350–353

**14a** Small snakes never more than 16 inches long, with no lower preocular and a straight-sided frontal (fig. i) . . . . . **15**

**14b** Snakes over three feet long as adults, with a small lower preocular (fig. a), and a frontal that is concave on the sides (fig. i) . . . . . **16**

**15a** Six supralabial scales, tail short, and no stripes along the face . . . . . *Virginia,* pp. 286–287

**15b** Seven supralabial scales, relatively long tail, and a dark and light stripe along the face . . . . . *Rhadinaea,* pp. 278–279

**16a** Usually seven, sometimes eight, supralabials and 15 scale rows just in front of the vent . . . . . *Coluber,* pp. 311–313

**16b** Usually eight supralabials and 13 scale rows just in front of the vent . . . . . *Masticophis,* pp. 314–315

**17a** No segmented rattle on the end of the tail . . . . . *Agkistrodon,* pp. 354–359

**17b** Segmented rattle on tail and nine large plates on top of the head . . . . .
*Sistrurus,* pp. 360–361

**17c** Segmented rattle on tail and several large plates, plus numerous small scales
on top of the head . . . . . *Crotalus,* pp. 362–365

### Brahminy Blind Snake (*Indotyphlops braminus*)

**Other names**: Common Blind Snake, flowerpot snake, *Ramphotyphlops braminus, Typhlops braminus*

**Description**: Blind Snakes are very small and entirely cylindrical with a **bluntly rounded head and tail**, the latter with a small spine on the tip. Overall, they are polished dark brown to nearly black, vaguely paler below and around the mouth. The tail is only about as long as it is wide. The **eyes are visible as dark dots that are entirely covered by a large shieldlike scale.** Blind snakes become overall silvery gray a few days prior to shedding their skin. There are **20 rows of nondifferentiated cycloid scales around the body**.

**Size**: Maximum length 8.0 inches (203 mm); adults usually 5.0–6.0 inches (127–153 mm); hatchlings approximately 2.3 inches (58 mm).

**Habitat**: In Louisiana, Blind Snakes occur in urban and suburban settings into which they have been introduced.

**Natural history**: Brahminy Blind Snakes usually remain in the soil but occasionally come to the surface during warm rains and may be found abroad or under surface objects. They are also called "flowerpot snakes" because they are frequently transported via the nursery industry in potted plants. They are unique among serpents in being parthenogenetic, which means that the species consists solely of females that reproduce asexually. Thus, a single snake, liberated from nursery products, can establish a population. Blind snakes lay one to seven (usually two to four) eggs and feed on termites and ant pupae and larvae. Blind snakes are not truly blind, but vision is probably limited to shades of dark and light.

**Distribution and status**: The Brahminy Blind Snake is native to southern Asia, though the boundaries of its native range have been blurred by its spread by man throughout the Orient. It has become established in parts of Africa, the East Indies, Australia, Mexico, and the southeastern United States. The first Louisiana specimen was found in New Orleans in 1996 by Dr. Robert Thomas of Loyola University. It has since been found in other parts of the New Orleans area, in Luling, Thibodaux, and Lafayette, and is sure to become established in other parts of the state.

99a adult, head at lower right (Orleans Parish)

99b anterior (India)    99c juvenile (Orleans Parish)

## Ring-necked Snake (*Diadophis punctatus*)

**Subspecies**: Southern Ring-necked Snake (*D. p. punctatus*): a single row of half-moon shaped dark spots down the midventer, neck ring split on the nape. Mississippi Ring-necked Snake (*D. p. stictogenys*): an irregular series of dark spots down the midventer, neck ring not split on the nape.

**Description**: Ring-necked Snakes are of moderate to slim build, with the head scarcely wider than the neck, and relatively short tails. Adults are **dark gray above and deep yellow below**. The ventral color is often more orange toward the tail. The base of each ventral scale has a central black spot or scattered black dots that form a line or irregular series. The top of the head to the middle of the upper labials is darker gray than the body and may be nearly black. There is a **distinct yellow collar around the dorsal neck that is connected to the ventral color** and bordered behind by a black margin. Hatchlings and juveniles are usually darker gray than the adults. The scales are smooth and in 15 rows around the body. The anal shield is divided.

**Size**: Maximum length 19 inches (482 mm), though rarely over 12.5 inches (315 mm) in Louisiana; adults usually 8.0–12.4 inches (203–316 mm); hatchlings 3.0–4.2 inches (76–107 mm).

**Habitat**: Ring-necked Snakes occur in wooded areas, including bottomland hardwoods, open pine flatwoods, and forested uplands.

**Natural history**: Ring-necked Snakes are usually found in leaf litter, and under and inside rotting logs and other ground cover. They are rarely encountered moving about in the open. They feed on earthworms, insect larvae, salamanders, and small skinks. Females lay a clutch of two to five (usually three or four) eggs. Ring-necked Snakes do not bite when handled. When molested, they may coil the tail and hold it downside up to expose the bright orange color of the underside, ostensibly to draw the attention of predators away from the head or as a warning of bad taste.

**Distribution and status**: Ring-necked Snakes occur in the southeastern part of Louisiana as far west as the Atchafalaya Basin. In northern Louisiana, it occurs from the Red River region eastward, with few records west of the Red River in Caddo, Calcasieu, Natchitoches, Rapides and Sabine Parishes. They are common in many parts of the state, with apparently stable populations.

100a adult (Catahoula Parish)

100b adult (Washington Parish)

100c venter (Catahoula Parish)

100d anterior (Santa Rosa Co., FL)

100e juvenile (East Baton Rouge Parish)

## Common Worm Snake (*Carphophis amoenus*)
**Other names**: Eastern Worm Snake

**Subspecies**: Midwest Worm Snake (*C. a. helenae*)

**Description**: Worm snakes are cylindrical, with a head that is not distinct from the neck, and a short tail. The snout is slightly flattened and pointed, and the **tail ends with a spinelike scale**. The eye is relatively small. The **upper half of the body is brown, the lower half pink. The brown dorsal color covers all but the first row of dorsal scales**. Juveniles may have darker backs than the adults. The **prefrontal and internasal shields are fused (one pair of scales on top of the snout)**. The scales are smooth and in 13 rows. The anal shield is divided.

**Size**: Maximum length 12.8 inches (324 mm); adults usually 6.9–11.1 inches (176–282 mm); hatchlings 3.0–4.1 inches (75–105 mm).

**Habitat**: Worm snakes occur in closed-canopy hardwood forest or mixed pine-hardwood forest, including hardwood bottoms.

**Natural history**: Worm snakes seem to spend most of their lives below the surface of the ground. Occasionally, they are discovered in leaf litter or under logs, especially when the surface is damp. Worm snakes lay a clutch of two to six eggs. When captured, worm snakes may wrap themselves about their captor's fingers and harmlessly poke the hand with their sharp tail tip.

**Distribution and status**: The Common Worm Snake occurs over most of the Florida Parishes, except for the Mississippi River floodplain, and there are no records from the pine flatwoods region above the north shore of Lake Pontchartrain. Due to the quantity of favorable habitat and regular discovery of Worm Snakes over recent decades, their populations are considered stable.

101a adult (East Baton Rouge Parish)

101b venter (DeKalb Co., AL)

101c anterior (DeKalb Co., AL)

101d juvenile (Washington Parish)

## Western Worm Snake (*Carphophis vermis*)
Other names: *Carphophis amoenus vermis*

**Description**: Worm snakes are cylindrical, with a head that is not distinct from the neck, and a short tail. The snout is slightly flattened and pointed, and the **tail ends with a spinelike scale**. The eye is relatively small. The **upper half of the body is dark brown or black, the lower half deep pink. The dark dorsal color covers all but the first two rows of scales**. The **prefrontal and internasal shields (two pairs of scales on top of the snout) are not fused**. The scales are smooth and in 13 rows. The anal shield is divided.

**Size**: Maximum length 15.4 inches (391 mm); adults usually 7.5–11.0 inches (190–280 mm); hatchlings 4.0–4.8 inches (100–121 mm).

**Habitat**: Western Worm Snakes occur in closed-canopy hardwood forest and potentially in mixed pine-hardwood forest.

**Natural history**: Western Worm Snakes seem to spend most of their lives below the surface of the ground. Occasionally, they are discovered in leaf litter or under logs, especially when the surface is damp. They lay a clutch of one to five (usually three) eggs and feed primarily on earthworms.

**Distribution and status**: The Western Worm Snake has been found in scattered localities in far northern Louisiana. Most Louisiana records are from Macon Ridge and the Bastrop Hills areas in Franklin and Morehouse Parishes. The only other record is of a few specimens from southern Caddo Parish found in the early 1900s. Most of the original forest of Macon Ridge has been cleared for agriculture. A Worm Snake was found in the Bastrop Hills in 2011, but all other Louisiana records date from prior to 1970. Due to its scarcity and habitat loss in Louisiana, the Western Worm Snake is a Species of Conservation Concern.

102a adult (Hempstead Co., AR)

102b venter (Hempstead Co., AR)

102c juvenile (Lyon Co., KS)

## Red-bellied Mud Snake (*Farancia abacura*)
**Other names**: aspique, pointe

**Subspecies**: Western Mud Snake (*F. a. reinwardtii*)

**Description**: Red-bellied Mud Snakes are of moderate build, with a head that is not distinct from the body, and with a **pointed, cone-shaped scale capping the tail tip**. The snout is bluntly rounded, and the eyes relatively small. They are **shiny black above**, and **below they possess alternating or connecting blocks of black and red**. The red extends upward onto the lower sides as 35–65 triangles or rectangles, which alternate with the black dorsal color. The labials, chin, and throat are yellow, dotted with black. The dorsal scales are smooth and in 19 rows. The anal plate is usually divided.

**Size**: Maximum length 90 inches (1,988 mm); adult males usually 29.3–46.9 inches (745–1,190 mm), females usually 34.1–76.3 inches (870–1,940 mm); hatchlings 6.0–10.6 inches (152–270 mm).

**Habitat**: Red-bellied Mud Snakes favor wet areas: marsh margins, hardwood bottoms and swamps, and pine flatwoods, as well as ditches and sloughs in agricultural lands.

**Natural history**: Red-bellied Mud Snakes are usually crepuscular or nocturnal, but during spring they may be found abroad in daylight. They are secretive, often remaining concealed in submerged leaf mats or near the entrances of burrows in shallow water, where they obtain their primary prey—amphiumas and sirens. When a Mud Snake captures one of these slippery salamanders, it coils its body tightly about its victim and delivers powerful bites along its length prior to swallowing it. Red-bellied Mud Snakes lay clutches of 15–50 eggs under surface objects or in pocketlike chambers, and the female remains coiled about the clutch until it hatches. Mud Snakes rarely bite, and when distressed they may expose the brightly colored underside of the tail. The sharp cone on the tail tip is mistakenly believed by some to be a stinger, but it has been observed that these snakes use this tail spine to aid in pinning or securing prey.

**Distribution and status:** The Red-bellied Mud Snake occurs statewide, except in brackish and salt marshes along the coast. Its populations are considered stable.

103a adult (Livingston Parish)

103b adult (St. Tammany Parish)

103c ventral (St. Martin Parish)

103d anterior (Livingston Parish)

103e juvenile (St. Martin Parish)

## Rainbow Snake (*Farancia erytrogramma*)

**Subspecies**: Common Rainbow Snake (*F. e. erytrogramma*)

**Description**: Rainbow Snakes have a head that is not distinct from the body, and they have a **spine on the tail tip**. The snout is bluntly rounded, and the eyes are relatively small. They are **polished black above, with a vertebral and two dorsolateral red stripes**. The two lowermost scale rows are yellow, red, or yellow with red centers. The **midventral zone is red, with a black spot on the outer edges and down the center of each ventral**, producing an appearance of two or three black lines. The throat, labials, and sides of the neck are yellow, and **each upper labial has a black spot in its center**. The top of the head is black with red zones along the sutures between the head shields. The dorsal scales are smooth and in 19 rows at midbody. The anal plate is usually divided.

**Size**: Maximum length 68.2 inches (1,733 mm); adults usually 34.6–50.6 inches (880–1,285 mm); hatchlings 5.6–8.8 inches (142–224 mm).

**Habitat**: Rainbow Snakes are tied closely to rivers and large streams, and inhabit bordering swamps and riverine forests.

**Natural history**: Rainbow Snakes may be either diurnal or nocturnal and are most often encountered as they forage in relatively clear water near riverbanks. When not in the water, they are usually under surface objects near shore or in burrows. Little is known about their natural history in Louisiana, but elsewhere in their range, Rainbow Snakes lay clutches of 10–52 (average of 32) eggs, which are deposited in chambers excavated by the female. Adults feed primarily on freshwater eels and occasionally on amphiumas, sirens, and frogs. Juveniles also eat tadpoles and earthworms. Like the Mud Snake, Rainbow Snakes seem never to bite when handled.

**Distribution and status**: Rainbow Snakes reach the western extent of their range in the Florida Parishes. The westernmost point is based on a reliable sighting in the Comite River, East Feliciana Parish. They have been found in a number of rivers and bayous (Amite, Tangipahoa, Lacombe, Bogue Falaya, Bogue Chitto, Pearl) but not in others between these. Despite enjoying a fairly extensive range, fewer than 25 Rainbow Snakes have been reported for Louisiana. Based on this scarcity and the lack of natural history details for Louisiana, the Rainbow Snake is a Species of Conservation Concern.

104a adult (Wakulla Co., FL)

104b adult (Laurens Co., GA)

104c ventral (roadkill) (Stone Co., MS)

104d anterior (Livingston Parish)

104e juvenile (Livingston Parish)

### Eastern Hog-nosed Snake (*Heterodon platirhinos*)
**Other names**: pine puffer, spreading snake

**Description**: Hog-nosed Snakes are relatively stout, with a **distinctive upturned snout that terminates as a ridged point**. All hatch with a spotted pattern. The dorsum is usually pale gray or pale brown, with a row of 14–24 squared brown blotches down the middle of the back, and an alternating row of oval, dark spots on each side.

There may be a reddish vertebral line and/or an orange wash, especially on the neck. Also **on each side of the neck is a large, elongate black blotch that originates from the temporal region**. The head bears a dark brown or black bar that crosses between the eyes and extends back to the corner of the mouth. Within a year or two of hatching, the snake may darken so that the markings are partially obscured by gray or brown, or the dorsum may become uniformly olive to shiny black. Other specimens retain the spotted pattern, and the ground color may be gray, tan, yellow, or orange. The underside is white, pale gray, or yellow, and grades to darker from the coalescence of gray blotches toward the tail. However, the underside of the tail abruptly returns to the pale color found toward the front of the snake. The dorsal scales are keeled and usually in 25 rows. The anal shield is divided.

**Size**: Maximum length 47 inches (1,194 mm); adults usually 25–33 inches (635–838 mm); hatchlings 5.7–8.1 inches (145–207 mm).

**Habitat**: Hog-nosed Snakes occupy most nonwetland habitats, though they may be found along swamp and marsh margins. They achieve their greatest abundance in well-drained woodlands and grasslands.

**Natural history**: Hog-nosed Snakes are primarily diurnal and are most often found abroad, either at rest or slowly prowling. They prefer to take refuge in burrows rather than beneath surface objects. They feed primarily on toads but are also known to prey upon other amphibians and, to a lesser extent, on lizards, rodents, insects, and spiders. Hog-nosed Snakes are adapted to eating toads by being immune to their toxic secretions and by possessing enlarged grooved teeth at the rear of the upper jaw. These teeth, irreverently called "toad poppers", will puncture the lungs of toads, which inflate themselves to prevent the snake from swallowing them.

Hog-nosed Snakes lay from 7–44 (average about 22) eggs in a clutch, and nesting sites include sand mounds and sawdust piles. Hog-nosed Snakes have a complex repertoire of defense mechanisms. When first alarmed, one of these snakes usually flattens, spreads its neck in cobralike fashion, and may even crawl about with its head and neck elevated. Should that behavior fail to thwart danger, they will roll on their back with mouth agape to appear dead. If set "upright," they will immediately turn belly-up again.

**Distribution and status**: Hog-nosed Snakes occur statewide, except for extensive areas of swamp and marsh along the southern coast. However, they may follow shell roads, levees, and natural ridges into those habitats. Hog-nosed Snakes were referred to as common, even abundant, during the mid-1900s, but have now become scarce over much of Louisiana and elsewhere. The reason for the sharp decline in numbers is unknown, and the Hog-nosed Snake is listed as a Species of Conservation Concern.

105a adult (Stone Co., MS)

105b adult (East Feliciana Parish)

105c subadult (Bienville Parish)

105d venter (Stone Co., MS)

105e anterior (Stone Co., MS)

105f juvenile (Catahoula Parish)

## Pine Woods Snake (*Rhadinaea flavilata*)
**Other names**: Pine Woods Littersnake, Yellow-lipped Snake

**Description**: The Pine Woods Snake is a small species of average build but with a relatively long tail. They are **reddish brown above, white to lemon yellow below**. There is a vague, slightly paler dorsolateral band on each side, and the lower sides grade to dull orange tan. The top of the head is usually a little darker than the back, and a **dark brown band with a pale upper margin passes through the eye from the snout to the rear of the jaw**. The labials are pale gray with black specks, and the chin and throat are white. The scales are smooth and in 17 rows. The anal shield is divided.

**Size**: Maximum length 16.1 inches (408 mm); adults usually 10.0–13.0 inches (254–330 mm); hatchlings 5.0–6.6 inches (127–167 mm).

**Habitat**: Pine Woods snakes inhabit pine flatwoods and pine-hardwood hammocks.

**Natural history**: Pine Woods Snakes are usually found under and within rotting pine logs or under the exfoliating bark of logs. They feed on small amphibians and lizards, which they subdue with toxic glandular secretions that are chewed into their victim until it is immobilized. They lay one to four eggs. Pine Woods Snakes are not known to bite.

**Distribution and status**: Pine Woods Snakes occur on low ground along the north shore of Lake Pontchartrain, ranging as far west as the middle of Livingston Parish. Fewer than 20 Pine Woods Snakes have been found in Louisiana. They are difficult to locate even when known sites are searched under favorable conditions. For these reasons, they are listed as a Species of Conservation Concern.

106a adult (St. Tammany Parish)

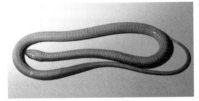

106b venter (St. Tammany Parish)

106c anterior (St. Tammany Parish)

## Dekay's Brown Snake (*Storeria dekayi*)
**Other names**: ground rattler

**Subspecies**: Midland Brown Snake (*S. d. wrightorum*): dark vertical bar behind eye, dark bars connecting most spot pairs across back. Marsh Brown Snake (*S. d. limnetes*): horizontal dark streak behind eye, spots on back tiny or absent. Texas Brown Snake (*S. d. texana*): dark spot or dark vertical bar behind eye, no dark bars connecting spot pairs across back.

**Description**: Dekay's Brown Snake is a small species of moderate build and with a head that is slightly distinct from the neck. They are tan, medium brown, grayish brown, or reddish tan above, with a slightly paler band down the middle of the back and on the lower sides. The top of the head is a little darker than the ground color, with a slightly darker patch on each side of the neck, and **black or brown marks directly below the eye. If lacking, there is a dark horizontal streak behind the eye.** The chin and throat are white, and the **belly is dull white to pale or pinkish beige, usually with a series of black dots on each side of the ventrals**. Dekay's Brown Snakes from the coastal marshes and prairie lack any additional markings, except for a horizontal black streak behind each eye. Elsewhere, the pale dorsal band is lined with small black spots, which are often connected in pairs by dark lines across the middle of the back. There is also a row of small dark spots on the lower sides. Such snakes have a vertical, rather than horizontal, dark bar behind each eye. Brown snakes often spread their sides in a defensive posture, and light marks on the interstitial skin, alternating with the dark spots, are exposed to produce a somewhat checkered pattern. Juveniles are gray with a pale band across the back of the head. The scales are keeled and in 17 rows at the middle of the body. The anal shield is divided.

**Size**: Maximum length 20.7 inches (527 mm); adult males usually 9.3–13.7 inches (237–348 mm), females usually 8.9–15.6 inches (228–395 mm); newborns 2.8–4.5 inches (72–114 mm).

**Habitat**: Dekay's Brown Snakes occupy most nonaquatic habitats in Louisiana, extending to brackish marsh and swamp margins, to urban settings, to upland forests.

**Natural history**: Due to their small size, Dekay's Brown Snakes are usually only discovered by looking under logs, in leaf beds, and under other surface cover. They are occasionally spotted foraging about the forest floor by day or crossing roads at night. This is one of several small snake species that thrive in landscaped neighborhoods. They feed on earthworms, slugs, snails, and soft-bodied insects. Snails are extracted from their shells by the relatively long teeth at the front of the jaws. Females produce a litter of 3–25 (usually 11–17) young. When threatened, this snake will often flare its body, spread the rear of its head to form a triangular shape, coil, and strike. However, the strikes seem to be a bluff, as they are done with the mouth closed.

**Distribution**: Dekay's Brown Snakes occur statewide, except in trackless coastal marsh. Their populations are considered stable.

107a adult, wrightorum (Chickasaw Co., MS)

107b adult, wrightorum (Lafayette Parish)

107c adult, texana (Natchitoches Parish)

107d adult, limnetes (St. Mary Parish)

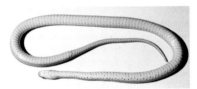
107e venter (St. Charles Parish)

107g juvenile (East Baton Rouge Parish)

107f anterior (East Baton Rouge Parish)

### Red-bellied Snake (*Storeria occipitomaculata*)

**Subspecies:** Florida Red-bellied Snake (*S. o. obscura*)

**Description:** The Red-bellied Snake is a small species of medium build with a head that is slightly distinct from the neck. Above, they are gray, reddish tan, yellow brown, or brown, with either a double row of small black spots or two dark lines along the middle of the back. A row of small black dots may be present on the sides. The  head is usually brown, often with black or gray mottling on the crown, and there is **a white spot below and slightly behind the eye.** There is often a pale collar or pale patches at the back of the head, though these may be indistinct. The chin is white with dark mottling, and the rest of the **underside is yellow, orange, or red.** Juveniles have a distinct yellow collar. The scales are keeled and in 15 rows. The anal shield is divided.

**Size:** Maximum length in the South 13.2 inches (335 mm); adult males usually 6.5–10.2 inches (164–258 mm), females usually 7.7–12.1 inches (195–308 mm); newborns 2.6–3.7 inches (65–93 mm).

**Habitat:** Red-bellied Snakes inhabit forested areas, from bottomland hardwoods to upland mixed pine-hardwood forests.

**Natural history:** Red-bellied Snakes are secretive and rarely seen abroad. Most often they are discovered under logs or other surface objects, or in leaf litter. On warm nights, they may be found on roads. They feed primarily on slugs, occasionally on earthworms, snails, and grubs. Females produce litters of 1–23 (usually 7–10) young. When captured, they may curl their lips upward in a threatening "sneer," though they do not bite; nor do they seem to coil and strike like the Dekay's Brown Snake.

**Distribution and status:** The Red-bellied Snake occurs in forested areas over much of the state but is absent from the coastal zone, prairie province, and much of the Mississippi Delta. Its populations are considered stable.

108a adult (Iberville Parish)

108b adult (East Feliciana Parish)

108c adult (St. Tammany Parish)

108d adult (Pointe Coupée Parish)

108e venter (Pike Co., MS)

108f venter (St. Tammany Parish)

108g anterior (Iberville Parish)

108h juvenile (Evangeline Parish)

## Rough Earth Snake (*Haldea striatula*)
**Other names:** *Virginia striatula*

**Description:** The Rough Earth Snake is a small species with a pointed head that is not distinct from the neck. The **dorsum is uniformly gray, brown, or reddish tan, and the underside is white to pale yellow.** On some individuals, the top of the head is slightly darker than the body, and there may be a slightly paler band across the back of the head. Juvenile coloration resembles that of adults, except that the pale band at the rear of the head is more distinct. There are **five supralabial scales.** The **scales are keeled** and in 17 rows at the middle of the body. The anal shield is divided.

**Size:** Maximum length 13.7 inches (348 mm); adult males usually 7.0–9.6 inches (177–244 mm), females usually 8.6–10.5 inches (219–267 mm); newborns 2.9–4.6 inches (74–117 mm).

**Habitat:** Rough Earth Snakes prefer well-drained wooded habitats but also occur in open grass, bottomland margins, and urban situations.

**Natural history:** Rough Earth Snakes are secretive, usually found only by searching in and under rotting logs, leaf litter, and other surface objects. They are difficult to locate in natural settings but can be locally abundant in urban landscapes. Favored haunts include vacant lots and yards with dense ornamental ground cover, such as Monkey Grass (*Ophiopogon*). They feed almost exclusively on earthworms but occasionally eat beetle larvae. Females produce litters of 2–13 (average 9) young. They do not bite when handled.

**Distribution and status:** The Rough Earth Snake occurs over much of Louisiana but is absent from the coastal marshes and the Mississippi/Atchafalaya Delta and floodplains. Their populations are considered stable.

109a adult (Livingston Parish)

109b adult (Natchitoches Parish)

109c adult (Lafayette Parish)

109d adult (Sebastian Co., AR)

109e venter (Sebastian Co., AR)

109f anterior (Santa Rosa Co., FL)

109g newborn (Cleveland Co., OK)

## Smooth Earth Snake (*Virginia valeriae*)

**Subspecies**: Western Smooth Earth Snake (*V. v. elegans*)

**Description**: Smooth Earth Snakes are small and of medium build, with a head that is not distinct from the neck. They are **reddish tan, brown, or gray, with or without a vague pale stripe down the middle of the back, and often with a scattering of black flecks.** The head is the same color as the body and is dotted with black "freckles." The **underside is white or pale yellow.** Juveniles are colored like the adults. There are **six supralabial scales**. The **scales are smooth** and in 17 rows. The anal plate is divided.

**Size**: Maximum length 15.5 inches (393 mm); adults usually 6.9–10.5 inches (174–266 mm); newborns 3.0–3.7 inches (76–95 mm).

**Habitat**: Smooth Earth Snakes occur in woodlands, usually those that are well drained, but also occur in pine flatwoods and forested bottomlands in the Florida Parishes.

**Natural history**: Smooth Earth Snakes are secretive and rarely seen unless they are uncovered beneath rotting logs and other surface objects. They are considered uncommon in northern Louisiana and the western Florida Parishes. However, in the pine flatwoods country north of Lake Pontchartrain, they are a common find during the winter and early spring. They are supposed to feed on earthworms, slugs, and soft-bodied insects. Females produce a litter of 2–14 (average of 6) young.

**Distribution and status**: The Smooth Earth Snake occurs in the Florida Parishes and in northern Louisiana in wooded uplands. East of the Red River it has been found as far south as Pineville, and west of the river it is reported from the Red Dirt area of Natchitoches Parish and northward. Its populations are considered stable.

110a adult (St. Tammany Parish)

110b adult (Hancock Co., MS)

110c ventral (Hancock Co., MS)

110d anterior (St. Tammany Parish)

110e newborns (Grant Parish)

## Glossy Swamp Snake (*Liodytes rigida*)
**Other names:** Glossy Crayfish Snake, *Regina rigida*

**Subspecies:** Delta Swamp Snake (*L. r. deltae*): one preocular scale on each side of the head. Gulf Swamp Snake (*L. r. sinicola*): two preoculars on each side of the head.

**Description:** Glossy Swamp Snakes are of moderate build, with the head scarcely distinct from the neck, and a shortened, rounded snout with oversized eyes. The top of the head and **dorsum are dark brown or dark olive, at times almost black in appearance.** There is a broad black band or paired black stripes down the middle of the back that are vaguely discernible. The labials, **underside, and lowermost scale row are dull white or yellow to dull orange.** A black line may be present along the outer margin of the ventrals, and there are **two rows of dark, crescent-shaped spots down the middle of the belly.** Populations around Lake Pontchartrain have a high incidence of entirely black (melanistic) snakes. The scales are keeled and glossy, and are in 19 rows at the middle of the body. The anal shield is divided.

**Size:** Maximum length 32.7 inches (830 mm); adult males usually 17.8–25.1 inches (452–637 mm), females usually 20.6–30.2 inches (522–767 mm); newborns 6.1–8 inches (155–202 mm).

**Habitat:** The Glossy Swamp Snake occurs in almost any habitat that contains freshwater wetlands, ranging from freshwater marsh and swamps to gum ponds in otherwise dry pine woodland.

**Natural history:** Glossy Swamp Snakes are active day or night, depending on temperature and hydrology. They are rarely observed foraging during the day and are usually found in saturated leaf mats, mats of water hyacinth, or under driftwood and other objects along the shores of flatwoods and gum ponds, swamps, and slack-water bayous. They feed almost exclusively on crawfish, though they occasionally eat amphibians. When tackling crawfish, these snakes use several coils to constrict and immobilize their prey, then eat them tail first. Females produce litters of 6–14 young. Swamp Snakes seem never to bite when captured.

**Distribution and status**: Glossy Swamp Snakes occur statewide, except for brackish and salt marshes along the coast, and there are no records for uplands in the Florida Parishes. They are difficult to detect in regions of the state in which wetlands are sparse, but their populations appear to be stable where suitable habitat is abundant.

111a adult (Ouachita Parish)

111b adult (Vermilion Parish)

111c venter (St. Martin Parish)

111d anterior (St. Charles Parish)

111e juvenile (Vermilion Parish)

## Graham's Crawfish Snake (*Regina grahamii*)

**Description:** Graham's Crawfish Snakes are of medium build with a head that is seemingly undersized for its body and is somewhat distinct from the neck. They are **gray or grayish brown on the upper back** and top of the head, usually with a slightly paler band or stripe down the middle of the back. The face, **underside, and the three low-**  **ermost scale rows are dull white to pale gray or tan**. The outer margin of each ventral is black, producing a black ventrolateral stripe on each side of the body. Usually, there is a **midventral line of brown or black spots posteriorly**. The scales are keeled and in 19 rows at the middle of the body. The anal shield is divided.

**Size**: Maximum length 47 inches (1,194 mm), though rarely over 40 inches (1,016 mm); adult males usually 19.7–33.3 inches (500–845 mm), females usually 25.4–36.3 inches (644–923 mm); newborns 6.0–11.4 inches (153–291 mm).

**Habitat**: Graham's Crawfish Snakes occur in wetlands in floodplains, river batture, and in freshwater marshes.

**Natural history**: Graham's Crawfish Snakes are usually only found when they are foraging in shallow wetlands in water that is less than two feet deep. Preferred sites include sloughs in river batture, vegetated roadside ditches, open swamp margins, and agricultural wetlands, such as rice and crawfish impoundments. When inactive, they seek refuge in crawfish burrows. They feed almost exclusively on crawfish, preferring those that have a soft exoskeleton right after shedding. When crawfish are scarce, they will feed on small fish. Females produce litters of 4–39 (average about 15) young. Crawfish Snakes rarely attempt to bite and are docile when handled.

**Distribution and status**: Graham's Crawfish Snakes occur in wetlands from the lower Mississippi River floodplain westward, the Red River Valley, and upper Mississippi Delta/Ouachita River bottoms. They remain abundant in much of their range and may benefit from certain agricultural practices. Their populations are considered secure.

112a adult (East Baton Rouge Parish)

112b adult (St. Martin Parish)

112c venter (Tensas Parish)

112d juvenile (Chambers Co., TX)

## Mississippi Green Water Snake (*Nerodia cyclopion*)

**Description:** Mississippi Green Water Snakes are
of medium to slightly stout build, with a head
that is distinct from the neck. They tend to have
an overall gray appearance with small, somewhat regular dark markings. The **ground color is
usually olive or gray, sometimes brown, and is
overlain by more than 50 short, vertical black**
**bars along the upper sides.** The bars may alternate near the middorsal
line or connect by means of diagonal dark markings. A secondary row of
spots, usually paler, occupies the lower sides. The head color is usually
about the same as the ground color and is unmarked. The **underside
begins as white or yellow on the chin, throat, and neck, where dark
gray marks begin to appear. By the middle of the underside, the light
and dark marks comingle to the point that, on the rear of the body, the
underside is dark gray or nearly black with the yellow reduced to spots
in the dark areas.** Young are colored like the adults, though the spotted
pattern may be more distinct. The scales are keeled and usually in 27 or
29 rows at midbody. The anal shield is divided.

**Size:** Maximum length 51 inches (1,295 mm); adult males usually 23.7–39.2
inches (603–995 mm), females usually 32.9–46.9 inches (835–1,190 mm);
newborns 7.5–12.0 inches (190–305 mm).

**Habitat:** Mississippi Green Water Snakes inhabit freshwater marshes,
cypress lakes, and bayous with abundant aquatic vegetation.

**Natural history:** Mississippi Green Water Snakes are diurnal or nocturnal,
depending on season and temperature. They are frequently seen basking
and foraging along marsh margins and on mats of aquatic vegetation. They
feed almost exclusively on fish, particularly types, such as centrachids,
that occupy a wide range in the water column. Females produce a litter
of 7–34 (average 18) young. Like most water snakes, this species bites vi-
ciously when captured and can produce shallow lacerations.

**Distribution and status:** The Mississippi Green Water Snake occurs over
most of the southern quarter of the state, aside from in brackish and salt

marshes, but to the north is restricted to the Atchafalaya, Mississippi, Red, and Ouachita River bottoms. They remain abundant in most places that they occur, and their populations are considered stable.

113a adult (St. Charles Parish)

113b adult (Cameron Parish)

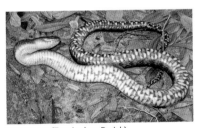

113c venter (Tangipahoa Parish)

113d anterior (St. Charles Parish)

113e juvenile (St. Tammany Parish)

## Diamond-backed Water Snake (*Nerodia rhombifer*)

**Subspecies**: Northern Diamond-backed Water Snake (*N. r. rhombifer*)

**Description**: Diamond-backed Water Snakes are of medium to robust build with a head that is distinct from the neck. The **ground color is tan to medium brown with vertical bars of dark brown or black on the sides that alternate with fewer than 40 short transverse bars that run down the middle of the back. The alternating bars usually connect on the upper sides to form a chainlike pattern.** The top of the head is unmarked, about the same shade as the ground color, and there are dark bars on the labial sutures. The **belly is pale yellow with numerous black semicircular marks that may form irregular rows on each side and down the midventer.** The young are colored like the adults. The scales are keeled and in 25 or (usually) 27 rows at the middle of the body. The anal shield is divided.

**Size**: Maximum length 69 inches (1,753 mm); adult males usually 29.2–41.8 inches (742–1,061 mm), females usually 35.6–58.2 inches (903–1,479 mm); newborns 9.1–13.8 inches (230–350 mm).

**Habitat**: Diamond-backed Water Snakes occur in wetlands, except for in brackish and salt marshes along the coast. Distribution in uplands is governed by the presence of permanent water bodies.

**Natural history**: Diamond-backed Water Snakes are tied closely to water and are rarely seen beyond an escapable distance from shoreline. It is the species most likely to be seen basking on vegetation overhanging water, into which the snakes drop when approached. They prefer large water bodies, such as lakes and river margins, but are also usually the first snake species to take up residence in man-made ponds in subdivisions and apartment grounds. These snakes feed almost exclusively on fish; rarely on amphibians or crawfish. Juveniles feed on a variety of fish species, but adults feed primarily on catfish and are known to swim to depths of over ten feet on foraging missions. Females produce litters of 10–62 (average about 20–24) newborns. Because of their tendency to form shoreline aggregations in springtime, there is a mistaken belief that these represent "nests of moccasins."

**Distribution and status:** Diamond-backed Water Snakes occur statewide, except in brackish and salt marshes along the coast. They are common to abundant over much of the state, and their populations are considered stable.

114a adult (Atchafalaya Basin)

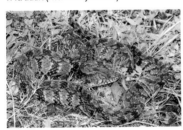
114b adult (St. Martin Parish)

114c venter (Vermilion Parish)

114d anterior (Livingston Parish)

114e juvenile (Atchafalaya Basin)

## Plain-bellied Water Snake (*Nerodia erythrogaster*)

**Subspecies**: Yellow-bellied Water Snake (*N. e. flavigaster*), Blotched Water Snake (*N. e. transversa*)

**Description**: Plain-bellied Water Snakes are of moderate build with a head that is distinct from the neck. They are born with a **pattern of closely spaced, squared, blotches down the back, which alternate with shorter, vertical blotches on the sides**. The blotches are dark brown against a ground color of grayish pink or rust. The top of the head is dark, with a dark band from the eye to the angle of the jaw. Over most of Louisiana, the snakes begin to darken during their second year of life and gradually become **uniformly dark olive to medium or very dark gray on the back**. As the snakes begin to darken, the existence of the blotches is reduced to transverse pale bars down the middle of the back, which eventually vanish (subspecies *flavigaster*). In Acadiana and westward, the juvenile pattern of blotches is retained in adults, but the ground color becomes tan or gray. The head of adults is unmarked, except for dark bars on the labial sutures (subspecies *transversa*). The underside of juveniles is dull yellow with dark markings at the bases of each ventral. In adults, the dark markings have faded, leaving a **plain yellow belly and a white chin**. The scales are keeled and in 23 rows around the middle of the body. The anal shield is divided.

**Size**: Maximum length 65.4 inches (1,661 mm); adult males usually 28.8–43.5 inches (731–1,106 mm), females usually 29.5–48.1 inches (749–1,221 mm); newborns usually 8.8–10.9 inches (223–277 mm).

**Habitat**: Plain-bellied Water Snakes occur in all Louisiana habitats, except for brackish and salt marshes.

**Natural history**: Of all of Louisiana's water snakes, the Plain-bellied Water Snake is the least tied to water. They favor small water bodies such as ponds and streams, and are often found foraging in woodlands or traversing areas between water bodies. They seem particularly adept at locating small garden ponds stocked with goldfish. Juveniles have a preference for small fish, whereas adults feed on both frogs and fish, and occasionally crawfish. Females produce a litter of 9–33 (average about 18–21) young.

**Distribution and status:** The Plain-bellied Water Snake occurs throughout Louisiana, except in the saline coastal marshes. Their populations are considered extensive and stable in the state.

115a adult flavigaster (West Feliciana Parish)

115b adult flavigaster (Natchitoches Parish)

115c adult flavigaster (St. Tammany Parish)

115d adult transversa (Lafayette Parish)

115e subadult transversa (Lafayette Parish)

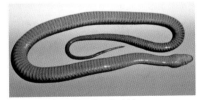
115f venter (Natchitoches Parish)

115g anterior (Natchitoches Parish)

115h juvenile (St. Tammany Parish)

## Salt Marsh Snake (*Nerodia clarkii*)

**Subspecies**: Gulf Salt Marsh Snake (*N. c. clarkii*)

**Description**: Salt Marsh Snakes are of medium build with a head that is slightly distinct from the neck. They are beige, pale gray, or pale tan with dark brown, dark gray, or black bands. A **broad dark band covers the upper dorsum, which is divided by a pale vertebral stripe or line. Another dark band runs along the middle of each side** and is usually connected to a dark band that passes through the eye on each side of the head. The margins of the mouth are black. The **underside is deep brownish red. A yellow or white patch occupies the middle of each ventral scale, and combined, these form a pale stripe down the middle of the belly.** Salt Marsh Snakes hybridize with Banded Water Snakes, and hybrids tend to have some vertical dark markings so that the pale bands may be broken into segments or streaks. The young resemble the adults. The scales are keeled and in 21 rows. The anal shield is divided.

**Size**: Maximum length 36 inches (914 mm); adult males usually 19.2–26.5 inches (488–674 mm), females usually 19.8–28.4 inches (502–721 mm); newborns 6.4–9.4 inches (163–240 mm).

**Habitat**: As their name implies, they inhabit salt and brackish marshes, and mangrove thickets.

**Natural history**: Salt Marsh Snakes may be diurnal or nocturnal, depending on season and hydrologic conditions. They are difficult to observe in marsh grasses but may be seen swimming among mangroves, basking on matted vegetation, or foraging in narrow passages in marshes. Salt Marsh Snakes feed primarily on fish, secondarily on crabs. Females produce a litter of from 2–22 (average of 11) young.

**Distribution and status**: Salt Marsh Snakes occur coastwide, from the Rigolets to the mouth of the Sabine River, including on the north shore of Lake Pontchartrain, and on offshore barrier islands. They have been insufficiently studied in Louisiana, but their abundance across the coast is regularly manifested by many live and dead snakes on roadways immediately after hurricanes, and their populations are considered stable.

116a adult (Lafourche Parish)

116b adult (Terrebonne Parish)

116c adult, hybrid with Southern Water Snake (Chambers Co., TX)

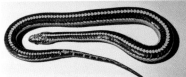

116d venter (Lafourche Parish)

116e anterior (Lafourche Parish)

116f juvenile (Orleans Parish)

## Southern Water Snake (*Nerodia fasciata*)
**Other names**: Banded Water Snake

**Subspecies**: Broad-banded Water Snake (*N. f. confluens*)

**Description**: Broad-banded Water Snakes are of medium build with a head that is distinct from the neck. The typical color pattern is **dark brown with 11–15 widely spaced, dull yellow or tan crossbands**. Often the dark zones have pale brown or tan centers on the sides, and these paler areas may connect with the crossbands to isolate the dark  areas into long, dark blotches. **In the eastern Florida Parishes, the pale zones may extend upward to meet at the vertebral line, thus bisecting the large dark areas into short dark crossbands.** In extreme cases **in the Florida Parishes, the entire dorsal surface may be pale tan or tan gray with a dozen short, dark crossbands.** The top of the head is dark brown to black, and the sides of the head are usually dull orange. In the eastern part of the state, there is a black band that runs from the eye to the rear of the jaw. There are usually dark bars on the labial sutures. Regardless of the complex dorsal patterns, all Broad-banded Water Snakes have a **white or yellow venter that is marked by alternating or paired, square blotches of red, red brown, or black that increase in density toward the tail**. Juveniles tend to be much more brightly marked than adults. The scales are keeled and in 23 rows at the middle of the body. The anal shield is divided.

**Size**: Maximum length 45 inches (1,145 mm); adult males usually 22.0–30.9 inches (558–785 mm), females usually 25.9–39.5 inches (659–1,004 mm); newborns 7.0–9.9 inches (179–252 mm).

**Habitat**: Broad-banded Water Snakes occur in most habitats in Louisiana other than salt and brackish marshes. Their preferred habitat is in and near water bodies in forested areas.

**Natural history**: Broad-banded Water Snakes are diurnal or nocturnal, depending on temperature and hydrologic conditions. They favor shallow water and are most often seen near water in closed canopy situations, such as swamps, forest sloughs, and bayous. They feed primarily on fish as juveniles, increasingly preferring amphibians and large fish as adults. In very shallow water (less than two inches), they will try to corral small fish and tadpoles by spinning about in a loose coil and lunging at prey as they become concentrated in the enclosing loop. Adult females produce litters of 7–39 (average of 20 or 21) young.

**Distribution and status:** The Broad-banded Water Snake occurs throughout Louisiana, except in extensive regions of salt and brackish marshes along the coast. They are common to abundant over most of the state, and their populations are considered stable.

117a adult (West Feliciana Parish)

117b adult (East Baton Rouge Parish)

117c adult (Lafayette Parish)

117d venter (East Baton Rouge Parish)

117e anterior (East Baton Rouge Parish)

117f juvenile (Bienville Parish)

117g juvenile (Jefferson Co., TX)

## Common Water Snake (*Nerodia sipedon*)

**Subspecies**: Midland Water Snake (*N. s. pleuralis*)

**Description**: Common Water Snakes are of moderate build with a head that is distinct from the neck. They have a **pale tan, gray, or orange ground color, with reddish to dark brown crossbands on the neck that are longer at middorsum than on the sides. At between one-quarter to one-half the length of the body, the crossbands**  **become offset, so that vertical bars on the sides alternate with longer middorsal blotches.** There is a dark bar from the back of the eye to the corner of the mouth and symmetric dark brown markings on the crown, but these may be absent in adults. The labials may or may not have dark bars on the sutures. The **underside is usually off-white with numerous dark brown crescent-shaped markings at the base of each ventral scale.** Newborns tend to be more brightly marked than adults. The scales are keeled and in 23 rows at the middle of the body. The anal shield is divided.

**Size**: Maximum length 59 inches (1,500 mm); adult males usually 23.7–29.3 inches (602–744 mm), females usually 26.2–34.5 inches (665–877 mm); newborns 7.2–10.9 inches (182–276 mm).

**Habitat**: Common Water Snakes inhabit rivers and streams in forested areas, usually in uplands.

**Natural history**: Common Water Snakes are diurnal or nocturnal, depending on water temperature. They are usually encountered along streams that are relatively clear and flowing, with sand and gravel bars. Prey consists primarily of fish, secondarily of frogs and tadpoles. Females produce litters of 6–45 (average about 20) young.

**Distribution and status**: The Common Water Snake ranges south from Mississippi into the northern half of the Florida Parishes, where it follows large streams and rivers to the edge of the flatlands. It also ranges southward, though sparingly, from the Ozarks and Ouachitas, and has been reported in the Ouachita River area in Ouachita Parish. Their populations appear to be secure in Louisiana.

118a adult (West Feliciana Parish)

118b adult (St. Francois Co., MO)

118c venter (East Baton Rouge Parish)

118d anterior (West Feliciana Parish)

118e juvenile (Washington Parish)

## Western Ribbon Snake (*Thamnophis proximus*)

**Subspecies**: Orange-striped Ribbon Snake (*T. p. proximus*), Gulf Coast Ribbon Snake (*T. p. orarius*)

**Description**: Western Ribbon Snakes are slender, with a relatively long tail, and a head that is distinct from the neck. They have a tan ground color in the coastal zone (subspecies *orarius*) and dark brown or black ground color elsewhere in the state (subspecies *proximus*). They have a **white,**

**yellow, or orange vertebral stripe and a pale lateral stripe on each side. The lateral stripes are on scale rows three and four,** and are bordered below by a dark band on scale rows one and two. One or two rows of black spots may be visible in the dark fields. The top of the head is brown or black with a **white parietal spot**. The labials, chin, and throat are whitish, and the underside grades to very pale sea green toward the tail. The **labials lack black suture marks**. Juveniles are colored like the adults. The scales are keeled and in 19 rows. The anal shield is not divided.

**Size**: Maximum length 48.5 inches (1,232 mm); adult males usually 21.6–29.3 inches (549–743 mm), adult females usually 27.4–40.9 inches (695–1,038 mm); newborns 8.6–10.6 inches (219–268 mm).

**Habitat**: Western Ribbon Snakes occur in nearly every habitat from freshwater marshes to upland pine-hardwood forests, occupying areas in and near wetlands.

**Natural history**: Western Ribbon Snakes are primarily diurnal but may be found after dark during hot weather. They are often observed actively prowling for food, especially around vegetated shallows and ground cover. They feed primarily on small frogs and secondarily on salamanders, tadpoles, and small fish. Females produce litters of 4–36 (usually 8–12) young. They may or may not bite when captured. If grabbed by the tail, they will often spin or twist their bodies until the end of the tail is severed, and roughly half of adults lack some portion of their tails.

**Distribution and status**: The Western Ribbon Snake occurs statewide, except in extensive zones of brackish and salt marsh, and is absent from the core zone of the Eastern Ribbon Snake in Washington Parish and much of St. Tammany Parish. They remain common to abundant in most areas of the state, and their populations are considered stable.

119a adult proximus (East Baton Rouge Parish)

119b adult proximus (St. Martin Parish)

119c adult orarius (Cameron Parish)

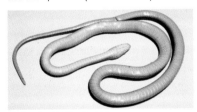
119d venter (Sabine Parish)

119e anterior (East Baton Rouge Parish)

119f juvenile (Big Thicket, TX)

# Eastern Ribbon Snake (*Thamnophis saurita*)

**Subspecies:** Common Ribbon Snake (*T. s. saurita*)

**Description:** Eastern Ribbon Snakes are relatively slender, with a head that is distinct from the neck. They are medium to dark brown with a **vertebral stripe and lateral stripe on each side that are dull white to dull yellow.** The **lateral stripes occupy scale rows three and four,** and are bordered below by a copper-colored band on  scale rows one and two and the outer margins of the ventrals. One or two rows of small black spots or dashes may be visible in the dark fields. The top of the head is brown with a **white parietal spot that is tiny or absent.** The labials, chin, and throat are whitish, and the underside grades to beige or very pale tan toward the tail. The **labials lack black suture marks.** Juveniles are colored like the adults. The scales are keeled and in 19 rows. The anal shield is not divided.

**Size:** Maximum length 40.9 inches (1,040 mm); adult males usually 20.2–27.7 inches (512–704 mm), adult females usually 24.4–30.2 inches (620–768 mm); newborns 5.9–9.1 inches (150–230 mm).

**Habitat:** Eastern Ribbon Snakes occur in wetlands or damp areas in pine flatwoods, bottomland hardwoods, bayhead swamps, and upland mixed pine-hardwood forest.

**Natural history:** Eastern Ribbon Snakes tend to be diurnal and are usually found in the vicinity of damp areas, bogs, flatwoods ponds, and stream seeps. They feed on small frogs and tadpoles, and occasionally on small fish. Females produce litters of 3–26 (usually 10–12) young. Like the Western Ribbon Snake, this species can also twist its tail off if grabbed.

**Distribution and status:** The Eastern Ribbon Snake is widely distributed in St. Tammany and Washington Parishes, but occurs in a few scattered localities in Tangipahoa, St. Helena, and East Feliciana Parishes. The eastern species is less common than the Western Ribbon Snake, and field surveys suggest a possible shallow decline in its numbers.

120a adult (Washington Parish)

120b adult (Escambia Co., FL)

120c venter (FL)

120d anterior (Winston Co., MS)

120e juvenile (Hinds Co., MS)

## Common Garter Snake (*Thamnophis sirtalis*)
**Other names**: garden snake

**Subspecies**: Eastern Garter Snake (*T. s. sirtalis*)

**Description**: Garter Snakes are of medium proportions, with the head moderately distinct from
the neck. In most of Louisiana, garter snakes
have a dark ground color with **a pale vertebral
stripe and a lateral stripe on each side. The lateral stripes occupy scale rows two and three**. The
ground color is usually dark brown with two al-
ternating rows of black spots. The interstitial skin, and sometimes certain
scale margins, have small white spots that become visible when the skin
is slightly stretched. The vertebral stripe is usually dull white but may be
yellow to orange or have a pale greenish tint. The lateral stripes are usually dull white to pale blue gray and are bordered below by a brown band.
The top of the head is brown to nearly black, with **a pale parietal spot**.
The pale labials are offset from the color of the top of the head and have
**dark vertical streaks along the labial sutures**. The chin and throat are
white, grading to pale blue gray or gray green on the venter. **Along each
side of the venter is a row of small black spots at the base of each ventral**. Garter snakes **from the eastern Florida Parishes often have a pale
tan or grayish brown ground color, and the alternating rows of black
spots give the snake a checkered appearance. Such snakes often have
indistinct or no stripes.** Juveniles resemble the adults in color pattern.
The dorsal scales are keeled and in 19 rows. The anal shield is not divided.

**Size**: Maximum length in Louisiana 38 inches (965 mm); adult males usually
16–24.5 inches (400–620 mm), females usually 17–30 inches (426–762
mm); newborns 5.4–7.1 inches (138–180 mm).

**Habitat**: Garter snakes occupy many habitats, from freshwater wetlands
to relatively dry pinelands. They are most often found in mixed hardwood-
pine and bottomland hardwood forests.

**Natural history**: Garter snakes are typically diurnal but may be crepuscular during summer. They feed primarily on earthworms, secondarily

on frogs and toads. In Louisiana, females give birth to 9–27 young. When threatened, garter snakes will often flair their jaws and partially flatten their bodies, which exposes the pattern of white flecks on the interstitial skin. They may or may not bite when captured.

**Distribution and status**: Garter snakes are widely distributed in the eastern part of Louisiana, except for the coastal marshes. West of the Atchafalaya Basin and Red River, there are few, widely scattered records, and garter snakes appear to be absent from most of the western half of the state. Their populations are considered stable, and they thrive in old, landscaped urban areas.

121a adult (Ouachita Parish)

121b adult (Evangeline Parish)

121c adult (Lafayette Parish)

121d adult (St. Tammany Parish)

121e adult (Washington Parish)

121f adult (St. Tammany Parish)

121g venter (St. Tammany Parish)

121h anterior (East Baton Rouge Parish)

121i juvenile (Ouachita Parish)

# North American Racer (*Coluber constrictor*)

**Other names**: Eastern Racer, blue runner, serpent noire, fouetteuse

**Subspecies**: Southern Black Racer (*C. c. priapus*), Eastern Yellow-bellied Racer (*C. c. flaviventris*), Buttermilk Racer (*C. c. anthicus*), Black-masked Racer (*C. c. latrunculus*), Tan Racer (*C. c. etheridgei*)

**Description**: Racers are slender, with a long tail and a head that is distinct from the neck. Juvenile racers are dull yellow to pale gray, with numerous, closely spaced transverse spots down the back. The spots are reddish brown with dark borders, and they coalesce and disappear toward the reddish brown tail. The belly, sides, and face are irregularly covered with dark dots. At about six to ten months of age, the entire spotted pattern begins to vanish as it coalesces with a darkening ground color, and the racers become uniformly colored above. The final dorsal color differs. Adult Racers from the Florida Parishes are **uniformly black above** (subspecies *priapus*); those from the upper and lower Mississippi Delta and the Atchafalaya Basin are **pale to medium gray with a black mask** (*latrunculus*); those from the southwest prairie and marsh country are **olive brown above, olive green on the sides, and yellow below** (*flaviventris*); those from the tributaries of the lower Sabine River are **tan** (*etheridgei*); and those from the hill country of northern and central Louisiana are **grayish to nearly blue black but develop dull white to pale tan spots that increase in number with age producing a speckled appearance** in adults (*anthicus*). The scales are smooth and in 17 rows. The anal shield is divided.

**Size**: Maximum length 70 inches (1,778 mm); adults usually 36.8–60.2 inches (935–1,530 mm); hatchlings 8.7–13.0 inches (220–331 mm).

**Habitat**: Racers occur in nonaquatic habitats.

**Natural history**: Racers are relatively common, diurnal, active predators that forage on the ground and in low shrubs. They feed on grasshoppers and other insects, frogs, lizards, small snakes, and, occasionally, rodents and small birds and their eggs. Females lay clutches of 7–29 eggs in rotted logs or within and under other moisture-retaining objects near the ground. Racers usually flee when approached but may alternately pull into a loose, striking coil and vibrate their tails against the ground. They readily bite when captured.

**Distribution and status**: Racers occur statewide, except in trackless areas of coastal marshes and swamps. They seem adapted to modified habitats, such as cutover woods and old fields, and their populations are considered stable.

123a adult priapus (Livingston Parish)

123b adult anthicus (Caldwell Parish)

123c subadult anthicus (Bienville Parish)

123d adult latrunculus (St. Martin Parish)

123e adult etheridgei (Tyler Co., TX)

123f adult flaviventris (Chambers Co., TX)

123g venter priapus (Livingston Parish)

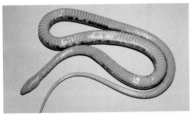

123h venter anthicus (Sabine Parish)

123j anterior (Winston Co., MS)

123i venter flaviventris (Waller Co., TX)

123k juvenile (Ouachita Parish)

## Coachwhip (*Masticophis flagellum*)
**Other names:** *Coluber flagellum*

**Subspecies:** Eastern Coachwhip (*M. f. flagellum*)

**Description:** Coachwhips are slender, with a long tail and a head that is distinct from the neck. They are **black to dark brown on the head and neck but become pale toward the middle of the body.** In the Florida Parishes, Coachwhips grade to pale tan or buckskin color on the posterior half of the body, but west of the Mississippi River they tend to be reddish tan to brick red toward the tail. The underside is white to black on the chin and throat, becoming dirty white posteriorly. The venter of snakes from western Louisiana is usually pink. Juveniles are tan with widely spaced, dark transverse markings on the neck, which break up into scattered brown spots that coalesce and disappear near the tail. The scales are smooth and in 17 rows. The anal shield is divided.

**Size:** Maximum length 102 inches (2,591 mm); adults usually 41.1–83.7 inches (1,035–2,126 mm); hatchlings approximately 15.3 inches (390 mm).

**Habitat:** Coachwhips occur in dry habitats, usually in uplands: pine-hardwood woodland and longleaf pine woodland and savanna.

**Natural history:** Coachwhips are active, diurnal predators, most often encountered as they bask or forage on open ground. They feed on grasshoppers, lizards, and other snakes, and less frequently on small birds and rodents. Females lay clutches of 4–24 (usually 12–17) eggs. Coachwhips usually flee when approached and will often ascend shrubs and small trees to escape. However, they can also take the offensive by coiling, striking, and vibrating their tails, hurling themselves with each strike in the direction of their perceived threat. Oddly, their next form of defense is to play dead by going into a limp coil, with the head partially concealed under the body.

**Distribution and status:** The Coachwhip occurs in the northern tier of the Florida Parishes and in upland portions of northern and central Louisiana, where it ranges south to Calcasieu, northern Jefferson Davis, and Evangeline Parishes. It is absent from the Red River floodplain and Mississippi Delta. Coachwhips are moderately common in semi-open habitats, and in such areas their populations seem stable.

124a adult (Jefferson Co., TX)

124b adult (Tangipahoa Parish)

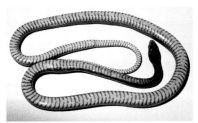

124c venter (Marion Co., FL)

124d venter (Sabine Parish)

124e anterior (Sabine Parish)

124f juvenile (Bienville Parish)

### Rough Green Snake (*Opheodrys aestivus*)
**Other names**: grass snake

**Subspecies**: Northern Rough Green Snake (*O. a. aestivus*)

**Description**: Rough Green Snakes are very slender, with a long tail and a head that is distinct from the neck. They are **bright green above, and white or yellow below** and on the labials. Hatchlings are gray above, white below. The scales are keeled and in 17 rows. The anal shield is divided.

**Size**: Maximum length 37.3 inches (947 mm); adult males usually 19.7–28.0 inches (501–712 mm), adult females usually 23.8–32.1 inches (604–815 mm); hatchlings 4.5–8.3 inches (114–210 mm).

**Habitat**: Rough Green Snakes favor highly vegetated habitats ranging from coastal marshes and scrubby old fields to mixed pine-hardwood forests.

**Natural history**: Rough Green Snakes are diurnal and tend to forage and rest in trees, shrubs, and vine tangles where they are well camouflaged—it is not unusual to find them in such habitat over a shallow wetland. They are often observed on open ground when crossing between vegetated spots but usually are otherwise overlooked. Chance encounters might imply that they are uncommon, but in favorable habitats they can occur in densities of 200 snakes per acre. They feed on spiders and insects, especially grasshoppers, katydids, and caterpillars. Females lay clutches of 1–14 (usually 5–7) eggs, usually in tree cavities, which may be used by more than one female. When encountered, especially in the open, these snakes remain still until prodded, at which point they become lively in their efforts to escape. They do not bite.

**Distribution and status**: Rough Green Snakes occur statewide, except for extensive zones of uniform brackish and salt marshes. Their populations are considered stable.

122a adult (Ouachita Parish)

122b adult (Vermilion Parish)

122c adult (Hardin Co., TX)

122d venter (East Baton Rouge Parish)

122e anterior (Livingston Parish)

## Southeastern Crowned Snake (*Tantilla coronata*)

**Description**: Southeastern Crowned Snakes are small, somewhat slender snakes with a head that is not distinct from the neck. They are **tan above, bright pink below**. The pink is replaced by white on the chin and throat. The top of the **head and mouth area are black, except for a whitish area below the eye and at the angle of the mouth. A dull white or dull yellow collar crosses the back of the head and is bounded behind by a dark crossband**. Hatchlings resemble the adults. The scales are smooth and in 15 rows. The anal shield is divided.

**Size**: Maximum length 13.0 inches (330 mm); adults usually 6.9–9.8 inches (174–250 mm); hatchlings 3.0–4.1 inches (76–104 mm).

**Habitat**: Southeastern Crowned Snakes occur in open pine woodland and mixed pine-hardwood forest.

**Natural history**: Southeastern Crowned Snakes are semifossorial and are usually only encountered under surface objects and under or inside rotting logs. They feed on centipedes, insect larvae, and earthworms. Females produce clutches of two or three eggs. Southeastern Crowned Snakes do not bite when handled.

**Distribution and status**: Southeastern Crowned Snakes occur in well-drained portions of the Florida Parishes as far west as the vicinity of the upper Amite River. They have been found at only one locality in Louisiana since the mid-1980s and for that reason are considered a Species of Conservation Concern.

125a adult (St. Tammany Parish)

125b adult (Wilson Co., TN)

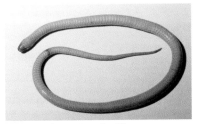

125c venter (Santa Rosa Co., FL)

125d anterior (Santa Rosa Co., FL)

125e juvenile (Wilson Co., TN)

## Flat-headed Snake (*Tantilla gracilis*)

**Description:** Flat-headed Snakes are small, somewhat slender snakes with a head that is not distinct from the neck. They are **tan or grayish tan above, paler on the lower sides, and bright pink below.** The pink is replaced by white on the chin and throat. The **top of the head is dark brown or grayish brown.** Hatchlings are brownish gray. The scales are smooth and in 15 rows. The anal shield is divided.

**Size:** Maximum length 9.8 inches (249 mm); adults usually 6.6–8.9 inches (168–225 mm); hatchlings 3.0–4.1 inches (77–104 mm).

**Habitat:** Flat-headed Snakes occur in open, well-drained pine woodland and semi-open mixed pine-hardwood forest.

**Natural history:** Flat-headed Snakes are semifossorial and are usually only encountered during warm, damp weather under surface objects, such as sandstone rocks, and under or inside rotting logs. They feed on centipedes, insect larvae, isopods, spiders, and scorpions. Females produce clutches of two to four eggs. They do not bite when handled.

**Distribution and status:** Flat-headed Snakes occur in well-drained portions of northern and central Louisiana on either side of the Red River lowlands. They have been reported as far south as northeastern Rapides Parish in the east and to the Peason Ridge region in Vernon Parish in the west. They are difficult to locate due to their fossorial habits, but there is an abundance of their preferred habitat in Louisiana. For these reasons, their populations are considered stable.

126a adult (Carroll Co., AR)

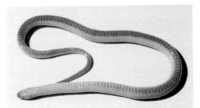

126b venter (Natchitoches Parish)

126c anterior (Natchitoches Parish)

126d juvenile (Madison Co., MO)

## Red Corn Snake (*Pantherophis guttatus*)
Other names: *Elaphe guttata*

Description: Red Corn Snakes are of medium build with a head that is distinct from the neck. Above, they are **pale gray brown to orange or orange tan with a row of 24–33 large, reddish brown to dull red blotches down the back**. The **blotches have darker borders and usually thin white margins.** Smaller blotches of similar color alternate with the larger ones on each side. The **first dark blotch on the neck has linear extensions forward along either side of the head that meet on the crown to form a point**. Another reddish band crosses between the eyes and extends back to the angle of mouth. The **underside is white with large, squared black markings**. The labials are white with black suture marks. Juveniles are very pale gray with a pale orange wash, and the blotches are dark red with black borders. The scales are weakly keeled on the top of the back and are in 27 rows. The anal shield is divided.

Size: Maximum length 72 inches (1,829 mm); adults usually 29.6–61.4 inches (753–1,560 mm); hatchlings 10.3–12.2 inches (263–311 mm).

Habitat: Red Corn Snakes favor open pine flatwoods, semi-open hardwood bottoms, and relatively dry upland forests. They can also be found in and around pastures and old fields.

Natural history: Red Corn Snakes are often diurnal but may be crepuscular or nocturnal during hot weather. They are more terrestrial than the other rat snakes and are usually found abroad on the ground or concealed in rotted stumps. They feed on small mammals and birds and their eggs. Females lay a clutch of usually 9–27 eggs. Red Corn Snakes will defend themselves by coiling and striking, and often bite when captured.

Distribution and status: The Red Corn Snake occurs throughout the Florida Parishes and also in areas just west of the Mississippi River in West Baton Rouge Parish and vicinity. It occurs on the salt domes and adjacent areas of St. Mary and Iberia Parishes, and the Sicily Island Hills, Catahoula Parish, as well. Their populations are considered stable over much of their range.

127a adult (Santa Rosa Co., FL)

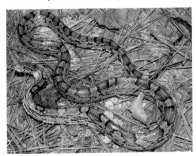

127b adult (Catahoula Parish)

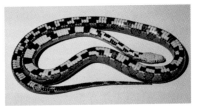

127c venter (St. Tammany Parish)

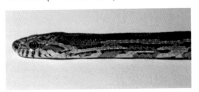

127d anterior (St. Tammany Parish)

127e juvenile (Catahoula Parish)

## Slowinski's Corn Snake (*Pantherophis slowinskii*)
**Other names:** Kisatchie Corn Snake, *Elaphe slowinskii*

**Description:** Slowinski's Corn Snakes are of moderate build with a head that is distinct from the neck. Above, they are **pale gray to gray brown with a row of 32–38 large dark brown to reddish brown blotches down the back**. The **blotches have darker borders but lack white margins.** Smaller blotches of similar color alternate with the larger ones on each side. The **first dark blotch on the neck has linear extensions forward along either side of the head that meet on the crown to form a point**. Another dark band crosses between the eyes and extends back to the corner of the mouth. The **underside is white with large, squared black markings.** The labials are white with black suture marks. Adults from the southeastern part of the range may have an orange cast to the ground color and reddish blotches, resembling the Red Corn Snake. Juveniles are very pale gray, often tinted with orange, and the blotches are dark reddish brown or brown with black borders. The scales are weakly keeled on the top of the back and are in 27 rows. The anal shield is divided.

**Size:** Maximum length at least 59 inches (152 cm); adults usually 28.4–50.3 inches (722–1,278 mm); hatchling length is not reported.

**Habitat:** Slowinski's Corn Snakes occur in longleaf pine forests and woodlands but will also occupy shortleaf or loblolly pine woodlands and mixed forest.

**Natural history:** Slowinski's Corn Snakes are diurnal but often crepuscular or nocturnal during hot weather. They are terrestrial and most often found active on the surface of the ground. They feed on birds and small mammals. Females produce clutches of 12–14 eggs. Slowinski's Corn Snakes, like Red Corn Snakes, will strike and bite when captured, and seem even more irascible.

**Distribution and status:** Slowinski's Corn Snakes are found in the uplands of central Louisiana on either side of the Red River Valley. In the east, they occur from Bienville Parish south to the Camp Livingston area in northeastern Rapides Parish. There is a record for Union Parish that needs corroboration. West of the river, they occur in western Natchitoches and eastern Sabine Parishes, southward to Evangeline Parish and the flat pinelands in northern Calcasieu Parish. Their populations appear to be stable.

128a adult (Natchitoches Parish)

128b adult (Rapides Parish)

128c venter (Vernon Parish)

128d anterior (Natchitoches Parish)

128e juvenile (Vernon Parish)

## Texas Rat Snake (*Pantherophis obsoletus*)

**Other names**: *Elaphe obsoleta lindheimeri*, *Elaphe obsoleta obsoleta*, Black Rat Snake, Western Rat Snake, chicken snake, oak snake, egg snake, serpent à z-oeufs, serpent à rat

**Description**: Texas Rat Snakes are relatively slim with a head that is distinct from the neck. Hatchlings are pale gray with a **row of 25–36 large, dark brown blotches down the back** and an alternating row of dark spots on each side. The **first dark blotch has linear extensions forward along either side of the head that end on the temples**. Another dark band crosses between the eye and extends back to the angle of mouth. When they are less than a year old, the ground color of the juveniles becomes yellowish tan, then continues to darken with age to yellowish brown, often becoming **dark brown, mingled with irregular markings of yellow and orange, giving the snake a calico appearance. In upland areas of northern and central Louisiana, the ground color and blotches become very dark gray to black, and the blotches are visible only by the presence of pale outlines**. In adults, the top of the head is dark brown, black, or gray, and the labials are dull white with a few dark suture marks. The **underside is white on the chin and throat, then becomes dirty white to yellow, with brown or black blotches that increase toward the tail so that the posterior underside is brown or gray**. The scales are keeled on the middle of the back and in 25 or 27 rows. The anal shield is divided.

**Size**: Maximum length 84.8 inches (2,153 mm); adults usually 41.1–77.3 inches (1,044–1,963 mm); hatchlings 13.0–17.6 inches (331–448 mm).

**Habitat**: Texas Rat Snakes occur in wooded and forested habitats, favoring those with an abundance of hardwoods.

**Natural history**: Texas Rat Snakes are arboreal and spend much of their time in large trees or crossing water or the surface of the ground between them. They take shelter in the hollows of trees and in snags. Their habit of climbing also enables them to take refuge in man-made structures that have an external entry, such as barn lofts, attics, and walls. They are primarily diurnal or crepuscular. They feed on small mammals and birds and their eggs, and juveniles may supplement their diet with lizards. Females produce a clutch of 7–22 eggs. At times, a Texas Rat Snake will deposit its clutch in the walls of a home, and some of the hatchlings end up inside. These snakes rely on camouflage and will usually remain motionless as one walks near or even steps over them. Once they feel the need to defend themselves, they will coil and strike while vibrating their tail on the ground.

**Distribution and status**: The Texas Rat Snake occurs along and west of the Mississippi River, and it is absent only from extensive areas of marsh and agricultural fields. It is distinguished from the Gray Rat Snake by genetic differences, and the geographic line of differentiation is approximate. Its populations are stable.

129a adult (Catahoula Parish)

129b adult (Ouachita Parish)

129c adult (Natchitoches Parish)

129d adult (St. Martin Parish)

129f venter (central LA)

129g anterior (Catahoula Parish)

129e adult (St. Martin Parish)

129h juvenile (Mississippi Co., MO)

## Gray Rat Snake (*Pantherophis spiloides*)

**Other names**: *Elaphe obsoleta spiloides,* chicken snake

**Description**: Gray Rat Snakes are relatively slim with a head that is distinct from the neck. Hatchlings are pale **gray with a row of 25–34 large, dark brown blotches down the back** and an alternating row of dark spots on each side. The **first dark blotch on the neck has linear extensions forward along either side of the head that end on the temples**.  Another dark band crosses between the eyes and extends back to the corner of the mouth. When they are less than a year old, the ground color of the juveniles becomes yellowish tan. It continues to darken with age to **yellowish brown, sometimes becoming gray or dark brown, mingled with irregular markings of yellow and orange, giving the snake a calico appearance**. In adults, the top of the head is dark brown or gray, and the labials are dull white with few dark suture marks. The **underside is white on the chin and throat, then becomes dirty white, with pale brown blotches that increase toward the tail so that the posterior underside is brown or gray**. The scales are keeled on the middle of the back and in 25 or 27 rows. The anal shield is divided.

**Size**: Maximum length 86 inches (2,184 mm); adults usually 43.3–69.6 inches (1,100–1,767 mm); hatchlings 12.0–15.5 inches (304–395 mm).

**Habitat**: Gray Rat Snakes occur in wooded and forested habitats, favoring those with an abundance of hardwoods.

**Natural history**: Gray Rat Snakes are arboreal and spend much of their time in large trees or crossing water or the surface of the ground between them. They take shelter in the hollows of trees and in snags. Their habit of climbing also enables them to take refuge in man-made structures that have an external entry, such as barn lofts, attics, and walls. They are primarily diurnal or crepuscular. They feed on small mammals and birds and their eggs, and juveniles may supplement their diet with lizards. Females produce a clutch of 7–23 eggs. At times, a Gray Rat Snake will deposit its clutch in the walls of a home, and some of the hatchlings end up inside. These snakes rely on camouflage and will usually remain motionless as one walks near or even steps over them. Once they feel the need to defend themselves, they will coil and strike while vibrating their tails on the ground.

**Distribution and status**: The Gray Rat Snake occurs along and east of the Mississippi River, where it is absent only from extensive areas of marsh. Their populations are stable.

130a adult (Tangipahoa Parish)

130b adult (Hancock Co., MS)

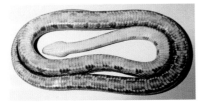

130c venter (East Baton Rouge Parish)

130d anterior (East Baton Rouge Parish)

130e juvenile (East Baton Rouge Parish)

## Eastern Pine Snake (*Pituophis melanoleucus*)

**Subspecies**: Black Pine Snake (*P. m. lodingi*)

**Description**: Black Pine Snakes are large snakes
of medium build, with a head that is somewhat
distinct from the neck and with a **pointed snout**.
Hatchlings are **tan with large, black saddlelike
blotches down the back**, which become diffuse
and patchy on the sides. The saddles may be close
together or separated by narrow black markings.

The **head and neck tend to be dark overall, with the saddles becoming
increasingly distinct toward the tail**. Within a year of hatching, the
snake's ground color changes to dark brown, making the snake appear as
though it has been tinted with shoe polish. East of the Pearl River, Black
Pine Snake adults are completely black, but that level of darkening has
not been observed in Louisiana. The underside is almost entirely dark
brown with scattered pale markings. The scales are keeled and usually in
31 rows. The anal shield is not divided.

**Size**: Maximum length 76 inches (1,930 mm); adults usually 48–64 inches
(1,219–1,626 mm); hatchlings 18.5–23.9 inches (474–608 mm).

**Habitat**: Black Pine Snakes favor uplands forested by old-growth longleaf
pine and hardwoods.

**Natural history**: Black Pine Snakes are diurnal and terrestrial. When not
actively foraging or thermoregulating, they reside in abandoned animal
burrows or root chambers of stumps. They feed primarily on rodents but
may also eat small rabbits and eggs of ground-nesting birds. Females
lay a clutch of five or six eggs. When they feel threatened, these snakes
present a provocative defense display by coiling as if to strike and, with
mouth open, producing a long, loud hiss. Despite this apparent ferocity,
they rarely bite when captured.

**Distribution and status**: The Black Pine Snake is limited to the southwest
corner of Alabama, southern Mississippi, and a corner of Louisiana in
Washington Parish. Two verified Louisiana records exist: one taken in
the 1930s a few miles southwest of Bogalusa and another found in 1965
a little northwest of Angie. There is an unverified report from 2005. No

intensive surveys have been conducted to locate additional snakes, except for systematic scoping of Gopher Tortoise burrows in the area of the two records. Black Pines Snakes are listed as Threatened under the Endangered Species Act.

131a adult (Perry Co., MS)

131b adult, preserved specimen (Walthall Co., MS)

131c venter, preserved specimen (Walthall Co., MS)

131d juvenile (Perry Co., MS)

## Louisiana Pine Snake (*Pituophis ruthveni*)

**Other names**: *Pituophis melanoleucus ruthveni,* hissing snake

**Description**: Louisiana Pine Snakes are large snakes of medium build, with a **pointed snout** and a head that is somewhat distinct from the neck. They are **dull yellow, pale tan, or beige with 30–37 large brown or black blotches on the back** and a row of smaller dark spots on each side.  There are often irregular dark markings between the blotches, especially on the neck, and the blotches may have paler brown centers. A dark band passes between the eyes and back to the angle of the mouth. The top of the head is often marked with dark spots, and the labials have dark suture marks. The **underside is pale yellow with few to many brown blotches,** usually along each side. Juveniles resemble the adults but have a slightly paler to orange-tinted ground color. The scales are keeled and in 29 or 31 rows. The anal shield is not divided.

**Size**: Maximum length 70.5 inches (1,790 mm); adults usually 48–59 inches (1,219–1,500 mm); hatchlings 20.5–21.9 inches (520–555 mm).

**Habitat**: Louisiana Pine Snakes are restricted to open longleaf pine woodland with loose, preferably sandy soil.

**Natural history**: Louisiana Pine Snakes spend most of their time in the burrows of Pocket Gophers, upon which they feed. Because they eat and thermoregulate in these shallow burrows, they have little need to come to the surface, so they are rarely seen. Though they feed primarily on gophers, they also eat cotton rats. Females produce a clutch of three to eight eggs. Like the Black Pine Snake, they elevate their foreparts and hiss loudly when threatened.

**Distribution and status**: The Louisiana Pine Snake occurs in several subpopulations: uplands in eastern Grant and northeastern Rapides Parishes, western Jackson and eastern Bienville to northern Natchitoches Parishes, and the vicinity of Natchitoches southward to western Rapides and Beauregard Parishes. In the past forty years, they have been found only on the north and southwest ends of Natchitoches Parish, in Bienville Parish, and on Fort Polk and vicinity. Due to their scarcity and their disappearance from many areas, the Louisiana Pine Snake cannot be removed from the wild except by permit and is a Species of Conservation Concern.

132a adult (Bienville Parish)

132b adult (Bienville Parish)

132c venter (Bienville Parish)

132d anterior (Bienville Parish)

132e juvenile (Bienville Parish)

## Scarlet Snake (*Cemophora coccinea*)

**Subspecies**: Northern Scarlet Snake (*C. c. copei*)

**Description**: Scarlet Snakes are of medium build, with a **pointed snout** and a head that is not distinct from the body. They are **pale gray or dirty white with 15–28 red saddles**. The saddles are bordered on either side by black crossbands. The several lowermost scale rows are spotted or mottled with black. The back of the head bears a dull yellow crossband, and the top of the head is red with a black crossbar just behind the eyes. The **underside is white**. Juveniles are more brightly colored than the adults. The scales are smooth and in 19 rows. The anal shield is not divided.

**Size**: Maximum length 26.4 inches (670 mm); adults usually 13.0–25.2 inches (330–640 mm); hatchlings 4.6–6.5 inches (115–165 mm).

**Habitat**: Scarlet Snakes are found in pine woodlands or relatively open pine-hardwood forests.

**Natural history**: Scarlet Snakes are fossorial and are rarely found abroad, except on roads at night. Unlike most Louisiana snake species, Scarlet Snakes have a peak of activity in June and early July, which may coincide with their feeding habits. They feed primarily on the eggs of reptiles but are also known to feed on lizards and small snakes. The rear maxillary teeth are enlarged and bladelike, which may assist in piercing the shells of the eggs. Fortunately, Scarlet Snakes are not known to bite. Females produce clutches of 2–11 (usually 4–7) eggs.

**Distribution and status**: Scarlet Snakes occur in the eastern Florida Parishes (east of the Tangipahoa River) and in uplands of northern and central Louisiana, mostly west of the Ouachita River, as far south as northwestern Calcasieu Parish. There are no records from Caddo or DeSoto Parishes. Scarlet Snakes are difficult to locate, but trapping surveys suggest that their populations are stable.

133a adult (Bienville Parish)

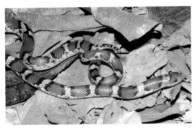

133b adult (Ouachita Parish)

133c venter (Wilson Co., TN)

133d anterior (Bienville Parish)

133e juvenile (Ouachita Co., AR)

## Scarlet King Snake (*Lampropeltis elapsoides*)

**Other names:** *Lampropeltis triangulum elapsoides*

**Description:** Scarlet King Snakes are of medium build, with a head that is scarcely distinct from the neck. They are **red with 11–17 series of white to yellow rings that are bordered on either side by black rings. The colors continue around the underside** but are slightly paler there. The first white ring encircles the back of the head and is bordered behind by a black ring and in front by a black crossband just behind the eyes. The **front of the head is red**. Juveniles are colored like the adults. The scales are smooth and in 19 rows. The anal shield is not divided.

**Size:** Maximum length 27.0 inches (686 mm); adults usually 17.0–21.9 inches (432–556 mm); hatchlings 5.0–6.2 inches (126–159 mm).

**Habitat:** Scarlet King Snakes occur in lightly wooded to forested areas, usually where pines are dominant or at least present.

**Natural history:** Scarlet King Snakes are secretive, rarely observed abroad by day, and crepuscular or nocturnal in warm weather. They are most often found under cover, especially under the bark of dead pines or inside rotting logs and stumps. They feed on lizards and small snakes. Females produce clutches of three to seven eggs. Scarlet King Snakes usually bite and chew when captured.

**Distribution and status:** The Scarlet King Snake occurs throughout the Florida Parishes, except in the bottomlands of the Maurepas, Bayou Manchac, and Mississippi River, where it is replaced by the Western Milk Snake. Scarlet King Snakes are difficult to find, so their status is tentatively considered stable, due to the extensive habitat availability.

134a adult (St. Tammany Parish)

134b adult (Okaloosa Co., FL)

134e juvenile (St. Tammany Parish)

134c venter (St. Tammany Parish)

134d anterior (Stone Co., MS)

## Eastern Milk Snake (*Lampropeltis triangulum*)
**Other names**: Red Milk Snake, *Lampropeltis triangulum syspila*

**Description**: Eastern Milk Snakes are of medium build, with a head that is scarcely distinct from the neck. They are **red with 13–17 series of white crossbands bordered on either side by black crossbands**. The **lower side of the red saddles extend only to the outer edge of the ventrals**. Otherwise, the underside is dull white with scattered black marks. A white crossband at the back of the head is bordered behind by a black crossband and in front by another black crossband at the level of the parietals. The **top of the head is red, and the end of the snout is pale**. There is **usually a black stripe behind the eye that connects with the black crossbar on the back of the head**. Juveniles are colored like the adults. The scales are smooth and in 21 rows. The anal shield is not divided.

**Size**: Maximum length outside of Louisiana 42.0 inches (1,067 mm); Louisiana adults usually 16.0–25.9 inches (406–657 mm); hatchlings 5.7–7.2 inches (144–183 mm).

**Habitat**: Eastern Milk Snakes occur in bottomland hardwood forest.

**Natural history**: Eastern Milk Snakes are secretive, rarely observed abroad by day, and crepuscular or nocturnal in warm weather. They are most often found under cover, especially in the bark of dead trees or inside rotten snags, logs, and stumps. They feed on lizards, small snakes, and occasionally shrews and small mice. Females produce clutches of four to nine eggs. Milk Snakes usually bite and chew when captured.

**Distribution and status**: The Eastern Milk Snake occurs in the upper Mississippi River Delta, at least as far southwest as southern LaSalle Parish. The boundary between it and the Western Milk Snake is not known but approximates the divide between the Tensas and Ouachita watersheds. Though much of their habitat has been cleared for agriculture, their populations appear to be stable in remaining tracts of forest.

135a adult (LaSalle Parish)

135b adult (Tensas Parish)

135c venter (LaSalle Parish)

135d anterior (Catahoula Parish)

135e juvenile (Tensas Parish)

## Western Milk Snake (*Lampropeltis gentilis*)
**Other names**: Louisiana Milk Snake, *Lampropeltis triangulum amaura*

**Description**: Western Milk Snakes are of medium build, with a head that is scarcely distinct from the neck. They are **red with a series of 12–22 white crossbands that are bordered on either side by black crossbands. The lower side of the red saddles may be bordered by black on the outer edge of the ventrals or extend partway onto the belly**. The midventral zone is dull white with scattered black marks. A white crossband at the back of the head is bordered behind by a black crossband. The **top of the head is black, and the end of the snout is white, black, or black with red or white spots**. Juveniles are colored like the adults. The scales are smooth and in 21 rows. The anal shield is not divided.

**Size**: Maximum length 31.0 inches (787 mm); adults usually 18.4–23.8 inches (468–604 mm); hatchlings approximately 5 inches (125 mm).

**Habitat**: Western Milk Snakes occur in bottomland hardwood and mixed pine-hardwood forests, usually in low areas.

**Natural history**: Western Milk Snakes are secretive, rarely observed abroad by day, and crepuscular or nocturnal in warm weather. They are most often found under cover, especially under the bark of dead trees or inside rotten logs, snags, and stumps. They feed on lizards and small snakes. Females produce clutches of three to nine eggs. Western Milk Snakes usually bite and chew when captured.

**Distribution and status**: Western Milk Snakes occur along the Red River Valley and bordering hills to the river's mouth, then southeastward along the lower Mississippi River floodplain and surrounding forested lands to near the mouth of the Mississippi. From there, they range west to the eastern part of the Atchafalaya region. They also occur in the forested portions of southwestern Louisiana from Vernon Parish southward to the Cameron Parish cheniers. Populations west of the Ouachita/Tensas River watershed divide in northeastern Louisiana appear referable to this species on the basis of head coloration. Their populations appear to be stable.

136a adult (Caldwell Parish)

136b adult (St. Martin Parish)

136c venter (Jefferson Parish)

136d anterior (Ascension Parish)

## Yellow-bellied King Snake (*Lampropeltis calligaster*)

**Subspecies**: Prairie King Snake (*L. c. calligaster*), Mole King Snake (*L. c. rhombomaculata*)

**Description**: Yellow-bellied King Snakes are of moderate build with a head that is scarcely distinct from the neck. They are **pale gray or dull yellow to tan or grayish tan with a row of 29–57 transverse, oblong blotches down the back** and a row of slightly smaller spots on each side. The **blotches are brown or reddish, usually with black borders and thin white edges**. The first dark markings on the neck are paired and elongate, extending from the temporal area to at least a head length onto the neck. A dark band passes between the eyes, back to near the angle of the mouth. The labials, chin, and **venter are whitish. The venter is marked by large, blocklike, pale brown markings. Snakes from northern and central Louisiana are often darker than those from elsewhere, especially as adults, and may be so dark brown to nearly black that the pattern is scarcely visible.** Juveniles are usually more brightly marked than adults. West of the Mississippi River, the scales are in 25 rows (subspecies *calligaster*) and east of the river are in 21 rows (*rhombomaculata*). The scales are smooth, and the anal shield is not divided.

**Size**: Maximum length 56.3 inches (1,430 mm); adults usually 31.5–44.1 inches (800–1,121 mm); hatchlings 6.9–12.1 inches (175–305 mm).

**Habitat**: Yellow-bellied King Snakes occur in pine forest, mixed pine-hardwood forests, both uplands and flatwoods, and occur in the open, former prairie country of Acadiana in areas now converted to pasture and agriculture.

**Natural history**: Yellow-bellied King Snakes are secretive and rarely seen except when they are crossing roads. In open country they can also be found under surface objects in early spring. They feed on rodents and shrews, and juveniles will also eat lizards. Females produce clutches of 4–21 (usually 9–15) eggs. They often bite when captured and may also coil and strike energetically when threatened.

**Distribution and status**: Yellow-bellied King Snakes occur in the eastern Florida Parishes, upland portions of northern and central Louisiana, and throughout southwestern Louisiana north of the marsh line and west of the Atchafalaya lowland. In western Louisiana, their populations appear stable. In eastern Louisiana, there are only a half-dozen records, and for that reason the subspecies *rhombomaculata* is considered a Species of Conservation Concern.

137a adult calligaster (Bienville Parish)

137b adult calligaster (Natchitoches Parish)

137c adult calligaster (Waller Co., TX)

137d adult rhombomaculata (Perry Co., MS)

137e adult calligaster (Garland Co., AR)

137f juvenile calligaster (Austin Co., TX)

## Black King Snake (*Lampropeltis nigra*)
**Other names**: Eastern Black King Snake, *Lampropeltis getula nigra*

**Description**: Black King Snakes are of medium build, with a head that is scarcely distinct from the neck. The juveniles are **black above**, with thin, transverse cream or yellow bars down the back, and a mottling of cream or pale yellow markings on the lower sides. As the snakes grow, many of the black scales develop yellow spots such that

the adult appears to be **heavily speckled with white or yellow**. The scales and shields of the head also bear light spots, and the labials are boldly barred. The underside is cream to pale yellow with blocklike black markings that are concentrated at the middle of the belly. The scales are smooth and in 21 rows. The anal shield is not divided.

**Size**: Maximum length 58 inches (1,473 mm); adults usually 28.8–53.7 inches (732–1,365 mm); hatchlings 9.3–11.3 inches (235–287 mm).

**Habitat**: Black King Snakes occur in all southeast Louisiana habitats, including urban areas, except extensive areas of swamp and trackless marsh.

**Natural history**: Black King Snakes are diurnal or crepuscular, most often found on the ground as they actively forage, or under surface objects. They occasionally climb shrubs and the rotted interior of snags in search of prey. They feed on rodents, other snakes, lizards, and turtle eggs. Females produce a clutch of 3–24 eggs. Black King Snakes usually do not coil and strike when threatened, but they do often bite when restrained.

**Distribution and status**: The Black King Snake occurs along and east of the Mississippi River– Atchafalaya River floodplains but is absent from trackless portions of the marsh. It is genetically differentiated from the Speckled King Snake, but inadequate genetic sampling has made the geographic boundary between the two species imprecise. There is some indication that Black King Snake populations may be declining in southern Louisiana, though they are still observed with regularity.

138a adult (Orleans Parish)

138b adult (Wilkinson Co., MS)

138c venter (East Baton Rouge Parish)

138d anterior (East Baton Rouge Parish)

138e juvenile (Tangipahoa Parish)

## Speckled King Snake (*Lampropeltis holbrooki*)
**Other names**: *Lampropeltis getula holbrooki*

**Description**: Speckled King Snakes are of medium build, with a head that is scarcely distinct from the neck. The juveniles are **black above**, with thin, transverse cream or yellow bars down the back, intermingled with pale specks, and a mottling of cream or pale yellow markings on the lower sides. As the snakes grow, many of the black scales develop yellow spots such that the snake appears to be **heavily speckled with white or yellow**, and the pale bars tend to break up into spots as well. The scales and shields of the head also bear light spots, and the labials are boldly barred. The underside is cream to bright yellow with extensive blocks of black, especially down the middle of the belly. Speckled King Snakes from the southwest marsh region often have brilliant orange yellow spots on the lower sides. The scales are smooth and in 21 rows. The anal shield is not divided.

**Size**: Maximum length 72 inches (1,829 mm); adults usually 27.3–56.0 inches (694–1,423 mm); hatchlings 8.0–11.7 inches (202–298 mm).

**Habitat**: Speckled King Snakes occur in nearly all Louisiana habitats, including urban areas, except extensive areas of swamp and trackless marsh.

**Natural history**: Speckled King Snakes are diurnal or crepuscular, most often found on the ground as they actively forage, or under surface objects. They occasionally climb shrubs and the rotted interior of snags in search of prey. They feed on rodents, other snakes, lizards, and turtle eggs. Females produce a clutch of 5–23 eggs. Speckled King Snakes usually do not coil and strike when threatened, but they do often bite when restrained.

**Distribution and status**: Speckled King Snakes occur along and west of the Mississippi–Atchafalaya River floodplains but are absent from trackless portions of the marsh. They are genetically differentiated from the Black King Snake, but inadequate genetic sampling has made the geographic boundary between the two species imprecise. There is some indication that Speckled King Snake populations may be declining in southern Louisiana, but they are still commonly observed.

139a adult (Allen Parish)

139b adult (Hardin Co., TX)

139c venter (St. Martin Parish)

139d juvenile (Evangeline Parish)

139e juvenile (Cameron Parish)

## Harlequin Coral Snake (*Micrurus fulvius*) VENOMOUS
**Other names**: Eastern Coral Snake, *M. f. fulvius*

**Description**: Harlequin Coral Snakes are relatively slender, with a head that is scarcely distinct from the neck. The color pattern consists of **alternating long rings of black and red, usually 13 or 14 pairs, each separated by a short yellow ring**. The red rings often contain black spots or blotches. The front of the head is black, and the rear of the head is encircled by yellow, which is followed by the first black body ring. The **first black ring does not reach forward to touch the posterior tips of the parietal scales**. The underside is similar in color to the back. Juveniles tend to be more brightly colored than adults. The dorsal scales are smooth and in 15 rows at midbody. The anal shield is divided.

**Size**: Maximum length 47.5 inches (1,207 mm), largest Louisiana individual 27.5 inches (699 mm); in Louisiana adults usually 18.9–26.1 inches (481–662 mm); hatchlings 6–6.5 inches (153–165 mm).

**Habitat**: Harlequin Coral Snakes inhabit forests, preferring well-drained areas. In all occupied terrain, there is a mixture of pines and hardwoods.

**Natural history**: The behavior of the Harlequin Coral Snake resembles that of the Texas form. They feed primarily on small snakes (Ring-necked and Crowned in Louisiana) and small skinks. In Louisiana, this species is known to lay 5–7 eggs but elsewhere lays 3–13. Despite tales to the contrary, coral snakes are highly venomous and will aggressively defend themselves by biting when captured. Their venom is neurotoxic, and initial bite symptoms may be subdued by a general lack of pain. Indications of the venom's potentially fatal effects can quickly follow and culminate in respiratory failure.

**Distribution and status**: The Harlequin Coral Snake occurs in the eastern Florida Parishes, as far west as the north shore of Lake Pontchartrain and the bluffs over the Amite River in northern St. Helena Parish. Fewer than 15 Harlequin Coral snakes are known from Louisiana, and the most recent was found in Washington Parish in 1984. Although the species probably persists in Louisiana, the paucity of records and lack of recent reports has warranted listing it as a Species of Conservation Concern.

140a adult (Perry Co., MS)

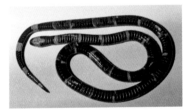

140b venter (Perry Co., MS)

140c anterior (Perry Co., MS)

## Texas Coral Snake (*Micrurus tener*) VENOMOUS

**Other names**: *Micrurus fulvius tenere*

**Description**: Texas Coral Snakes are relatively slender with a head that is scarcely distinct from the neck. The color pattern consists of **alternating long rings of black and red, usually 10–13 pairs, each separated by a short yellow ring**. On the back, the scales of the red rings are often overlain by black stippling or spots. The front of the head is black, and the rear of the head is encircled by yellow, which is followed by the first black body ring. The **first black ring extends far enough forward to cover the posterior tips of the parietal scales**. The underside is similar in color to the back, except that the red areas may or may not have black spots and blotches. Juveniles tend to be more brightly colored than adults. The dorsal scales are smooth and in 15 rows at midbody. The anal shield is divided.

**Size**: Maximum length 47.7 inches (1,213 mm), largest Louisiana individual 32.4 inches (822 mm); adult males usually 20.0–27.2 inches (504–690 mm), females usually 23.1–30.9 inches (587–786 mm); hatchlings 6–6.5 inches (153–165 mm).

**Habitat**: Texas Coral Snakes inhabit forests and open woodlands, preferring well-drained areas. In nearly all occupied terrain, there is a mixture of pines and hardwoods. An exception occurs in the fringes of Acadiana, where these snakes occupy swamp margins and wooded floodplains that finger through open country.

**Natural history**: Texas Coral Snakes are secretive predators that search for prey in and around rotted logs, leaf litter, and other vegetative debris piles. Except for in very hot or cold weather, they are most active at midmorning and late afternoon. They feed primarily on small snakes (Red-bellied, Flat-headed, Earth) and small skinks, which they subdue by chewing venom into their prey. They lay 3–12 eggs, probably in June or early July. Despite tales to the contrary, Texas Coral Snakes are highly venomous and will aggressively defend themselves by biting when captured. Their venom is neurotoxic, and initial bite symptoms may be subdued by a general lack of pain. Indications of the venom's potentially fatal effects can quickly follow and culminate in respiratory failure.

**Distribution and status**: The Texas Coral Snake inhabits much of western Louisiana but is absent from the marshes, the Mississippi Delta, and the Red River Valley. It enters the open flatlands of Acadiana along the Houston, Mermentau, and Vermilion Rivers. It is rarely encountered due to its secretive nature, but observations have been regular and persistent for decades, and populations are considered stable.

141a adult (Natchitoches Parish)

141b adult (Catahoula Parish)

141c venter (Acadia Parish)

141d anterior (Vernon Parish)

141e juvenile (Rapides Parish)

## Copperhead (*Agkistrodon contortrix*) VENOMOUS

**Other names**: Southern Copperhead, sonnette de canne

**Description**: Copperheads are relatively stout snakes with a head that is distinct from the neck. They are **beige to orange tan with 12–16 darker, hourglass-shaped markings down the back. The hourglass markings are longest on the lower sides and shortest at the middorsal line— markings are dull orange to coppery brown with broad, even, dark brown borders**. The end of the tail grades to dark gray or black. The top of the head is colored as the dorsum, with a **distinctly pale face**. The underside is white on the chin and along the sides, and beige near the center. There are about a dozen, large brown spots along the sides of the belly that alternate between the bases of the hourglass marks, and there are often lighter brown patches toward the middle. Juveniles are less brightly marked than adults, often with a vague gray tint, and the **end of the tail is bright yellow**. The scales are keeled and in 23 rows. The anal shield is not divided.

**Size**: Maximum length 52.0 inches (1,321 mm); adult males usually 20.0–48.0 inches (509–1,218 mm), adult females usually 23.2–40.6 inches (590–1,030 mm); newborns 8.5–11.1 inches (215–283 mm).

**Habitat**: Copperheads occur in all wooded habitats in Louisiana except for permanent swamps and coastal cheniers, and they favor hardwood forests.

**Natural history**: Copperheads are diurnal during spring and fall but become crepuscular or nocturnal during hot weather. Difficult to detect due to their camouflage pattern, they are usually found in a resting coil or on the prowl in ground cover. They are primarily terrestrial but are known to climb shrubs and trees. They are both sit-and-wait and active predators. They feed on small mammals, birds, frogs, and grasshoppers but also feed seasonally on cicadas and their larvae during emergence. Females produce litters of 4–16 (usually 6–11) young. Copperheads are quick to bite when molested and will bite by lashing back and forth if pinned. Though their venom has the lowest toxicity of the five Louisiana pit vipers, any Copperhead bite should receive immediate medical attention. Most bites are to the feet of those who walk about barefoot on hot nights.

**Distribution and status**: Copperheads occur throughout wooded portions of the state, including in forested river bottoms that finger into the otherwise open country of the marsh and prairie. They have vanished from large deforested tracts, such as in the Mississippi Delta, but remain common, even abundant in most forested regions of the state. Their populations are considered stable.

142a adult (Madison Parish)

142b adult (Rapides Parish)

142c adult (Ouachita Parish)

142d venter (Plaquemines Parish)

142e anterior (Perry Co., MS)

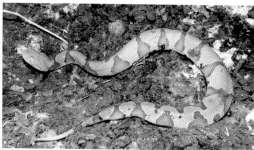

142f juvenile (St. Martin Parish)

## Cottonmouth (*Agkistrodon piscivorus*) VENOMOUS

**Other names**: Western Cottonmouth, *Agkistrodon piscivorus leucostoma,* stumptail moccasin, water moccasin, mudflower, congo

**Description**: The Cottonmouth is a stout, robust snake with a head that is distinct from the neck. The ground color of adults is **usually some shade of brown, ranging from tan to blackish brown. They have 10–15 darker crossbands that are a little shorter at middorsum than on the lower sides and usually a little longer than the interspaces. The crossbands have irregular edges, are dark brown to black with paler brown centers**, and often have irregular black markings within. Some adults may appear dark gray in general, with vague brown markings. The top of the head is brown to black, and a **black band passes along the side of the head from in front of the eye to the rear of the jaw**. A pale line is usually present at the top of the black band, and another below the band borders the mouth. The lower jaws are marked by dark patches, and the rest of the chin and throat are usually dirty white. The dark crossbands of the back extend onto the outer edges of the belly, which is overlain by dark patches that increase posteriorly to produce a nearly black underside toward the tail. The ground color of juveniles is pinkish tan or dull orange tan. The crossbands are dark brown with tan centers, and the **end of the tail is bright yellow**. The distinct crossbanded pattern of juveniles usually becomes increasingly obscured with age, by darkening of the ground color and crossbands. The scales are keeled and in 25 rows. The anal shield is not divided.

**Size**: Maximum length 62.0 inches (1,575 mm); adult males usually 24.0–49.5 inches (610–1,257 mm), females usually 23.5–36.3 inches (596–923 mm); newborns 6.8–11.8 inches (173–299 mm).

**Habitat**: Cottonmouths occur in nearly every habitat in Louisiana, from mangrove thickets on barrier islands and rice fields to upland forests.

**Natural history**: Cottonmouths are primarily ambush predators and may be found coiled along forest sloughs or facing into streams on log jams awaiting prey. They are often found casually swimming in shallow streams and swamps or in resting coils near cover. They are not restricted to water and may be found crossing overland in subdivisions or wooded ridges. Unlike most water snakes, Cottonmouths favor closed-canopy areas with shallow water and rarely bask over water. Most of their activity is terrestrial, but they occasionally ascend shrubs, vine tangles, palmettos, and snags. They feed on small mammals, birds, other snakes, amphibians, fish, and carrion. Females give birth to 2–16 (usually 4–10) young. Cottonmouths are considered aggressive, though it would be more appropriate to term them *defensive*. They rely on camouflage to escape detection but when disturbed will coil, gape their mouths to expose the pale inner lining, and vibrate their tails. If cornered or separated from a safe retreat such as water, Cottonmouths may resort to striking and advancing toward a perceived threat. They are dangerously venomous.

**Distribution and status**: Cottonmouths occur statewide, including on the barrier islands. They are relatively common in many places, and their populations are considered stable.

143a adult (Livingston Parish)

143b adult (Washington Parish)

143d subadult (East Baton Rouge Parish)

143c adult (Wilkinson Co., MS)

143e venter (St. Martin Parish)

143g juvenile (West Feliciana Parish)

143f anterior (Wilkinson Co., MS)

## Pygmy Rattlesnake (*Sistrurus miliarius*) VENOMOUS

**Other names**: ground rattler

**Subspecies**: Western Pygmy Rattlesnake (*S. m. streckeri*)

**Description**: Pygmy Rattlesnakes are small, moderately stout snakes with a head that is distinct from the neck and with a **tiny rattle on the end of the tail**. The ground color is **gray, pale tan, or beige. There are 23–35 black spots down the top of the back, each about as long as or shorter than the space between them**. A corresponding dark spot occurs on the lower sides, and a darker smudge may alternate with the spots on the middle of each side. There is usually a dull reddish or orange stripe down the back, and the **end of the tail is black**. The head is colored like the body, with a pair of dark bands on top of the back of the head. Another dark band, running from the eye to the rear of the jaw, connects with its fellow atop the snout. The margin of the mouth is also dark. The underside is white to pale beige, darkest toward the middle, with few tan markings to numerous black spots. Juveniles are colored like the adults. The scales are keeled and in 21 rows. The anal shield is not divided.

**Size**: Maximum length 25.1 inches (638 mm); adults usually 11.2–20.3 inches (285–517 mm); newborns 4.8–6.5 inches (121–165 mm).

**Habitat**: Pygmy Rattlesnakes occur in palmetto-hardwood forests, pine flatwoods, and mixed pine-hardwood uplands.

**Natural history**: Pygmy Rattlesnakes are ambush predators that remain coiled near cover much of the time. They are very difficult to spot and are usually found when moving between resting sites. They appear to occur in local, spottily distributed population groups and are most often encountered in the fall. They feed on frogs, lizards, snakes, centipedes, and, rarely, small mammals. Females produce litters of 3–18 young. Despite their small size, Pygmy Rattlesnakes are dangerously venomous.

**Distribution and status**: Pygmy Rattlesnakes occur in several disjunct populations in Louisiana. They occur in much of northern and central Louisiana west of the Mississippi Delta, as far south as Evangeline and northern Calcasieu parishes. They also occur in the Florida Parishes and on high ground south and east of New Orleans. Local populations occur on the salt dome islands of St. Mary and Iberia Parishes, and along the low slopes between the Atchafalaya lowlands and Vermilion River in the vicinity of Lafayette. Pygmy Rattlesnakes are rarely encountered, but recent captures suggest that their populations remain stable.

144a adult (St. Tammany Parish)

144c adult (Natchitoches Parish)

144b adult (St. Tammany Parish)

144d venter (Morehouse Parish)

144e anterior (St. Tammany Parish)

144f juvenile (Nevada Co., AR)

## Eastern Diamondback Rattlesnake (*Crotalus adamanteus*)
### VENOMOUS

**Description**: Eastern Diamondback Rattlesnakes are large, robust snakes with a head that is distinct from the neck and a **segmented rattle on the end of the tail**. The ground color is tan to medium brown or brownish gray, slightly paler toward the tail. On the back are **25–28 brown diamonds with wide black borders. Each diamond is edged with a row of whitish to dull yellow scales**. On the front of the body, each diamond touches a similarly colored triangle on the lower sides, and the ground color of the middle sides may have irregular dark blotches. The dorsal **diamonds contact each other on most of the body, but toward the tail the markings tend to fade so that there are only black outlines. The tail has alternating black and pale rings**, and the end of the tail is black. The color of the top of the head is similar to the ground color. Just **in front of and just behind the eye are whitish stripes that angle down back to the mouth line**, between which is a dark zone. The chin and throat are white, and the underside of the body is dull yellow with a dusky midventral zone. Juveniles are colored like the adults. The scales are keeled and in 29 rows. The anal shield is not divided.

**Size**: Maximum length 99 inches (2,515 mm); adult males usually 49.0–74.8 inches (1,245–1,900 mm), females 45.3–64.0 (1,150–1,625 mm); newborns 11.8–17.9 inches (300–455 mm).

**Habitat**: Diamondback Rattlesnakes inhabit pine woodlands that may be intermingled with hardwood strips and hammocks. They occur in slash pine–palmetto flatwoods, as well as in open longleaf pine uplands.

**Natural history**: Diamondbacks are diurnal but may be crepuscular in hot weather. Individuals may winter in one area and then move to foraging areas during the active season. They are most often encountered when migrating between their seasonal ranges. They are ambush predators and spend a lot of time coiled in places likely to support prey. Juveniles feed on small rodents, while adults eat rabbits, rats, squirrels, and ground-nesting game birds. Females produce litters of 7–21 young. Diamondbacks rely on camouflage to avoid detection but will coil, rattle, and strike if molested. They are dangerously venomous.

**Distribution and status:** Reliable, historical reports for the Diamondback include sightings in the North Shore region of Lake Pontchartrain (late 1800s), but all other reliable reports are from northern Tangipahoa Parish and Washington Parish. There are only four confirmed records since 1995, and no population has been located in the state. For that reason, the Eastern Diamondback Rattlesnake may not be taken in Louisiana without permit and is considered a Species of Conservation Concern.

145a adult (Forrest Co., MS)

145b venter (Forrest Co., MS)

145c juvenile (Forrest Co., MS)

## Timber Rattlesnake (*Crotalus horridus*) VENOMOUS
**Other names**: Canebrake Rattlesnake, *Crotalus horridus atricaudatus*, serpent à sonnette

**Description**: Timber Rattlesnakes are large, ro-bust snakes with a head that is distinct from the neck and a **segmented rattle on the end of the tail**. The **ground color is pale tan or gray, beige, or yellowish. There are 19–30 dark brown to nearly black crossbands on the body that have slightly paler centers. Those on the neck are dis-connected on the upper sides to form a dorsal blotch with an adjacent blotch on each side. The crossbands are often angled rearward along the vertebral line, and all are widely spaced from their fellows.** Most Timber Rattlesnakes have a reddish middorsal stripe. The **body darkens toward the tail, which is entirely black**. The head is colored like the body, except for a wide, dark brown band that runs from the eye back to the angle of the jaw. The underside is whitish to beige, with a slightly darker midventral zone that is fringed by diffuse, dark gray markings. Juveniles are similar in color pattern to the adults, though are usually grayer. The scales are keeled and in 23 or 25 rows. The anal shield is not divided.

**Size**: Maximum length 74.5 inches (1,892 mm); adult males usually 45.9–70.0 inches (1,165–1,778 mm), females usually 44.8–57.9 inches (1,138–1,470 mm); newborns 14.4–15.5 inches (365–395 mm).

**Habitat**: Timber Rattlesnakes prefer hardwood or mixed pine-hardwood forests, whether upland or bottomland. They are absent from swamps, cleared tracts, and pure pinelands.

**Natural history**: Timber Rattlesnakes winter in tree cavities, log hollows, stump holes, and other secluded sites below or near the surface of the ground. At the start of the active season, they often move to foraging areas that may be some distance from their winter quarters. They are ambush predators that coil in spots likely to yield prey, such as around palmetto thickets, large logs, brush piles, or in trees or shrubs. They periodically move from one spot to another, and during hot weather they may move at night. It is during their travels that they are most often seen. They feed on rabbits, squirrels and other rodents, and quail. Females produce litters of

5–17 (usually 7–11) young, usually every other year. Timber Rattlesnakes rely on camouflage to avoid detection and typically do not rattle or strike until disturbed. Their venom is dangerously potent.

**Distribution and status**: Timber Rattlesnakes occur in forested portions of northern and central Louisiana, and along the Mississippi River and adjacent bottomlands at least as far as Triumph, Plaquemines Parish. They also occur in forested areas on the east side of the Atchafalaya Basin as far as Terrebonne and LaFourche Parishes, and on the salt dome islands of St. Mary and Iberia Parishes. They are absent from the open country and pinelands of southwestern Louisiana, as well as exclusive pine woodlands of the eastern Florida Parishes. Timber Rattlesnakes disappear when large forest blocks are fragmented, and little is known of the requirements to maintain viable populations. They appear to occur in stable numbers in many areas but have vanished from others. They are a Species of Conservation Concern.

146a adult (Catahoula Parish)

146b adult (Allen Parish)

146c subadult (Catahoula Parish)

146d venter (Ouachita Parish)

146e juvenile (Ouachita Parish)

# Glossary

**Adpressed**: Placed along the side of the body

**Anal shield**: A large platelike scale immediately anterior to and partially concealing the cloacal aperture in snakes

**Bridge**: The portion of a turtle's shell that joins the plastron and carapace

**Carapace**: The upper part of a turtle's shell

**Chenier**: An elevated ridge of land within marsh

**Core growth center**: The portion of each scute on a turtle's shell from which growth rings (annuli) originate

**Costal groove**: A vertical furrow along the sides of the trunk of most salamanders that is positioned adjacent to each rib

**Crepuscular**: Active around dawn or dusk

**Crossband**: A transverse marking that does not completely encircle a part of the body

**Cycloid**: Scales that are smoothly semicircular and overlapping

**Diurnal**: Active during daylight

**Dorsal/Dorsum**: The upper surface of an animal, and pertinent elements

**Dorsolateral fold**: A ridge of skin that runs along the boundary between the back and sides of some frogs

**Estivate**: Pass hot, dry periods in a state of dormancy or inactivity

**Florida Parishes**: The part of Louisiana lying east of the Mississippi River and north of Lakes Maurepas and Pontchartrain

**Fossorial**: Digging and/or burrowing

**Ground color**: The general coloration upon which additional aspects of color pattern exist

**Labials**: Scales that line the margin of the mouth in squamates (Squamata)

**Lacustrine**: Pertaining to lakes or ponds

**Lateral**: The side of an animal or pertaining to the sides

**Lateral fold**: A longitudinal fold of scale-covered skin on the lower sides

**Laterally compressed**: Somewhat flattened from side to side

**Lentic**: Lacks flow or current

**Longitudinal**: Running lengthwise on the body

**Lotic**: Flowing

**Marginals**: The scutes around the perimeter of a turtle's carapace

**Median**: Running longitudinally in the center of the body

**Metamorph**: An amphibian that exhibits remnant features of the larval state

**Metamorphosis**: The transformation from a larval to an adult form

**Nasolabial groove:** A groove that runs from the nostril under the upper lip of some salamanders

**Ocelli**: Eyelike patterns of rings with darker or paler central markings

**Paravertebral**: Adjacent to the vertebral line

**Parietal scale(s)**: A single or paired, platelike scale on the crown

**Parietal spot**: A pale mark that straddles the suture between the parietal scales of snakes

**Parotoid gland**: An enlarged, usually elongate, raised gland behind the eyes of toads

**Plastron**: The portion of a turtle's shell covering the underside of the body

**Rugose**: Rough in texture

**Sacral hump**: The raised area in the middle of the back of anurans

**Scute**: A large scale or plate as in those covering a turtle's shell

**Serrate**: A saw-toothed appearance

**Snout-vent length**: Length of the head and body from the tip of the snout to the rear of the cloacal aperture

**Thermoregulate**: To adjust body temperature by moving between areas of higher and lower temperature

**Tympanum**: The eardrum, a membrane covering the middle ear cavity in the skull

**Vent**: The cloacal aperture or orifice

**Venter/Ventral**: The lower surface of an animal, and its pertinent elements

**Vermiculations**: Irregular, wormlike markings

**Vertebral**: Located along the spine of an animal

# References

Altig, R., and R. McDiarmid. 2015. Handbook of larval amphibians of the United States and Canada. Ithaca: Cornell University Press. 345 pp.

Boundy, J. 2006. Snakes of Louisiana. 2nd ed. Baton Rouge: Louisiana Department of Wildlife and Fisheries. 40 pp.

Buhlmann, K., T. Tuberville, and W. Gibbons. 2008. Turtles of the Southeast. Athens: University of Georgia Press. 252 pp.

Crother, B., et al. 2012. Scientific and standard English and French names of amphibian and reptiles of North America north of Mexico, with comments regarding confidence in our understanding. Society for the Study of Amphibians and Reptiles, Herpetological Circular 39. 92 pp.

Dixon, J., and T. Hibbitts. 2013. Amphibians and reptiles of Texas (with keys, taxonomic synopses, bibliography, and distribution maps). 3rd ed. College Station: Texas A & M University Press. 460 pp.

Dodd, C. 2013. Frogs of the United States and Canada. 2 vols. Baltimore: Johns Hopkins University Press. 982 pp.

Dorcas, M., and W. Gibbons. 2008. Frogs and toads of the Southeast. Athens: University of Georgia Press. 238 pp.

Dundee, H., and D. Rossman. 1989. The amphibians and reptiles of Louisiana. Baton Rouge: Louisiana State University Press. 300 pp.

Ernst, C., and E. Ernst. 2003. Snakes of the United States and Canada. Washington, DC: Smithsonian Books. 668 pp.

Ernst, C., and J. Lovich. 2009. Turtles of the United States and Canada. 2nd ed. Baltimore: Johns Hopkins University Press. 827 pp.

Fouquette, M., and A. Dubois. 2014. A checklist of North American amphibians and reptiles. The United States and Canada. 7th ed. Vol. 1: Amphibians. Tempe: M. J. Fouquette. 613 pp.

Gibbons, W., and M. Dorcas. 2005. Snakes of the Southeast. Athens: University of Georgia Press. 253 pp.

Gibbons, W., J. Greene, and T. Mills. 2009. Lizards and crocodilians of the Southeast. Athens: University of Georgia Press. 235 pp.

Green, D., L. Weir, G. Casper, and M. Lannoo. 2013. North American amphibians: Distribution and diversity. Berkeley: University of California Press. 340 pp.

Holcomb, S., et al. 2015. Louisiana state wildlife action plan. Baton Rouge: Louisiana Department of Wildlife and Fisheries.

Lannoo, M., ed. 2005. Amphibian declines: The conservation status of United States species. Berkeley: University of California Press. 1094 pp.

Liner, E. 2005. The culinary herpetologist. Salt Lake City: Bibliomania! 382 pp.

Mitchell, J., and W. Gibbons. 2010. Salamanders of the Southeast. Athens: University of Georgia Press. 324 pp.

Petranka, J. 1998. Salamanders of the United States and Canada. Washington, DC: Smithsonian Institution Press. 587 pp.

Powell, R., R. Conant, and J. Collins. 2016. Peterson field guide to reptiles and amphibians of eastern and central North America. Boston: Houghton Mifflin Harcourt. 512 pp.

Reichling, S. 2008. Reptiles and amphibians of the southern pine woods. Gainesville: University Press of Florida. 252 pp.

Trauth, S., H. Robison, and M. Plummer. 2004. The amphibians and reptiles of Arkansas. Fayetteville: University of Arkansas Press. 412 pp.

Van Dijk, P., J. Iverson, A. Rhodin, B. Shaffer, and R. Bour. 2014. Turtles of the world: Annotated checklist of taxonomy, synonymy, distribution with maps, and conservation status. 7th ed. Chelonian Research Monographs 5:329–479.

# Credits for Photographs

**Christopher Austin:** 34b, 108b

**Charles D. Battaglia:** Sabine Map Turtle (page vi), Common Five-lined Skink (page xiv), Marbled Salamander (pages 32–33), Box Turtle (page 154), 33b, 49c, 132e, 133d

**David Beamer:** 10d

**Richard Bejarano:** American Alligator (pages 150–151), 73b, 74a

**Jeff Boundy:** Copperhead (page viii), Intermediate marsh, salt marsh, pine flatwood, hardwood flatwood, longleaf pine savanna, upland longleaf pine, loblolly pine-hardwood slope, calcareous prairie, bottomland hardwoods, cypress-tupelo swamp, coastal liveoak, river, stream, lake, gum pond, woodland slough, abandoned sugarcane field, loblolly pine plantation (pages 7–19), Four-toed Salamander (page 34), 1a, 1b, 3a, 3c, 3d, 4c, 4d, 5a, 5b, 8a, 9d, 10a, 10b, 11a, 11d, 12a, 12c, 13a, 13c, 13d, 14a, 14b, 15a, 15d, 16a, 17a, 18a, 18b, 18c, 19a, 19c, 20a, 20d, 21a, 21e, 21f, 22a, 22b, 23a, 23d, 24a, 24b, 25a, 26a, 26d, 27a, 27b, 27e, 28a, 28b, 28c, 28f, 29a, 30b, 30c, 30d, 30e, 30f, 31a, 31e, 32a, 32b, 33a, 33c, 33d, 37a, 37b, 38b, 40a, 40c, 43a, 43b, 44d, 45c, 46a, 49a, 50a, 50b, 50c, 50f, 51a, 51e, 53a, 53b, 53e, 56b, 56j, 57c, 58e, 58f, 62a, 62c, 62d, 63c, 66a, 67a, 69b, 69c, 69g, 70a, 70c, 71b, 72d, 76b, 76d, 78c, 78f, 79c, 80d, 82a, 82b, 85a, 85d, 86a, 86d, 86e, 88a, 89a, 89e, 90a, 90c, 91a, 91c, 91d, 93e, 93f, 94a, 96d, 96f, 97a, 98b, 98c, 98e, 99b, 100d, 101a, 101b, 101c, 103a, 103b, 103d, 104d, 105a, 105b, 105c, 105d, 105e, 106a, 106b, 106c, 107a, 107e, 107f, 107g, 108a, 108c, 108d, 108e, 108f, 108g, 109a, 109b, 109f, 110a, 110d, 110e, 111a, 111d, 112a, 113a, 113d, 113e, 114c, 114d, 115a, 115f, 115g, 115h, 116a, 116d, 116e, 117a, 117b, 117d, 117e, 117f, 118a, 118c, 118d, 118e, 119a, 119d, 119e, 120a, 120c, 120d, 121d, 121e, 121f, 121g, 121h, 122d, 122e, 123a, 123b, 123c, 123h, 123j, 124b, 124c, 124d, 124e, 124f, 125a,

125c, 125d, 126b, 126c, 127a, 127c, 127d, 128a, 128c, 128d, 129a, 129f, 129g, 130a, 130c, 130d, 130e, 131b, 131c, 132a, 132b, 132c, 132d, 134a, 134c, 134d, 134e, 135a, 135c, 135d, 136c, 136d, 138b, 138c, 138d, 138e, 139a, 140a, 140b, 140c, 141a, 141c, 141d, 142a, 142b, 142d, 142e, 143a, 143b, 143d, 143f, 143g, 144a, 144e, 145a, 145c

**Kurt Buhlmann:** 57f

**John L. Carr:** Green Tree Frog (page 84), Prairie Fence Lizard (page 224), Eastern Hog-nosed Snake (page 258), 1c, 2c, 2e, 2f, 3b, 4e, 5c, 6e, 17f, 34a, 38a, 39a, 39b, 42a, 42d, 54b, 56a, 56e, 56f, 56g, 56i, 57a, 57b, 57d, 57e, 58c, 58g, 58h, 58i, 59d, 62b, 62e, 62f, 63b, 63d, 64c, 64d, 65a, 65b, 65d, 65e, 66b, 66c, 66e, 67c, 67e, 67f, 67g, 67i, 68b, 68c, 68d, 68e, 68f, 68g, 68h, 68i, 69e, 69f, 70b, 70e, 70f, 70g, 76a, 76e, 78b, 78g, 79a, 79d, 79e, 79f, 79g, 80c, 80e, 80g, 83f, 89d, 96c, 98a, 98f, 105f, 113b, 119c, 121a, 121i, 122a, 123k, 127b, 127e, 129b, 133b, 135e, 136a, 137b, 141b, 142c, 144d, 146c, 146e

**Donna L. Dittman:** 69d

**Kyle L. Elmore:** 6d, 112d, 116c, 122c, 123e, 123f, 123i, 137c, 137f, 139b

**Kevin Enge:** 104a, 104b

**Dino Ferri:** 99a

**Andy Ford:** 96g

**Kathy Gault:** 73d

**Brad M. Glorioso:** Green Anole (pages ii–iii), 2b, 4b, 6a, 7b, 7d, 10c, 11c, 13b, 13e, 14c, 15b, 17b, 19b, 20e, 21b, 24c, 24d, 24e, 26b, 27c, 27f, 28d, 28e, 29e, 30a, 31c, 31d, 31h, 32c, 32d, 32e, 32h, 37c, 38c, 38f, 39d, 41a, 41b, 41c, 42b, 42c, 42f, 43d, 43.1a, 43.1b, 43.1c, 43.1d, 43.1e, 44c, 45b, 46b, 46c, 46d, 46e, 49d, 51b, 52e, 53c, 54a, 54c, 56c, 56h, 58a, 61c, 64b, 66d, 67b, 67d, 67h, 69a, 71a, 71c, 73c, 76c, 78e, 80a, 80b, 80f, 81a, 81b, 81c, 81d, 83b, 83c, 83d, 83g, 84a, 84c, 85b, 86c, 87a, 87b, 89f, 89g, 92a, 92b, 92d, 92e, 93b, 93c, 93d, 94b, 96a, 96b, 96e, 97d, 100e, 103c, 114a, 114e, 115b, 115c, 115d, 115e, 116f, 117c, 118b, 119b, 119f, 120e, 121b, 122b, 123d, 125b, 125e, 126d, 129c, 129e, 129h, 133c, 137a, 138a, 139c, 139e, 142f

**David Heckard:** 84b, 84d, 87e, 87f, 99c

**Jeromi Hefner:** 2a, 4a, 5e, 6b, 12b, 15c, 15e, 17d, 20c, 21c, 23b, 25b, 26e, 27d, 28g, 28h, 29c, 29d, 31b, 31f, 31g, 32f, 32g, 34c, 34d, 34e, 35a, 35b, 38d, 38e, 39c, 40b, 41d, 41f, 42e, 43c, 48a, 48b, 49b, 50c, 50d, 51c, 51d, 51f, 52a, 52c, 53d, 53f, 64a, 68a, 70d, 78a, 83a, 83e, 86b, 87c, 87d, 89b, 89c, 92c, 93a, 97b, 97c, 98d, 100a, 100b, 101d, 103e, 107b, 107d, 108h, 109c, 110c, 114b, 117g, 120b, 121c, 124a, 129d, 130b, 134b, 136b, 143e, 146a, 146d

**Timothy A. Herman:** 18d

**Sam Holcomb:** 79b

**Brian J. Hutchinson:** 77a

**John B. Jensen:** 61a, 91b

**Robert L. Jones:** 60e

**Jennifer Y. Lamb:** Bayhead (page 15), 16c, 16e, 16f, 17e

**James R. Lee:** 104c, 131a, 131d

**Stephanie D. Lee:** 145b

**Peter V. Lindeman:** 59b, 59c, 59e, 59f, 60a, 60b, 60c, 60d

**Louisiana Department of Wildlife and Fisheries:**
   Todd Baker: 78d
   Amity Bass: 133a
   Dave Butler: 74b, 74c, 74d
   Ruth Elsey: 55a, 55b, 55c, 55d
   Beau Gregory: 7a
   Judy Jones: shortleaf pine-hickory (page 10)
   Keri Landry: 72a, 72b, 72c
   Chris Reid: coastal prairie (page 8), river batture (page 14)
   Michael Seymour: 65c
   Mickey Miller: 54e
   W. Parke Moore III: 54d

**Jacob Loyacano:** 6c, 6f, 6g

**Morrison Baker Mast:** 77b

**Roderic B. Mast:** 73a

**Armin Meier:** 104e

**Brad Moon:** 2g, 8b, 8c, 8d, 16b, 16d, 17c, 20b, 21d, 23c, 26c, 29b, 41e, 44a, 44b, 45a, 52b, 52d, 56d, 58b, 58d, 85c, 90b, 100c, 107c, 110b, 111b, 111c, 111e, 112b, 112c, 113c, 116b, 128e, 135b, 139d, 143c, 144c, 146b

**Donald Newman:** 137d

**Matt Pardue:** 59a

**Wayne Parker:** 65f

**Kory G. Roberts:** 1d, 2d, 5d, 7c, 9a, 9b, 9c, 11b, 25c, 33e, 36a, 36b, 36c, 37d, 37e, 39e, 47a, 47b, 47c, 61b, 61d, 63a, 63e, 90d, 94c, 94d, 94e, 95a, 95b, 102a, 102b, 109d, 109e, 126a, 133e, 137e, 144f

**Don Shepard:** 14d

**Steve Shively:** 128b, 141e

**Greg Sievert:** 47d, 71d, 75b, 75c, 88b, 102c, 109g

**Kimberly Terrell:** 91e, 144b

**John A. Tupy:** 48c

**U.S. Fish and Wildlife Service:** 74e, 75d

**Christopher Williams:** 49e

# Index